THE BUCKET LIST
NORTH AMERICA

First published in the United States of America in 2021 by
Universe Publishing, a division of
Rizzoli International Publications, Inc.
300 Park Avenue South
New York, NY 10010
www.rizzoliusa.com

2021 2022 2023 2024 / 10 9 8 7 6 5 4 3 2 1

ISBN: 978-0-7893-4102-0
Library of Congress Control Number: 2021934381

Visit us online:
Facebook.com/RizzoliNewYork
Twitter: @Rizzoli_Books
Instagram.com/RizzoliBooks
Pinterest.com/RizzoliBooks
YouTube.com/user/RizzoliNY
Issuu.com/Rizzoli

Conceived, designed, and produced by the Bright Press,
an imprint of the Quarto Group
The Old Brewery, 6 Blundell Street
London N7 9BH, United Kingdom
T (0)20 7700 6700
www.QuartoKnows.com

Publisher: James Evans
Editorial Director: Isheeta Mustafi
Managing Editor: Jacqui Sayers
Art Director: James Lawrence
Senior Editor: Caroline Elliker
Project Manager: Angela Koo
Design: JC Lanaway
Picture Research: Jane Lanaway, Katie Crous

Printed in Singapore

Horseshoe Canyon,
Grand Canyon, Arizona

THE BUCKET LIST
NORTH AMERICA

1000 Adventures Big and Small

United States • Canada • Mexico • The Caribbean

PAUL OSWELL and KATH STATHERS

UNIVERSE

HOW TO USE THIS BOOK

This book is divided into three main areas—the United States,
Canada, and Mexico and the Caribbean. The United States is
further divided into the regions of West, Midwest, South, and
Northeast, with a separate chapter for each of these. Locations
are given at the start of each entry. These provide a town or
area, as well as the relevant territory, state, or country. If you
have a specific location in mind, simply turn to page 406 to
search for it in the index.

COLOR CODE

Each entry number in the book has been given a color
that relates to one of seven categories, as shown below,
allowing you to select activities based on the type
of experience you're interested in.

■ Sport   ■ Culture   ■ Animals   ■ History

■ Journeys   ■ Outdoors   ■ Food and drink

Dakota Badlands at sunrise

CONTENTS

INTRODUCTION

When it comes to "bucket list" travel items—experiences that we'll remember for the rest of our lives—there's nowhere quite like North America. Here, all things are possible, including leaving the planet entirely (although that's the preserve of the superrich). For the rest of us, though, there's still a universe of opportunities. In this book, we've researched and selected 1,000 of these experiences, all of them completely within the reach of the ordinary traveler who wants to form extraordinary memories.

What makes North America such a wonderful destination? One obvious factor is the sheer diversity of the landscape. Here you can traverse the icy tundra of Alaska, admire the great plains of the Midwest, sleep under the stars in the Mexican desert, or island hop around the Caribbean. The breadth of cultural attractions is also a thing of wonder. Where else can you see state-of-the-art technology at a space center, wander amid centuries-old Mayan architecture, and ride the world's most thrilling roller coasters?

Whether your dream vacation is getting off-grid on a scenic hiking trail, immersing yourself in history and art, indulging in a tour of culinary specialities, or searching out a city's hidden secrets, this list has something for you. From Canada to Cuba, and Miami to Mexico, we've picked out the cream of what every region has to offer. We've included the famous— from the Grand Canyon and the Las Vegas Strip—alongside lesser-known roadside attractions and hidden beaches. What these experiences have in common is that they will leave a lasting impression.

The majority of this book was completed during the Covid-19 pandemic, so many of the establishments mentioned in the text were closed at the time of writing. We hope that business will resume for all of them once travel restrictions ease, but the sad likelihood is that not all will recover, so always check that facilities are still operational before planning an activity. Above all, let this list be your inspiration. All you need is an adventurous spirit and an open mind—this incredible continent will do the rest. Happy, safe, and memorable travels to you all.

PAUL OSWELL AND KATH STATHERS

A Californian spring superbloom

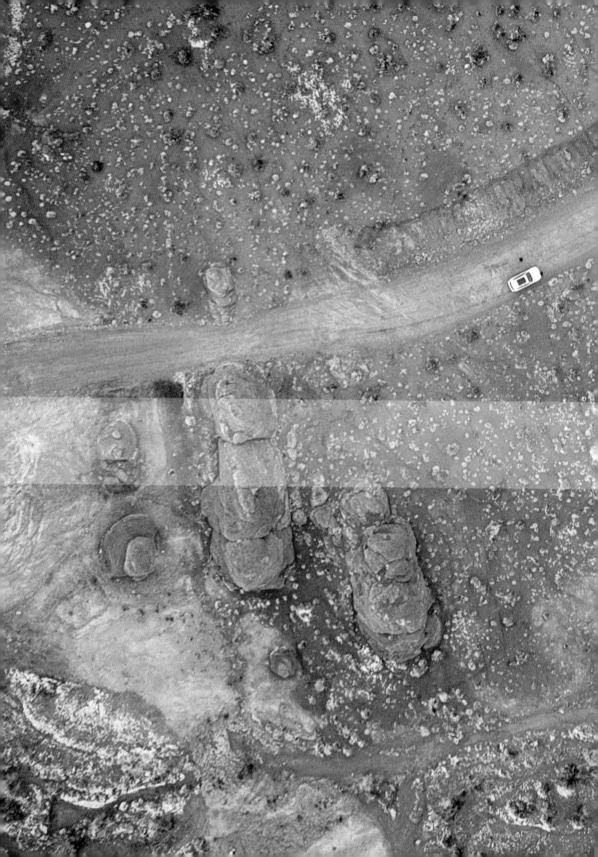

1
US WEST

3 Ice art at Fairbanks

UTQIAGVIK, ALASKA

1 Stay awake for a day that never ends

In early May, the sun sets for the last time each spring in Utqiagvik. So begins almost ninety days of continuous daylight for the United States' most northerly point. Spot houses with windows blacked out to help people sleep. Or visit from November to January, when the sun never rises.

KING ISLAND, ALASKA

2 See the abandoned stilt village of Ukivok

Located on tiny King Island, off the coast of Alaska, this haunting village was once home to a secluded but thriving Ukivokmiut fishing community. Having been inhabited for thousands of years, it was abandoned fifty years ago, yet still clings precariously to the steep cliffside.

FAIRBANKS, ALASKA

3 Become part of an ice sculpture

The Aurora Ice Museum, at Chena Hot Springs Resort, is the world's largest year-round ice environment. It's constructed from locally sourced ice—1,000 tons—and the temperature is kept at 25°F (–7°C). Witness elaborate carvings of jousting knights, polar bears, and a two-story snowball fight.

5 Dall ewe, Denali National Park

STEEP CREEK, ALASKA

4 Marvel at color-changing salmon

Pay a visit to Steep Creek from mid-July through October to catch sight of sockeye salmon swimming back to the fresh water of their beginnings in order to spawn a new generation. At this time, their bodies take on a brilliant red hue, and their heads become a darkish green.

DENALI NATIONAL PARK AND PRESERVE, ALASKA

5 Count an alternative Big Five

With wolves, moose, grizzly bears, caribou, and Dall sheep, Alaska has a Big Five to rival Africa's (lions, leopards, rhinos, elephants, buffalo). This list has a long association with hunters, but happily today's generation comes armed with cameras and Instagram accounts. You'll find these creatures in the national park surrounding Denali, North America's highest peak. Dall sheep are particularly plentiful in the mountainous regions, sheltering from less nimble predators. If you get close enough, you can calculate a ram's age by counting the rings on its horns.

DENALI NATIONAL PARK AND
PRESERVE, ALASKA
6 Climb North America's highest peak

Just one thin road cuts through
some 6 million ac (2.5 million
ha) of wild nature here,
surrounded by alpine tundra
and snow-topped mountains.
Denali looms over the park,
the continent's tallest peak at
just over 20,000 ft (6,000 m).
It's possible to scale it, but by
experienced climbers only.

KODIAK ISLAND, ALASKA
7 Admire the speed of the sei whale

Despite its impressive 20 ton
(18 tonne) weight, this whale
can charge through the oceans
at speeds reaching 30 mph
(50 kmh), twisting and turning,
and scooping up gigantic
mouthfuls of plankton as
it goes.

ANCHORAGE, ALASKA
8 Feel Alaska's beating heart

You'll feel utterly immersed
in Alaskan heritage at the
Alaska Native Heritage
Center, named one of America's
Cultural Treasures by the Ford
Foundation. Chronicling more
than 10,000 years of Alaskan
Indigenous history and culture,
it provides exhibitions and
demonstrations to bring this
culture to a wider audience.

6 Snowy peaks of Mt. Denali

ANCHORAGE, ALASKA

9 Psych yourself up to take a polar plunge

People get their thrills in all manner of ways, and in this part of the world, one of the most bracing activities is to dive into the icy polar waters. It might sound like the last thing people would want to involve themselves in, but every year at Goose Lake in Anchorage, hundreds of participants line up to take the iciest of icy dips, all to raise money for good causes. Outlandish costumes are encouraged, and the dip is only for a few seconds, though it may feel like a lot longer.

ANCHORAGE, ALASKA

10 Ride the train from Anchorage to Fairbanks

Few train lines offer quite such epic views as the railroad between Anchorage and Fairbanks. The journey takes almost twelve hours, crossing mighty bridges, rolling through Denali National Park, encompassing the majestic scenery of the Nenana River Gorge, and skirting the edges of blue lakes and flowing streams. Many visitors break the journey up rather than completing it in one go, stopping at Talkeetna to climb Mt. Denali, or at Denali National Park for whitewater rafting or a wildlife safari.

SEWARD, ALASKA
11 Get up close to a mighty glacier

The Kenai Fjords National Park covers a huge area of Alaskan wilderness, including the 700-sq-mi (1,813-sq-km) Harding Icefield from which forty glaciers flow out. Many people visit the ice field in a day—it's an epic adventure to walk to and on a glacier, before returning to the comfort of Seward overnight. It's also possible to camp out in the park—whether in the campsite at Exit Glacier or wild in the backcountry—to enjoy the true emptiness of the wilderness and a sky full of stars.

SEWARD, ALASKA
12 Sample the biggest crab legs in the world

King crabs truly deserve their name. The biggest of the species, the red king crab, can reach a leg span of 5 ft 11 in (1.8 m) and weigh a whopping 28 lb (12.7 kg)—as much as a cocker spaniel. They live off the Alaskan coast and are a prized catch for the region's fishing fleet and a taste sensation for diners. Several Seward restaurants offer them on the menu, but many locals swear by Ray's Waterfront. Enjoy a plate of legs, served simply with butter and lemon dips. Lip-smackingly good!

CORDOVA, ALASKA
13 Spot a gathering of bald eagles

America's national bird is more prevalent in Alaska than anywhere else in the United States. With its distinctive white head and brown body, it seems to epitomize the early American settlers' pioneering spirit, though it was a spiritual symbol for Alaskan Indigenous people long before. Each year around fall, roughly 3,000 bald eagles congregate on the Chilkat River north of Haines to take advantage of a late run of salmon. Watching them soar over the river and perch feeding on a rock is a mesmerizing experience.

GLACIER BAY NATIONAL PARK AND PRESERVE, ALASKA
14 Kayak your way through an icy wilderness

Only 350 years ago, Glacier Bay was a shallow valley with villages along its river. By 1750, glaciers had forged from the head of the valley to the sea, obliterating the villages. A blink of an eye later in geological terms, those glaciers have retreated, leaving a turquoise fjord, surrounded by mountains. To kayak here, with glacier fragments floating by, is a magical experience and living geography lesson rolled into one.

SKAGWAY, ALASKA
15 Take a panoramic route through the mountains

The White Pass and Yukon Route was built in 1898 to move equipment and passengers during the Gold Rush. A century later, a heritage railway service climbs around 3,000 ft (900 m), surrounded by glaciers, gorges, and waterfalls. The line stretches for 110 mi (177 km), with various sightseeing options available—most of which make use of original parlor cars for added ambience. Passengers can complete round trips or be dropped off for a few days' camping in the wilderness.

14 Kayaking in Glacier Bay

16 Inside the Mendenhall Ice Caves

JUNEAU, ALASKA

16 Reach the heart of a glacier

Breathtaking blue walls shimmer inside a partially hollow glacier at the stunning Mendenhall Ice Caves. To add to the excitement, you must kayak to the glacier, then ice-climb over it to reach the caves!

SITKA NATIONAL HISTORICAL PARK, ALASKA

17 Watch millions of herring spawn

The arrival of spring on Sitka Sound is heralded each year by a phenomenon of nature that sees the sea turn a foamy, milky white with herring eggs. As adult herrings make their annual visit to the shallows to spawn, they are pursued by whales, seals, and fishermen.

VARIOUS SITES IN ALASKA

18 Try heli-fishing

If long hikes aren't your thing but fishing in pristine wilderness is, heli-fishing is the solution. Arrive at your remote—but often luxurious—lodging, where a guide will escort you to your own personal stretch of a river to see if the salmon are biting. Salmon runs go from May to September, with king salmon arriving first and staying until the end of July.

KAUA'I, HAWAII
19 Snorkel along the Nā Pali Coast

With its steep cliffs and remote location, the Nā Pali Coast, northwest Kaua'i, is pretty inaccessible. And that's exactly why it's so unspoiled and beautiful. The coastline is peppered with caves and arches and a stunning array of rock colors. Above water it's stunning; below the surface it's buzzing, ablaze with colorful corals and teeming with schools of fish. At any moment a Hawaiian green turtle might swim by, and on the boat journey back, you're often joined by dolphins.

KAUA'I, HAWAII
20 Cycle down a volcanic canyon

Often described as the Grand Canyon of the Pacific, Waimea Canyon is a riot of orange and pink lava beds, dotted with verdant green vegetation. At 10 mi (16 km) long and 3,000 ft (914 m) deep, there are many ways to explore it. By car, you can reach amazing views. A hike takes you to refreshing waterfalls and lush forests. But a truly unforgettable trip is to arrive at the canyon's rim to watch the sunrise, then hop on a bike for a downhill cruise along the canyon to the coast.

KAUA'I, HAWAII
21 Glide down the Wailua River

The Wailua is the island of Kaua'i's largest navigable river. Traveling up it via canoe or kayak is a popular activity due to both the accessibility and the unmissable scenery that the location offers. It's a very easy, nontechnical waterway, and several types of canoe and kayak are readily available for rental. The main route is around 2 mi (3.2 km) long and takes visitors past a traditional Hawaiian village, through lush forests, and then on to the scenic Uluwehi Falls.

19 Marine life on the Nā Pali Coast

22 Hang ten at Waikiki

Hawaii and surfing go together like a mai tai and a cocktail umbrella. Waikiki Beach, with its 2-mi (3.2-km) stretch of sand and gentle waves, used to be the surfing playground for Hawaiian royalty. Now it's the surfing playground of the world and a great place to learn. You'll also spot historic buildings like the Moana Surfrider Hotel—a throwback to a bygone age.

23 Indulge in a traditional luau

Just about every movie set in Hawaii features a luau—a lavish feast with a show of music and dancing and, in Hollywood at least, brightly colored shirts. The tradition dates to the early nineteenth century, when rules for men and women eating separately were abolished. Today's luaus feature all kinds of food, but traditionally they included a meat dish containing the leaves of the luau (taro) plant.

HONOLULU, O'AHU, HAWAII

24 Learn hula

Study the spirit, grace, and history of the ancient form of hula, the well-known Hawaiian dance that preserves the stories, traditions, and culture of the islands. Traditional hula is usually accompanied by chanting and drumming; modern hula features contemporary music. Honolulu's Royal Hawaiian Center offers free lessons.

O'AHU, HAWAII

25 Ascend a stairway to heaven

Almost 4,000 steps take you up Hawaii's luscious Ko'olau mountain range. Despite a "no trespassing" sign and a guard stationed at the bottom, many people risk a fine to climb the phenomenal Haiku Stairs, installed in the 1940s to reach a radio station at the summit.

PEARL HARBOR, O'AHU, HAWAII

26 Pay your respects at Pearl Harbor

Before 8 a.m. on December 7, 1941, the skies above Pearl Harbor filled with Japanese warplanes raining bombs and bullets on the naval fleet. The attack lasted for two hours, destroyed 20 US warships and 300 airplanes, and killed 2,403 sailors, soldiers, and civilians. It goaded the United States into joining World War II. A memorial to the USS *Arizona* floats above the remains of the ship, which sank with 1,177 onboard—a moving tribute to the horrors of war.

25 Ascending the Haiku Stairs

O'AHU, HAWAII

27 Experience the tranquility of floating lanterns

As the sun sets on Memorial Day, more than 6,000 candlelit lanterns bearing remembrances and prayers illuminate the ocean at Ala Moana Beach Park. Despite the crowds, the serene movements of the lanterns on the water bring feelings of peace as loved ones who have passed are remembered.

MAUI, HAWAII

28 Hawaii drive-o!

Life, someone once said, is about the journey, not the destination. Nowhere is that sentiment truer than on the winding roads of Hawaii's spine-tingling Hana Highway. With the glittering ocean to one side, and lush rain forest and waterfalls to the other, it's a drive-through paradise. Take in more than 600 curves and fifty-five bridges on the road that's carved into Maui's precipitous coastline.

27 Memorial Day lanterns in Hawaii

30 Swimming with spinner dolphins

29 Take a trip to the "House of the Sun"

A Hawaiian legend claims that the Sun slept in the crater of Haleakala, hence its nickname: "House of the Sun." The crater of this dormant volcano on Maui is 7 mi (11.3 km) across, and it's one of the best places on Earth to catch a sunrise. Once the day has begun, take the chance to explore its moonlike features, or dip into its wild scrubland, packed full of birds and other animals.

30 Take a spin with spinner dolphins

Spinner dolphins are named for the high spinning leaps they perform. They are best watched in the mornings, when they playfully interact with each other. The clear waters and white sands of Hawaii's bays make it easy for them to keep an eye out for predators—sharks mainly. As they have never been hunted by people here, they often approach boats, providing an even more interactive experience.

31 Watch volcanoes erupting in front of you

There is something primal about the natural power of a volcano spilling lava. On the "Big Island" of Hawai'i, you can see the lava flowing at Hawai'i Volcanoes National Park or the Kalapana viewing area, with the Halema'uma'u crater particularly striking at sunset.

HAWAI'I, HAWAII
32 Stargaze at Mauna Kea

Some of the world's most advanced observatories are stationed at the peak of this mountain; the geographic location and lack of light pollution make it the perfect spot to gaze upon the Milky Way. Private sunrise and sunset tours take visitors to stargaze alongside these facilities, with planets, expansive star systems, and the glories of the universe all on display.

OLYMPIC NATIONAL PARK AND FOREST, WASHINGTON
33 Visit the home of the gods

Mt. Olympus, the highest peak in this national park, owes its name to the English voyager John Meares, who thought it looked like a home fit for the gods, and so named it after its Greek counterpart. It's a stunning park to explore, with several peaks over 7,000 ft (2,000 m), ancient rain forests, and thousands of years of human history.

SAN JUAN ISLANDS, WASHINGTON
34 Tour artists' studios on the San Juan Islands

Take a ferry from the Washington State Ferry terminal and explore these islands by bicycle. The rocky shorelines and quaint villages draw artists from all over.

32 Mauna Kea's night sky

MT. BAKER, WASHINGTON

35 Cut a perfect line in powder snow

The resort with the most snow in the world is surely the destination to head to when you're planning to leave a perfect track down the mountain. So make your way to Mt. Baker, where, in nature's huge expanse, you can create a simple wavy line in the snow.

PUGET SOUND, WASHINGTON
36 Salute a legend of the deep

The largest recorded giant octopus measured a whopping 30 ft (9 m) across, but its more average brethren tend to reach 16 ft (5 m), with a 30 ft arm span—still big enough, though, to swap their regular diet of fish and lobster for the occasional shark. Puget Sound is a popular site for divers wanting to view the behavior of these intelligent creatures, including using camouflage to disguise themselves as intricate pieces of coral.

SEATTLE, WASHINGTON
37 View the world from space (needle)

A sculpture of a dancer, a doodle on a napkin, and a revolving bar in Hawaii all influenced the designs of Seattle's iconic Space Needle, conceived as the centerpiece of the 1962 World's Fair. Delays in the design process, followed by the search for a suitable location, meant that the structure was built in just eight months, in time for the fair, for which it was crowned with a gas torch that lit up at night in the colors of the rainbow. If you ascend the needle, the observation level now includes a glass floor and walls for fantastic views across Seattle and to the mountains beyond.

36 Diving to view a giant octopus

37 Seattle's Space Needle, seen from Kerry Park

SEATTLE, WASHINGTON

38 See all that Pike Place Market has to offer

One of this market's founding principles, when established in 1907, was to give consumers the opportunity to meet producers. That still holds true, and today you'll find farmers, craftspeople, vegetable stalls, small restaurants, buskers, and quirky stores selling everything from miniature cars to magic tricks, collectible comics, and handmade candy. It's also known for its Gum Wall—a brick wall with a tradition of chewing gum "tributes" that is now a tourist attraction in its own right. The tradition persists, despite a cleanup in 2015.

SEATTLE, WASHINGTON

39 Grab a coffee in Seattle

Seattle's love affair with coffee started in the 1950s with the opening of its first coffee shops. It gathered pace in the 1960s when the California company Peet's Coffee started to explore different beans, leading to the opening of the first Starbucks in Seattle in 1971 (its first shop in Pike Place Market is still there). Coffeehouse culture truly mushroomed with the arrival of hippies who sought out places to gather and discuss ideas, sheltered from Seattle's slightly chilly climate. Today there are hundreds of independent coffee shops and many coffee roasting companies.

38 Gum Wall, Pike Place Market

39 Coffee at Pike Place Market

40 Dance performance at Seattle's Olympic Sculpture Park

SEATTLE, WASHINGTON
40 See downtown art

Seattle's 9-ac (3.6-ha) Olympic
Sculpture Park is a fabulous
place to spend an afternoon.
At first glance, it's like many
public parks—with native plants,
fun seating areas, and waterfront
views. But this park also houses a
world-class collection of outdoor
sculptures by artists ranging
from Richard Serra to Louise
Bourgeois, and complemented
by the regular staging of
performance art and live
music events.

LEAVENWORTH, WASHINGTON
41 Discover your inner Bavarian

There's been tourism in
Leavenworth since the town
built a ski jump in 1929, and in
the 1960s the Alpine quotient
was stepped up. Nestled in
the Cascade mountain range,
the town now resembles a
Bavarian village. As well as the
architecture, there's a 100 ft
(30 m) maypole, a nutcracker
museum, and restaurants selling
the best Wiener schnitzel and
sauerkraut this side of Munich.

WALLA WALLA, WASHINGTON
42 Sip your way through Walla Walla

The quaint town of Walla Walla
has become an epicenter of wine
tourism in Washington State—
the downtown area boasts around
forty tasting rooms. Amble down
Main Street and sample cuvées
from some of the state's top
producers, such as Rotie Cellars
and nearby Seven Hills Winery
and Charles Smith Wines.

45 Creating sand art on Cannon Beach

MT. RAINIER NATIONAL PARK, WASHINGTON

43 Look out from the Mt. Fremont Lookout

One of this park's top trails is the hike to Mt. Fremont Lookout, a two-story cabin built in 1934 for wildfire watchmen. Look out for marmots and chipmunks on the way. At 4,226 ft (1,288 m) above sea level, the watchtower's balcony provides 360-degree views. Bring binoculars to spy mountain goats, black bears, and elk. On a clear day, you'll even see Seattle's Space Needle.

METHOW VALLEY, WASHINGTON

44 Say you've seen an ermine's winter coat

The beauty of an ermine in its white winter coat (with black tail tip) is one of winter's pleasures—unless you're its prey, which it hunts ferociously all year round. In summer its coat turns brown.

CANNON BEACH, OREGON

45 Explore a haystack on a beach

Oregon has 363 mi (584 km) of coastline. There are dunes, fabulous cliffs, a ghost forest—where the stumps of ancient trees rise in the surf—and the beautiful white sands and bumpy sea stacks of Cannon Beach. Haystack Rock is the largest, and an iconic landmark. At low tide, it's a mesmerizing place to watch the antics of the sea creatures in its rock pools and lose yourself for hours.

YACHATS, OREGON
46 See the sea drain into a giant well

There's an unassuming part of the Oregon coast in the Siuslaw National Forest—scenic in its own right, with waves crashing onto moss-covered rocks and the panorama of Cape Perpetua. However, a strange rock formation creates what is known as the "drainpipe of the Pacific," or more impressively "Thor's Well." A large hole has formed and water spills through it at a frightening pace, looking like the ocean is draining into the land.

PORTLAND, OREGON
47 Savor the timeless tradition of tea

The Tao of Tea in the Tower of Cosmic Reflections, within the Lan Su Chinese Garden, pairs the beauty of the garden with the elegance of the Chinese tea ceremony. This two-story teahouse is run by a Portland-based company that promotes the art and culture of tea, focusing on fine organic brews from around the world.

PORTLAND, OREGON
48 Feast from legendary food carts

In the last few decades, Portland has become a food-centric destination. Many culinary trends have started here, and some have really stuck—the proliferation of food carts being one success story. Every kind of cuisine is represented, from gourmet burgers and barbecue to esoteric dishes such as Chinese crepes. Most remain speciality operations and have really refined their menus. Go early to avoid lunch crowds.

46 Thor's Well at high tide

50 Benson Bridge, Multnomah Falls

51 Willamette Valley vineyard

PORTLAND, OREGON
49 Lose yourself in Powell's City of Books

When we say "lose yourself," we mean both figuratively and literally. This Portland institution is the largest independent bookstore in the world, weighing in at four stories and a whole city block. Over 1 million new and used books are on sale across a whopping 3,500 different sections. There's also an exciting Rare Books room, which stocks sought-after autographed first editions and other collectibles. A one-stop shop for bookworms.

COLUMBIA RIVER GORGE, OREGON
50 Feel the spray of Multnomah on your face

Over 2 million people visit this region every year, making it the most popular recreational site in the Pacific Northwest. Just thirty minutes from Portland, Multnomah Falls is 611 ft (186 m) high, and the water falls with exhilarating ferocity. For a close-up view, walk a couple hundred feet up the paved trail to Benson Bridge, which spans the falls at the first tier's base. Rainwater, an underground spring, and melted snow mean the water falls year-round.

WILLAMETTE VALLEY, OREGON
51 Taste a pinot noir in Willamette Valley

Oregon has long had a thriving wine industry, and while high-profile regions such as Sonoma in California get much of the press, there's a wealth of great wines and scenic trails here. Almost two-thirds of the winemakers are in this valley, and it has become one of the world's leading producers of high-quality pinot grapes. Wine regions also usually come with great restaurants and scenery, and Willamette Valley is no exception, with an abundance of both.

CASCADE LAKES, OREGON

52 Canoe the Cascade Lakes by moonlight

Wanderlust Tours' canoe tours seek out the quiet of the shimmering waters of central Oregon's Cascades region by the light of the moon. Paddle beneath a blanket of stars in a clear sky, as your senses soak up the sights and sounds of the night and attune to the natural world around you. Afterward, return to shore for a welcome beer or hot chocolate.

BEND, OREGON

53 Investigate Bend's top breweries

Boneyard is a hop-focused brewery that pours pints and tasters of its iconic West Coast styles at a pub in downtown Bend. Bottles and crowlers are available to go. Meanwhile, the original outpost of the 10 Barrel Brewing Company features dozens of West Coast–style ales and lagers with bar food served in generous portions. And one of Bend's oldest breweries, the laid-back Bend Brewing Company, has an outdoor patio where you can knock back surprisingly modern styles—think juicy IPAs and dry-hopped pilsners.

53 Outdoor entertainment at 10 Barrel Brewing Company

CRATER LAKE NATIONAL PARK, OREGON
54 Hike into a volcanic crater

Crater Lake is a beautiful natural feature that appeared around 7,700 years ago. Witnessed by the area's Klamath Tribes, the 12,000-ft (3,658-m) volcano Mt. Mazama erupted and collapsed in on itself. Over the next few hundred years, the crater this left slowly filled with melting snow water and rainfall, creating a lake 2,000 ft (600 m) deep. The surrounding park is great hiking country, with waterfalls, meadows, and forests. And imagine arriving at the peak for your first view of the almost perfectly round, magical, deep blue lake.

ASHLAND, OREGON
55 Search out the Bard in Oregon

The prestigious Oregon Shakespeare Festival dates from 1935 and has roots even further back. The Chautauqua movement brought culture and entertainment to rural areas of the country in the late nineteenth century, and the town's first theater was erected in the very spot where the festival now happens. From February to October, the festival includes over 800 performances of classic and contemporary plays. They're not limited to Shakespeare's works, but the Bard is certainly a strong presence in the program every year.

55 Evening performance at the Oregon Shakespeare Festival

PRAIRIE CREEK REDWOODS STATE PARK, CALIFORNIA

56 Drive the Newton B. Drury Scenic Parkway

In 1993, a diversion through Prairie Creek Redwoods State Park in Humboldt County was opened to honor the eponymous director of the National Park Service. The drive takes you through a glorious old-growth redwood forest, the trees towering on either side and providing a home to wild Roosevelt elk.

NAPA VALLEY, CALIFORNIA

57 Design your own wine

Your dreams of becoming a master blender really can become a reality at the Hess Collection's blending sessions. You'll learn about the craft from the experts, then blend and sip your way to your ideal cuvée. Afterward, you'll even have the opportunity to design a label for your wine, resulting in a completely bespoke bottle.

NAPA VALLEY, CALIFORNIA

58 Tour wine country by train

When you're in the heart of America's best wine-producing region, the last thing you need is a car limiting your enjoyment. A trip on the Napa Valley Wine Train solves that problem. Capturing the luxury of a bygone era, it takes you on a 36-mi (58-km) loop through the vineyards, serving a gourmet meal onboard and stopping for tours with winemakers.

SONOMA, CALIFORNIA

59 Dance the day away in Sonoma

Immerse yourself in good music, top wine, and great vibes at the family-friendly Huichica Music Festival. Bring a blanket, grab a glass, and chill out to a lineup of bands at Gundlach Bundschu Winery's amphitheater, or sway to the music inside the Old Redwood Barn.

SAN FRANCISCO, CALIFORNIA

60 Investigate some classic murals

In the mid-1980s, murals started appearing in San Francisco's bohemian Mission District. Gracing the walls of Balmy Alley, they reflected political movements in Central and South America. They now loom over the sidewalks on every street—huge, colorful scenes of every description celebrating the varied cultures of this corner of town.

SAN FRANCISCO, CALIFORNIA

61 Spend the night in the slammer

The threat of a night in Alcatraz used to send a shiver down the spine of hardened criminals. It's now a popular tourist attraction, and it's possible to sleep in a cell—although only 600 people get the chance per year—thanks to the charity Friends of the Golden Gate. Spots are secured by lottery. If you get picked, prepare to bunk up on a small bed in spooky conditions.

56 Touring the Newton B. Drury Scenic Parkway

62 See the famous "Painted Ladies"

The Painted Ladies of San Francisco aren't people but houses. It's a term that refers to Victorian and Edwardian properties painted with three or more colors that show off their architectural details. A few of them line up along Postcard Row at Hayes and Steiner Streets, the high-rises in the background providing photogenic contrast.

63 Wind up (or down) Lombard Street

Beautiful to look at, although fiendish to drive with its tight, snaking bends, Lombard Street is one of the most cinematic streets in the United States. You'll have time to see and smell its fabulous flower beds when in season, as the street's eight hairpins restrict drivers to a 5-mph (8-kph) speed limit.

64 Hitch a ride on a cable car

The cable cars trundling up the steep hills of San Francisco are an enduring and iconic sight. At their peak, there were twenty-three cable car lines in the city, but many were destroyed by the huge earthquake of 1906. Today, just three routes remain. They run through many popular spots for visitors, including Fisherman's Wharf, Nob Hill, and Ghirardelli Square, offering fabulous views over the bay—and bucketloads of nostalgia—as you travel.

65 See the sights of the 49-mi drive

In 1939, San Francisco hosted the Golden Gate International Exposition. The festival showcased, among other things, the city's two new bridges: the San Francisco–Oakland Bay Bridge and the Golden Gate Bridge. A driving route was devised to show off the city's attractions. Its 49 mi (79 km) take in City Hall, the Palace of Fine Arts, Grace Cathedral, Fisherman's Wharf, and a host of celebrated local sights. It ends on Treasure Island, which was built for the exposition.

66 Eat your way around Chinatown

San Francisco's Chinatown is the oldest in North America, dating back to 1848. Some 15,000 residents live within two dozen square blocks, and the neighborhood is densely packed with restaurants. The origins of American Chinese cuisine are here, and it's fun to hop between eateries trying dozens of classic dishes.

67 Cycle over the Golden Gate Bridge

A perfect day: Rent a bike at Fisherman's Wharf, pedal along the handsome shore and across the iconic bridge, savoring the views of the bay. On the other side, Sausalito is a picturesque, arty enclave where you can grab some lunch—and the boat ride back is a real pleasure, too.

THE STREETS OF SAN FRANCISCO

Cable car on California Street

Painted Ladies

Lombard Street

CARMEL-BY-THE-SEA, CALIFORNIA

68 Spend the day in California's quaintest village

Covering one square mile, Carmel-by-the-Sea is a laid-back, picturesque village that pops out of the forest and overlooks the sea. In the early twentieth century it was a popular spot for writers and artists, and in 1910, the *San Francisco Call* reported that 60 percent of its houses had been built by people connected to the arts. A walking tour takes in these storybook-style homes, often constructed from local stone or recycled bricks. Don't miss Tor House, built by poet and writer Robinson Jeffers, with the help of a local stonemason.

MONTEREY, CALIFORNIA

69 Go deep at Monterey Bay Aquarium

Experience the combination of an unrivaled Pacific Coast location and incredible exhibits—including great whites, sea otters, bluefin and yellow tuna, stingrays, and penguins—that make this one of the most visited and fun attractions in the United States. Exhibits about its former Cannery Row location are fascinating, too.

BIG SUR, CALIFORNIA

70 Retreat from it all at the Esalen Institute

Steeped in the countercultural ethos of the 1960s, the Esalen Institute offers spiritual retreats, workshops, and digital detoxes with a side order of Californian bohemianism. Fed by a hot spring, its famous thermal baths sit on a ledge above the North Pacific, overlooking the dramatic coastline.

70 Esalen Institute

BIG SUR, CALIFORNIA
71 Explore the Pacific Coast Highway

Hugging the coastline between San Francisco and San Diego, this is quite possibly one of the world's best road trips. At every moment the highway offers epic views of mountains or sea, and stop-offs ranging from surfing beaches to forests of giant redwoods. It can be driven in ten hours—or made to last for an unforgettable ten days.

SAN SIMEON, CALIFORNIA
72 See Hearst's "Enchanted Hill"

William Randolph Hearst was the founder of Hearst Communications and the man behind Hearst Castle, which nestles in the hills above San Simeon. It was architect Julia Morgan who helped Hearst realize his life's ambition to re-create the castles he'd visited in Europe as a child—as a place to house his art collection.

YOSEMITE NATIONAL PARK, CALIFORNIA
73 Conquer a dome

Yosemite's Half Dome is one of the world's most iconic rock formations. Celebrated in the beautiful photos of Ansel Adams, it is majestic always, but spectacular at sunset. The 8-mi (13-km) hike from the valley floor to its summit is steep but worth it, and climbing the dome's near-vertical face is every rock climber's dream.

YOSEMITE NATIONAL PARK, CALIFORNIA

74 Witness a waterfall transformed into a wall of fire

Among the many spectacular waterfalls in Yosemite National Park is the seasonal Horsetail Fall, which appears on the east side of El Capitan as the snow melts. Some years, when there's been just the right amount of snow and it melts at just the right time of the month and the skies are perfectly clear, nature conspires to turn the cascade of icy water into a seeming cascade of fire. The phenomenon is caused by February's setting sun catching the falls at just the right angle, and it only happens for a few days each year.

YOSEMITE NATIONAL PARK, CALIFORNIA

75 Tick America's smallest bear off your list

Black bears are North America's smallest and most common bear—yet no less appealing for that. In Yosemite there are only black bears, and despite their name, many of them have brown coats.

YOSEMITE NATIONAL PARK, CALIFORNIA

76 Hear the roar of some mighty falls

Yosemite has some of the country's oldest hiking trails. The Yosemite Falls Trail was built between 1873 and 1877, and is a strenuous 7-mi (11-km) hike up 2,700 ft (823 m) of elevation. Determination is rewarded with spectacular views, and hikers can cool down in the mists that rise off the falls. You can also take the easy route and, from ground level, admire the two tiers that rise up 2,425 ft (739 m), with the torrents falling into the Merced River.

JAMESTOWN, CALIFORNIA

77 Have a go at panning for gold

Try your hand at a simple process that's been used since Roman days and that prompted the famous Gold Rush of the mid-nineteenth century. At places like Jamestown, gold-panning prospectors can still use a basic pan and experience the thrill of potentially striking it rich.

71 Big Sur's Pacific Coast Highway

80 Setting up camp in Lone Pine

ANCIENT BRISTLECONE PINE
FOREST, CALIFORNIA
78 Walk among the world's oldest trees

The ancient bristlecone pine trees in California's White Mountains are the oldest trees on Earth— so old that their gnarled trunks appear to hold the wisdom of the ages (the dense wood twisting around on itself is a defense mechanism against insects and disease). There are two groves— Schulman and Patriarch, which are at their most surreal in early morning light.

SEQUOIA NATIONAL PARK,
CALIFORNIA
79 Be awestruck by a mighty redwood

Nothing is quite as humbling as walking among the giant redwoods and sequoias of Sequoia National Park. In this giant forest there are more than 8,000 of these ancient trees, whose trunks stretch hundreds of feet into the sky. The largest tree on Earth (by volume) can be found here, too—General Sherman, which is more than 2,000 years old.

LONE PINE, CALIFORNIA
80 Climb the highest peak in the Lower 48

To stand at the highest point in the United States, you'd have to head to Alaska, but in California, you can stand at the peak of the contiguous United States (or the Lower 48 states) on the summit of Mt. Whitney. Hikers favor the Mt. Whitney Trail, which can be done in a day, but most people pack a tent and take two days. Don't forget to bear-proof your supplies; bears and marmots live in these hills.

82 Geometric salt flats at Badwater Basin

DEATH VALLEY NATIONAL PARK, CALIFORNIA
81 Find yourself in an unexpected sea of wildflowers

Death Valley got its name from gold prospectors crossing this desolate area on their way to seek their fortunes in California. Ironically, the valley floor is very far from dead. The soils contain millions of wildflower seeds and each spring, some will erupt into bloom—only for a short time; the seeds know that life is harsh and more easily survived underground than above. Every ten years or so, conditions conspire for millions of the seeds to erupt at once, leading to a superbloom that covers the desert floor. Reds, yellows, pinks, and whites carpet the hillsides in one of nature's most life-affirming spectacles.

DEATH VALLEY NATIONAL PARK, CALIFORNIA
82 Brave the surreal salt flats of Badwater Basin

At the southern end of Death Valley is the lowest point of the United States—Badwater Basin, 282 ft (86 m) below sea level. The rainwater that falls on the surrounding mountains filters through mineral-rich rocks and comes to rest here in temporary lakes. These slowly evaporate in the heat, leaving behind crystallized minerals. During thousands of years of this process, minerals have built up on the desert floor, creating 200 sq mi (518 sq km) of salt flats. The geometric shapes shimmer in the sunshine, creating an otherworldly white landscape. There's a simple mile-long hike out to the flats, so plan your arrival for sunset for epic memories.

87 Sunset on a Malibu beach

PAINTED HILLS, DEATH VALLEY NATIONAL PARK, CALIFORNIA
83 Color yourself surprised at rainbows within the rocks

Much of the natural splendor in Death Valley National Park is stark and brutal. However, there are more conventional shows of beauty at certain points among the rocks. A loop off Furnace Creek brings you to Artists Palette, where turquoise, red, yellow, and purple pigmentations shine from the slopes. Head to Zabriskie Point for another rock-based rainbow effect.

CARRIZO PLAIN, CALIFORNIA
84 Feel brave tracking a giant kangaroo rat

You don't have to be all that brave! Despite its name, the giant kangaroo rat is one of the sweeter-looking rodents. It's only 6 in (15 cm) long and jumps around on its hind legs.

SOLVANG, CALIFORNIA
85 Enjoy a Danish Day

Solvang was founded by Danish immigrants in 1911 so that they could embrace the religion and education of their homeland. By 1947 the idea to re-create a Danish village really took off, with the addition of windmills and a copy of the *Little Mermaid* statue. Head here for California's best Danish pastries and lots of fun on Danish Days.

SANTA BARBARA, CALIFORNIA
86 Soar over the Pacific

Who doesn't fancy flying like a bird? Try the peace of a glider, its huge wingspan holding you gently aloft, thousands of feet above the California coast. Spiral your way up a thermal to gain height as you glide above the landscape, taking in the coast below, the vineyards, the lakes, and even Michael Jackson's Neverland Ranch.

MALIBU, CALIFORNIA
87 Choose your favorite Malibu beach

Malibu has around three dozen beaches. Some, such as Surfrider Beach, are named for popular activities, though water sports are available at many. There are also lesser-known public beaches, hidden by rocky outcrops, such as Lechuza and El Matador beaches, and hugely popular, wide sandy beaches like Zuma.

83 Shifting colors in the Painted Hills

88 Santa Monica Pier's Pacific Park

89 Hollywood Walk of Fame

SANTA MONICA, CALIFORNIA
88 Submit to pier pressure

The West Coast landmark of Santa Monica Pier is over a century old and was completed as the first concrete pier in the region in 1909. Its reputation as the best fishing spot in Santa Monica contributed to its initial popularity and you still find people fishing there today. The pier is immediately recognizable thanks to the looming Pacific Park Ferris wheel, as well as the West Coaster—both part of the Pacific Park amusement park. Among other unmissable entertainment options are Playland Arcade, Trapeze School Los Angeles, and the famous historic carousel.

LOS ANGELES, CALIFORNIA
89 Tread the Hollywood stars

You're nobody in Hollywood until you've got a star, and any wannabe actor, singer, or musician who moves to the city must walk among more than 2,500 five-pointed stars along the Hollywood Walk of Fame and fantasize. Located along fifteen blocks of Hollywood Boulevard and Vine Street, it's a great place to promenade, spotting favorite names from movies, TV, music, radio, and theater. It began as a collection of eight stars in 1956, and twenty stars are added every year, making it an ever-expanding attraction that celebrates LA as a world-famous culture hub.

LOS ANGELES, CALIFORNIA

90 Take in a concert at the Hollywood Bowl

Set in a natural amphitheater in the Hollywood Hills, the Hollywood Bowl is an outdoor concert venue that exudes style. It began life in the 1920s with a few benches in front of a simple stage and is now an 18,000-seater auditorium under the stars, with wooden benches in front of an iconic elliptical stage. Don't just go for the show: Make a night of it and pack a picnic to enjoy beforehand, surrounded by the nature of the hills in one of the Bowl's many picnic areas. Don't forget to look up and enjoy the stars in the sky as well as those on the stage.

LOS ANGELES, CALIFORNIA

91 Brush up on modern art at the Broad

The Broad opened in 2015, its honeycomb exterior complementing the modernist architecture of downtown LA. Its 2,000 exhibits are a who's who of modern art, with works by Andy Warhol, Cindy Sherman, and Roy Lichtenstein. Memorable installations include Yayoi Kusama's *Infinity Mirrored Room* and a nine-screen video installation by Ragnar Kjartansson.

LOS ANGELES, CALIFORNIA

92 Trek to the stars and beyond!

The nine letters of the Hollywood sign are among the most recognizable in the world. They were originally erected as a temporary advertisement for a local real-estate company, but were left up due to popular demand. Visitors can join a tour, drive, or even hike to the sign from the Bronson Canyon entrance to Griffith Park, or from Griffith Observatory. It's an A-list feeling, looking out over the affluent Hollywood Hills.

96 Infinity pool at Laguna Beach

LOS ANGELES, CALIFORNIA

93 Join a studio audience and watch a TV show taping

Most visitors to Los Angeles want to experience at least a slice of entertainment-industry glamour, but unless you're well connected or happen to spot a movie star over lunch, it's mostly at a distance. Hundreds of TV shows are filmed here, though, and many of them require live studio audiences. Most tapings take place in Burbank and each show has its own process for free tickets; the best plan is to apply via their websites as far in advance as possible.

LOS ANGELES, CALIFORNIA

94 Take in a cinematic view

After the Hollywood sign, the unlikely landmark of the Griffith Observatory, looking out over LA, has become one of the city's most iconic sites. Built in 1935, the observatory has a publicly accessible telescope, and some 7 million people have peered through the lens. The building has also been featured in several well-known movies, and location sequences in the James Dean movie *Rebel Without a Cause* (1955) cemented its fame. The Planetarium and its show (which runs eight to ten times daily) is also a much-loved attraction.

PALM SPRINGS, CALIFORNIA

95 Experience 360-degree scenery on a tramway

There are many aerial tramways in the world, and their leisurely pace always provides an ideal way to experience the landscape. The Palm Springs Aerial Tramway has a big difference, though—it's the largest rotating tramway in the world. Take in the natural splendor as you travel 2.5 mi (4 km) along the cliffs of Chino Canyon, on a ten-minute ride to the wilderness of Mt. San Jacinto State Park.

LAGUNA BEACH, CALIFORNIA

96 Seek refuge at the Pearl Laguna

This calm well-being retreat focuses on yoga and nature. You'll find it nestled among the trees in Laguna Canyon, just minutes from the idyllic Laguna Beach.

SAN DIEGO, CALIFORNIA

98 Go around the wildlife world in one day

Despite the amazing documentaries available, nothing quite matches seeing wild animals at leisure in their (almost) natural setting. San Diego Zoo Safari Park has 300 species, so a visit leaves you feeling like you've toured the world. From the Africa Tram, marvel at how tall a giraffe really is, while in the Walkabout Australia section, see just how a baby kangaroo lives in its mother's pocket. That leaves 298 . . .

SAN DIEGO, CALIFORNIA

97 Reach new heights at Balboa Park

This huge urban park contains seventeen museums, multiple gardens, and the renowned San Diego Zoo. Make sure to climb 125 steps to the top of the California Tower in the Museum of Us for some stunning views.

99 Hugging the coast on the *Pacific Surfliner*

SAN DIEGO, CALIFORNIA
99 Let the train take the strain

There aren't many views easier on the eye than the California coastline. Taking the *Pacific Surfliner* lets you sit back and enjoy said views between San Diego and San Luis Obispo. Sip a drink while you savor the cruise through Anaheim and Los Angeles—without the traffic of the freeway. Idyllic coastal scenery awaits as you pass Solana Beach, San Juan Capistrano, and Grover Beach. One tip: make sure you book the "surf" side when buying your ticket.

CAMPO, CALIFORNIA
100 Walk all the way from Mexico to Canada

The spellbinding Pacific Crest Trail winds through California, Oregon, and Washington State on a 2,650-mi (4,260-km) trek covering the length of the United States. Start at Campo on the Mexican border, and you'll traverse deserts, forests, mountain ranges, canyons, glacial lakes, and volcanoes on this magnificent journey.

CLEARWATER NATIONAL
FOREST, IDAHO
101 Strip off in nature

Plunging into a natural hot
spring is one of life's true joys.
The Jerry Johnson springs in
Idaho's Clearwater National
Forest are an easy mile-long walk
from the Northwest Passage
Scenic Byway (itself, a beautiful
drive). There are three springs—
one (usually the hottest, but
submerged until water levels drop
in late summer) feeds a pool at
the foot of a waterfall, another
feeds several linked pools just
beyond the waterfall, and the
third spring is in a peaceful
meadow, offering views through
the pines up to the mountains.

SAWTOOTH NATIONAL
RECREATION AREA, IDAHO
102 Seek solitude in a wilderness

With almost 740,000 ac
(300,000 ha) to explore, there's
space enough here to choose
your own adventure and get fully
off-grid. There are over 700 mi
(1,100 km) of hiking trails,
forty peaks rising over 10,000 ft
(3,050 m), and more than 300
high-elevation alpine lakes.
You'll have plenty of space to
make memories, which might
include paddleboarding on
Redfish Lake against the
backdrop of picture-perfect
mountains or taking a soak
in the Sunbeam Hot Springs.

BOISE, IDAHO
103 Appreciate a Rockies sunset

Table Rock might not look
far in terms of distance, and the
most popular trail is a moderate
3.7-mi (6-km) loop. However,
the incline to the summit of
this striking granite dome is a
little more demanding, with an
elevation gain of 746 ft (227 m),
and you'll need to look out for
rattlesnakes. There's a huge
white cross to say you've
arrived—illuminated at night,
it can be seen from most parts
of Boise. Time it right and
you'll be rewarded with an
evocative sunset and views
over the Rockies.

103 Table Rock's cross at sunset

SUN VALLEY, IDAHO

104 Visit America's first ever ski resort

Sun Valley was transformed from a sleepy mining village into
a world-class resort in 1936, when Union Pacific Railroad
chairman Averell Harriman hired an Austrian count to find
the perfect American valley for the purpose. It had to be
near railroad tracks, but remote enough not to be overrun by
weekend skiers. The count found Sun Valley. Since it opened,
its beautiful setting, well-designed lodges, and the world's
first chairlifts have attracted celebrities from Marilyn Monroe
to Ernest Hemingway.

CRATERS OF THE MOON NATIONAL
MONUMENT AND PRESERVE, IDAHO
105 Listen for the sounds of love

When it comes to the mating season, the sage grouse knows how to stage a spectacular show—one that you can witness at Idaho's Craters of the Moon national preserve. Males strut around their leks—the breeding grounds that generations return to every year—fanning their tail feathers and puffing out two neck sacs that then deflate with whooshing air, pops, and whistles.

CRATERS OF THE MOON NATIONAL
MONUMENT AND PRESERVE, IDAHO
106 Gaze into an abyss from a volcanic eruption

Volcanic rock formations are usually associated with Iceland or tropical islands in the South Pacific, but volcanoes formed parts of America, too. In this preserve there are almost 400 sq mi (1,000 sq km) of otherworldly lava fields. These are dramatic enough, but most people come to see the King's Bowl crater and Great Rift, the deepest rift in the Earth's crust anywhere on the planet.

BLACKFOOT, IDAHO
107 Discover the potato

Every place has something that makes it special. For Idaho, the combination of fertile soil, clean water and air, and the climate means a perfect environment for growing potatoes. These humble tubers are big business in this part of the world—so much so that there's a museum dedicated to all things potato. At the Idaho Potato Museum, brush up on potato history and agriculture, watch spud-focused short films, and see the world's largest collection of potato mashers and the world's biggest potato chip!

GLACIER NATIONAL PARK, MONTANA
108 Cycle the Going-to-the-Sun Road

A Native American legend has it that when Sour Spirit returned to the sun after coming down to teach the Blackfeet how to hunt, he left his image on a mountain as inspiration—hence the name of Going-to-the-Sun Mountain. It rises above the easternmost section of this amazing road through Glacier National Park. Covered in snow for much of the year, sections are open to bikes before cars, and it's a delight of hairpins, spectacular bridges, glacial lakes, and the unforgettable Logan Pass.

GLACIER NATIONAL PARK,
MONTANA
109 Paddleboard on a glacial lake

Carved by glaciers, the 10-mi
(16-km) long Lake McDonald is
the largest of this national park's
lakes. Explore by paddleboard
for peace and amazing views.
In summer, you might spot
the colors of the park's Garden
Wall's wildflowers shimmering
in the distance, before jumping
in for a refreshing swim.

JOCKO VALLEY, MONTANA
110 Find enlightenment with a thousand Buddhas

Nestled in a remote valley,
the Garden of One Thousand
Buddhas was created to counter
global negativity. The park
contains 1,000 hand-cast
Buddha statues set out in a
design based on the eight-spoked
dharma wheel, symbolizing the
awakening of wisdom. Visitors
of all faiths are welcome.

MISSOULA, MONTANA
111 See where a river runs through it

One of the most stunning movies
about life in Montana is 1992's
A River Runs Through It, directed
by Robert Redford. It's based on
the semiautobiographical novel
by Norman Maclean, who grew
up in Missoula, and is a love
letter to the local landscape,
family bonds, and the joy of
fishing. Visit to feel the power
of the landscape for yourself.

110 Garden of One
Thousand Buddhas

BUTTE, MONTANA

112 Eat noodles at the country's longest-running Chinese restaurant

The gold mining rush of the late nineteenth century brought a diverse population to Montana, including a newly arrived Chinese population. Chinese restaurants began to spring up quickly, and one such place has managed to stay open ever since. Pekin Noodle Parlor was established in 1909, and moved to its current location in 1911, making it the oldest known continuously operating Chinese restaurant in the United States. Slide into one of the distinctive orange booths and order up a plate of history.

BOZEMAN, MONTANA

113 Get your nerd on at the American Computer and Robotics Museum

Computers may seem a thoroughly modern phenomenon, but the exhibits at this museum take visitors on a journey that goes back some 4,000 years. It turns out that the Babylonians practiced a form of text messaging, and that early weaving looms provided a blueprint for what became punched memory cards for early software packages. Exhibits include a reconstruction of an ancient Greek astronomy computer, the first handheld calculator, and the first Apple home computers.

CROW AGENCY, MONTANA

114 Stand where Custer took his last stand

The event goes by a few names— the Battle of the Little Bighorn, Battle of the Greasy Grass, and Custer's Last Stand. It was on the site of the Little Bighorn Battlefield National Monument that the Lakota Sioux and Cheyenne warriors inflicted a great defeat on the 7th Cavalry Regiment of the US Army. The infamous "last stand" only lasted a couple of hours according to the last living witnesses, such was the overwhelming firepower. An obelisk now marks the spot.

VARIOUS SITES IN MONTANA

115 Work up some cabin fever in a rural retreat

In the 1920s and 1930s, the Forest Service in Montana built a couple of hundred cabins as field headquarters for rangers working on trails, fires, and forestry projects. Some have been retained for their original use, but many can be rented for a real back-to-basics woodland stay. The cabins are typically basic log structures, with beds, a stove, and an outhouse, and while they're not in the "glamping" arena, they provide shelter and feed into a pioneering spirit that suits the adventurous.

YELLOWSTONE NATIONAL PARK

116 Come on in—the water's perfect

If you've spent a hard day hiking in Yellowstone National Park, you can probably think of nothing better than rolling up to a hotel and soaking in a luxurious hot tub. If you're willing to compromise on the luxury element just a little, though, you can enjoy soothing warm waters right here in nature. Boiling River, just 3 mi (5 km) from the park's North Entrance, is where a large hot spring enters the Gardner River and the hot and cool waters mix into a bathlike temperature.

WILDLIFE SIGHTINGS IN YELLOWSTONE NATIONAL PARK

Bison

Hunting ospreys

Grizzly bear

118 Yellowstone gray wolves

YELLOWSTONE NATIONAL PARK

117 Beware of grizzlies

The head and shoulders of a grizzly emerging from the meadows will make you catch your breath. For a large and dangerous carnivore, grizzlies are very endearing, with their lolling stride, curious faces, and nurturing ways with their young. The grizzly is a subspecies of brown bear, but because the hair on its back and shoulders is often tipped with white, it looks grizzled, and the name has stuck. As with most nature spotting, there's no guarantee of seeing one, but if you do, never approach it—just back away slowly without running. Always be careful around these wild, dangerous animals.

YELLOWSTONE NATIONAL PARK

118 Learn about evolution at the world's first national park

Yellowstone National Park is home to many animals, but most remarkable has been the successful reintroduction of predators. Gray wolves and cougars were wiped out by early settlers, resulting in large numbers of elk but few other species. In 1995 the gray wolf was reintroduced; it hunted the elk, which made the elk move around more. As areas were less continuously grazed, there was more plant growth, which led to more birdlife and beavers—then otters, fish, and amphibians. The wolves also hunted coyotes, leading to more mice and rabbits, which then attracted hawks, weasels, foxes, and badgers. Yellowstone offers a glimpse into the wonders of nature before people tried to manage it.

YELLOWSTONE NATIONAL PARK
119 Marvel at steaming geysers

Hundreds of thousands of years ago, the land that most of Yellowstone National Park sits on was inside the crater of a volcano. Although there are no longer volcanic eruptions, there is still plenty of thermal activity bubbling up to the surface in the form of geysers—hot springs heated by underground rocks until pressure causes them to explode in fountains of water or steam. The most famous is Old Faithful, which erupts up to 180 ft (55 m) into the sky every half hour to two hours.

YELLOWSTONE NATIONAL PARK
120 Awaken your artistic urges

The entire Yellowstone experience is a bucket-list item, but once there, some vistas are more alluring than others. Artist Point Trail leads to the eponymous observation spot, one that is known as a "marquee" overlook—a standout example among the many world-class panoramas on offer within the park. A deep V-shape of orange rocks merge to frame a powerful waterfall, and it's a sight that cries out to be appreciated and at least photographed, if not painted.

YELLOWSTONE NATIONAL PARK
121 Be dazzled by a rainbow-hued spring

With its rings of green, yellow, and orange leaking into the landscape around a circle of deep blue, Yellowstone's huge Grand Prismatic Spring looks as much like an artist's creation as it does a natural hot spring. The colors around the edge are caused by heat-loving bacteria that live in the water—different colors for different heat levels, which is why as the water gets shallower and cooler, the colors change. The rich blue center is due to depth— the spring could swallow a ten-story building.

GRAND TETON NATIONAL PARK, WYOMING
122 Pay homage to Mormon homesteaders

In the late nineteenth century, as their population expanded, Mormon settlers from Idaho arrived in what is now the Grand Teton National Park. Working together by hand and with teams of horses, they created an irrigation system of levees and dikes, some of which remain today. There were once twenty-seven homesteads in Mormon Row, but now just a few remain, their wooden structures among the long prairie grass creating an evocative image of a bygone era.

122 Pioneer home in Mormon Row

124 *Wapiti Trail*, National Museum of Wildlife Art

126 Jackson Hole's Big Red

JACKSON HOLE, WYOMING
123 Don't spring for a hotel

Jump into a natural spring, with the Rockies as your backdrop. There are plenty of high-end hotels here, and many doubtless have mountain views and hot tubs, but it's way more exciting (and economical) to treat yourself to a natural experience. Around 30 mi (48 km) south of Jackson, the Granite Hot Springs are a collection of geothermally heated pools that have drawn visitors since the 1930s. Surrounded by the Bridger-Teton National Forest and the picturesque Rockies, it beats a penthouse suite any day.

JACKSON HOLE, WYOMING
124 See an art museum set in a hillside

A rustic cabin in the quiet Jackson Hole countryside isn't the first place you'd look for a national museum, but the National Museum of Wildlife Art isn't just any museum. The exterior looks like an ancient fortification emerging from the rock itself. Opened in 1994, it has amassed 5,000 pieces of wildlife art, from Native American bird stones that are 2,500 years old, to works by masters such as Georgia O'Keeffe and Andy Warhol. Fourteen galleries of majestic animal artworks await.

JACKSON HOLE, WYOMING
125 Get fly at Snake River

Ocean fishing can be fun and exciting, zipping along on the seas and chasing down the fastest fish. Although more sedate and peaceful, fly-fishing can also be hugely rewarding and involves a different set of skills. Snake River in Jackson Hole is one of the country's premier spots to try your hand, and several local companies offer fully accompanied sessions. Let an expert show you how to fix your lure and bait, and cast off against the backdrop of some of the region's most stunning mountain scenery.

128 Devils Tower National Monument

JACKSON HOLE, WYOMING
126 Take the easy way up a mountain

In just nine minutes, Jackson Hole Aerial Tram—or Big Red, as it's fondly known—will take you from Teton Village up 4,139 vertical ft (1,262 m) to the top of Rendezvous Mountain. From the peak, you can enjoy fabulous 360-degree views over the Rockies and, depending on the season, take your pick of hiking routes back down, or tackle every skier's or boarder's favorite challenge, the Rendezvous Bowl. Before you leave the peak, head to Corbet's Cabin for its world-famous waffles.

CODY, WYOMING
127 Get to know the man behind a legend

At the Buffalo Bill Center of the West, five museums bring the Wild West back to life. Born William Cody, Buffalo Bill earned his nickname from supplying buffalo meat to workers on the Kansas Pacific Railway. Legend has it that in eighteen months, he shot 4,282 buffalo. His fame comes from the show he created, *Buffalo Bill's Wild West*, a circuslike attraction that toured the United States and Europe with tales of cowboy and cowgirl sharpshooting adventures and skirmishes with Native Americans.

CROOK COUNTY, WYOMING
128 Discover the devil is in the detail

Jutting out of the prairies that surround Wyoming's Black Hills, Devils Tower is a dramatic rock formation that has long been considered sacred by Northern Plains Indigenous people. Thousands of parallel cracks give the tower—technically a butte—a ridged appearance, and tourists and expert climbers alike are drawn to the strange patterns. Such is the tower's importance and beauty that it was made the first US national monument on September 24, 1906, by President Theodore Roosevelt.

CHEYENNE, WYOMING
129 Saddle up for the world's largest outdoor rodeo

Since 1897, Cheyenne has celebrated its Old West roots with a festival that is now a multiday event: Cheyenne Frontier Days. Every July, thousands make the pilgrimage, and one of the main draws is the Professional Rodeo Cowboys Association rodeo. Nine daily performances include bull, saddle, and bareback bronco competitions, with all manner of entertainment between rounds.

MESA VERDE NATIONAL PARK, COLORADO
130 Sense the magic of rock art

There is nothing like ancient rock art to help you feel the connection between a land and the people who lived on it thousands of years ago. In this national park there are geometric designs carved into rocks. Because shadows fall across them in a specific way at the winter solstice, archaeologists believe that the Ancestral Pueblo people who lived here used the designs to follow the seasons and plan their crops. Who needs iCalendar?

NEAR CORTEZ, COLORADO
131 Stand in four US states at the same time

Four Corners Monument—where Utah, Colorado, New Mexico, and Arizona meet—is the only place in the United States where you can stand in four states at the same time. Photographs of straddling, on-all-fours poses on the monument are practically compulsory, so get snapping.

ASPEN, COLORADO
132 Play golf on a mountaintop

You don't need an excuse to ride the Silver Queen Gondola to the top of Aspen Mountain—the experience and views are enough. But in summer, if you're looking for a good reason to take the gondola up to the 11,212-ft (3,417-m) summit, treat yourself to a round of disc golf at the top. The game originated in Canada in the 1900s and is essentially golf, but instead of hitting a ball into a hole in as few strokes as possible, the aim is to throw a disc into a basket. There's a full eighteen-hole course on Aspen Mountain.

DENVER, COLORADO
133 Feel the thrill of chasing a tornado

The usual inclination when a storm is coming is to head inside, but if you're of a daring disposition, you can head in the other direction and experience one firsthand. Storm chasing—going after tornadoes and hurricanes—can be thrilling but dangerous, so it's not recommended without an experienced and responsible guide in a suitable vehicle. Tours run from Denver into "Tornado Alley." Each storm is different and poses a unique set of thrills and risks—but emerge unscathed, and you'll have a new understanding of nature's power.

133 Tempest Tours Storm Chasing Expeditions

DENVER, COLORADO
134 Take afternoon tea at the Brown

The gorgeous Italian Renaissance atrium is the heart of Denver's historic and celebrated Brown Palace Hotel, and it's also considered the perfect setting for afternoon tea. While enjoying the traditional refreshments, accompanied by the gentle sound of a harp playing in the background, you can admire the way the stained-glass ceiling—eight stories above you—drapes its shimmery light over the Florentine arches and gold-filigreed balcony panels.

DENVER, COLORADO
135 Make tracks for a vintage rail station

Union Station is the main transportation hub for the Mile High City, and there's been a station here since 1881. The building is a fine example of Romanesque Revival architecture; the facade alone is worth seeing. The entire site was renovated in 2013, and now offers a wide range of dining and shopping options as well as a farmers' market. For the full experience, stay at the Crawford Hotel, located in the building's upper levels.

DENVER, COLORADO
136 Redefine your view of a rock concert

Few venues are as rock and roll as Red Rocks Amphitheatre outside Denver. Carved into a natural amphitheater between two huge rocks, the site seats 9,500 people, and its perfect acoustics have echoed to the sounds of everyone from Diana Ross to the Beatles to Mumford & Sons, whose video for "I Will Wait" was recorded here. The venue also hosts an Easter Sunrise Service every year—a spiritual service with songs, sermons, and views.

134 Taking tea at the Brown

135 Christmastime at Union Station

GOLDEN, COLORADO
137 Sip gold in Golden

Opened in 1873, the Coors Brewery is the world's largest single-site brewery. Book a self-paced tour and see the malting, brewing, and packaging processes, as well as enjoying samples along the way. At the end, view historic photos, beer cans and bottles, and other memorabilia. A gift store has all your T-shirt, glassware, and bottle-opener needs. The brewery encourages you to soak up Golden's outdoor spirit, with dozens of hiking, kayaking, and adventure opportunities nearby.

MAROON BELLS, COLORADO
138 Document a view through the seasons

The changing seasons offer a great meditation on nature and the circle of life, and by revisiting the same location every day, week, or month to document its changes through words, painting, or photography, the observer can learn a huge amount. An iconic spot always helps, and Maroon Bells is an ideal place for this exercise. With its much documented mountains reflected in Maroon Creek, it's certainly the most photographed spot in Colorado.

THROUGHOUT COLORADO
139 Make the world your oyster in the Rockies

Don't worry if you have an aversion to seafood—the oysters found here have never seen an ocean. The local delicacy known as Rocky Mountain oysters also go by the names of "cowboy caviar" and "Montana tendergroins," the latter hinting at their origins. For transparency, they're bull testicles that are skinned, coated in flour, and deep-fried. They're more delicious than they sound, so discard your preconceptions. Vegetarians get a pass.

136 Evening performance at Red Rocks Amphitheatre

VARIOUS SITES IN COLORADO

140 Book yourself into an authentic dude ranch

Thanks to the romanticism of the Old West, many visitors to regions like Colorado want an authentic cowboy experience. Luckily, it now takes less commitment than in the past, with a network of "dude ranches" available—working farms that allow guests to live a cowboy life for a while. Activities include cattle drives, outdoor cookouts, and horseback riding, plus they'll throw in the hats and accessories to keep things as authentic as possible.

BLACK ROCK DESERT, NEVADA

141 Enter the world of Burning Man

A crazy, bewildering, but never boring experience— tens of thousands descend on the desert, set up a temporary city dedicated to art and self-expression, then head off a week later without leaving a trace. The central theme of Burning Man is to selflessly give over one's talents for the enjoyment of all— sculpture, building, performance, and elaborately decorated cars are all central to the experience. Join in and witness the event's centerpiece: a ritual burning of a huge wooden man on Saturday.

LAKE TAHOE, NEVADA

142 Take a catamaran trip on an alpine lake

Traveling by wind power across Lake Tahoe is the best way to take in the scenery here. You don't have to know how to sail; a crew can look after that while you lie on the webbing and spot perfect coves or watch clouds drift by. In a spot with so much action to be had, in the form of hikes, skiing, and water sports, why not slow down and drift?

GOLDFIELD, NEVADA

143 Drive by a car forest

Formerly home to infamous lawmen Wyatt and Virgil Earp, Goldfield now hosts a postapocalyptic skyline of around forty upended vehicles: the International Car Forest of the Last Church. This artwork represents individuality and the renouncement of organized religion—equally, it's simply a vibrant stop along Highway 95's sea of brown desert.

AREA 51, NEVADA

144 Go alien hunting

There is no guarantee that a trip to the heartland of Earth's extraterrestrial activity will result in alien sightings, but it's certainly a unique experience. Enjoy Area 51 on a kitsch level—travel along Extraterrestrial Highway before grabbing an alien burger and a peek at the Black Mailbox of rancher Steve Medlin, the unofficial meeting point for UFO enthusiasts.

141 Burning Man festival

147 Las Vegas's Venetian Resort

146 Tim Burton exhibition at the Neon Museum

LAS VEGAS, NEVADA
145 Bet it all on black

You can't visit Vegas without trying your luck on the slots or taking a seat at a blackjack table—after all, it's what the town is known for—so step onto the Vegas Strip, where 4 mi (6 km) of casinos are waiting to part you from your money. You'll find casinos to suit every taste and a dazzling array of accommodation options.

LAS VEGAS, NEVADA
146 Wander among the old signs of Sin City

There's likely no bigger concentration of neon signs in the world than in Vegas. Many of its most famous examples were made by the Young Electric Sign Company, and their storage facility has developed into the Neon Museum, where old signs retire. Just beyond Fremont Street, where Las Vegas has its roots, you can wander among an outdoor display called the Neon Boneyard. Its 150 decommissioned signs relive the city's glory days.

LAS VEGAS, NEVADA
147 Travel the globe in a day

Vegas casinos have to really stand out to attract foot traffic, which has led to the most famous sights in the world springing up. Don't worry if a flight to Europe is too costly—many international landmarks have been faithfully re-created within a handy square mile. The Statue of Liberty, Eiffel Tower, Great Pyramids, and the canals of Venice are all accessible; you can even ride in a gondola as your guide sings opera. It might be the only cheating approved of in Vegas.

BLACK CANYON, NEVADA

148 Give a damn about mighty engineering

It took almost half a century of planning and construction, but in 1936, the United States completed one of the most enduringly loved engineering projects in history— Hoover Dam. Six and a half million tons of concrete may not sound enticing, but once you witness the scale of the project, it's hard not to get emotional. Take a guided tour or learn about its story via ample interpretive signs. Save time for the Mike O'Callaghan–Pat Tillman Memorial Bridge for the best views.

VALLEY OF FIRE STATE PARK, NEVADA

149 Celebrate scenery on fire

With its rich, red outcrops, it's not hard to see how the Valley of Fire State Park got its name. Just 50 mi (80 km) from Las Vegas, the park tells the story of what happens to soft rock over years of wind and rain. There are stunning waves of rock, banded in pink and red hues, and intriguingly shaped forms such as the Elephant Rock and the Beehives, as well as caves and arches. Stay for sunset to watch the scenery catch fire.

149 Valley of Fire State Park

SALT LAKE CITY, UTAH
150 Admire a temple (from the outside only)

Salt Lake Temple stands at the heart of Temple Square, an icon of the Church of Jesus Christ of Latter-day Saints. Wandering around its exterior (the interior is for devotees only), you sense the dedication of the pioneers who built this huge structure from local stone over forty years. Spot Mormon symbols in the stonework, including the All-Seeing Eye, the Big Dipper, and the Earth, Sun, and stars.

GREAT SALT LAKE, UTAH
151 Unwind on the *Spiral Jetty*

Spiral Jetty is a 1,500-ft (4,572-m) long sculpture created by Robert Smithson from natural materials. Take a stroll on the coil that juts out of the northeastern shore of the Great Salt Lake, although be warned—it's sometimes submerged, depending on water levels.

151 Robert Smithson's *Spiral Jetty*

PARK CITY, UTAH
152 Pick the next Tarantino

Every January, Park City buzzes with actors, directors, and paparazzi as the Sundance Film Festival comes to town. Run by Robert Redford's company and named after his character in *Butch Cassidy and the Sundance Kid*, this is America's largest independent film festival, seeking the best in that year's clutch of filmmakers. Be the first to spot new talent: The likes of Quentin Tarantino and Jim Jarmusch are both past winners.

154 Dining at the Solitude Mountain Resort

155 Ancient art in Nine Mile Canyon

SNOWBASIN, UTAH

153 Identify the calls of owls

Utah's aspen groves are a rich hunting ground for forest owls. Sit out at night and listen to their calls: a low-pitched *boop* for a flagellated owl, a staccato Morse code for the whiskered screech owl, a high-pitched *too-too-too* for the northern saw-whet owl, and a low-pitched, resonating *hoo* for the great gray owl.

SOLITUDE MOUNTAIN RESORT, UTAH

154 Dine out in the snow

Follow a guide on a snowshoe adventure through a moon- and lantern-lit forest to an intimate dining experience in a traditional Mongolian yurt.

CARBON COUNTY, UTAH

155 Cruise along a 40-mi art gallery

Nine Mile Canyon is a strange name for a canyon that's 40 mi (64 km) long, but even stranger are the artworks framing the road. The ancient Fremont people created hundreds of drawings between 400 and 1400 CE that are still visible. You'll see hunting scenes, bison, and what look like ancient astronauts!

ARCHES NATIONAL PARK, UTAH

156 Inspect God's stonemasonry

"God is a stonemason," they say around here, and walking beneath the majestic natural arches, spires, and pinnacles that have been hewn from the rock in this national park, it's hard not to believe they're right. You can hike or ride a mountain bike around the 73,000 ac (29,542 ha) of arches, and sunrise and sunset are especially magical times as radiance fills the sandstone crags and illuminates incredible horizons. There are 2,000 arches, the most famous being Landscape Arch—a 306-ft (93-m) whopper that must be seen to be believed.

COLORADO RIVER, UTAH

157 Have a whitewater ride on the Colorado

The sheer variety of whitewater rafting that the Colorado River is blessed with means that you can pick your thrill level, like skiers who choose between gentle Danish trails or death-defying black slopes. On the Colorado, you can bubble along on relatively placid waters or thunder down a spill-a-minute stretch of rampaging rapids—and most likely end up in the water at least once. With wonderful views along the way, it's also a great environment to chill out in once all the water cannoning has come to an end.

BRYCE CANYON NATIONAL PARK, UTAH

158 View the "hoodoo" that they do so well

There are some places on this planet that truly resemble something out of a science fiction movie. Luckily, some of these otherworldly experiences are possible in the continental United States. Hoodoos, for instance, are strange-looking rock pillars, typically between 5 and 150 ft (1.5–45 m) high, resembling natural totem poles. They're abundant in the northern section of Bryce Canyon National Park, with some examples that are ten-stories high and like nothing else you'll see in nature.

156 Sandstone formations of Arches National Park

157 Whitewater rafting on the Colorado River

159 Passing through the Narrows, Zion National Park

ZION NATIONAL PARK, UTAH
159 Navigate the Narrows at Zion

There are almost endless ways to experience the raw beauty of Zion National Park, and the compact gorge known as "the Narrows" is one of the most spectacular. Don some suitable footwear and wade upstream along the Virgin River from the Temple of Sinawava. You'll be rewarded with huge, rugged red walls that loom over you, each corner a new scene of geological wonder.

LAKE POWELL, UTAH
160 Steer a houseboat across Lake Powell

In the right light, Lake Powell can look like you're cruising on Mars. Rock formations jut out of the blue water that seeps its way into rugged canyon after rugged canyon. The lake is actually a reservoir, formed with the building of the Glen Canyon Dam. In addition to water sports and hiking, it also offers a popular line in houseboats— giving you the perfect way to see the lake and somewhere to stay.

PAGE, ARIZONA
161 Get loopy about the curves of another canyon

If you've consumed any media about the natural splendor of the Grand Canyon State, you'll probably have seen images of the famous Antelope Canyon. This awe-inspiring sandstone slot canyon attracts hikers and climbers from across the globe, thanks to its monumental, wavelike structure and the way that the amazing looped walls capture the sunlight. Guided tours are compulsory.

162 The Wave, Coyote Buttes

COYOTE BUTTES, ARIZONA
162 Ride "the Wave" in a red canyon

It's hard to believe that the sweeping red-rock formation of Paria Canyon ("the Wave") is naturally formed, such is the designed appearance of its undulating, surreal stripes. It's been carved out by a kind of wave-making machine, however, as first water, then wind, steadily altered the ancient Jurassic-era sandstone into the mind-blowing formations seen today. If you're lucky enough to get a permit, it's worth every second of the three-hour hike to get there. Go at midday when few shadows fall for the ultimate bucket-list photo shoot.

MONUMENT VALLEY, ARIZONA
163 Gallop a horse like a cowboy

If it's good enough for John Wayne, it's good enough to go on the cowboy fantasist's bucket list. Monument Valley is a western movie come to life; characterized by those vast sandstone buttes, its 2 sq mi (5 sq km) are as familiar to most moviegoers as Manhattan. Get on horseback with a tour guide—and optional ten-gallon hat—and it's frankly impossible not to have a private little cinematic moment.

GRAND CANYON, ARIZONA

164 Hike to the bottom of the Grand Canyon and back up again

The Grand Canyon is one of Earth's most impressive geological formations, hewn into shape over millennia by the Colorado River. The classic hike is the rim-to-the-river-and-back trip. A full descent starts from an elevation of around 10,000 ft (3,048 m), carefully winding down the trails. It can be bone jarring, but the solitude and wilderness make it worthwhile. And there are plenty of animals to spot, including bald eagles, beavers, coyotes, bobcats, tarantulas, six kinds of rattlesnakes, and even mountain lions. After staying overnight in the canyon, the return trip is far more demanding than the descent, so a hike should be carefully planned; more than 250 people are rescued annually!

GRAND CANYON, ARIZONA

165 Navigate the Grand Canyon by raft

Of all the ways to see the Grand Canyon, floating through on a river raft has to be one of the more unique. Trips take from three days to two weeks, depending on how far you go. By day you'll drift through towering rock formations, bracing yourself for the adrenaline hit as you run the rapids, stopping off for hikes into the side canyons and to swim in the peaceful waters. By night you'll sleep on sandy beaches, under the Milky Way, counting the shooting stars overhead. Truly an epic way to explore this epic location.

164 Skywalk view over the Grand Canyon

165 Canyon rafting

WILLIAMS, ARIZONA

166 Preserve a canyon by traveling in old-fashioned style

With something as beautiful and natural as the Grand Canyon, the last thing you want is a traffic jam around the rim and choking fumes at every viewpoint. The Grand Canyon Railway departs from Williams every morning, returning in the afternoon, and is estimated to keep 50,000 cars away per year. It's also a fabulous throwback in time with restored carriages—some with viewing domes—musicians playing Old West tunes, and cowboys to spot out of the wide windows.

SEDONA, ARIZONA

167 Find inspiration in Sedona

Sedona has long attracted spiritual seekers who believe that the area is full of vortices channeling Earth's energetic power, allowing you to tap into the frequencies of the universe. Considered North America's New Age capital, the town has more than its fair share of crystal stores, aura-reading psychics, and spiritual classes. The real beauty of the place, however, lies beyond town, where striking, rust-colored sandstone formations and soaring blue skies induce awe and inspire even the most skeptical.

PHOENIX, ARIZONA

168 See a botanical garden in the middle of a desert

The 140-ac (57-ha) Desert Botanical Garden in Phoenix celebrates the Arizona desert's natural beauty, from the dramatically towering cacti and brilliant wildflowers to hosts of strangely shaped succulents and unexpectedly lush trees.

PHOENIX, ARIZONA

169 Learn from the Heard

With twelve exhibition galleries, sculpture gardens, and a contemporary gallery, you're bound to find inspiration at the Heard Museum. It's been collecting, preserving, and presenting Native American stories since it opened in 1929. There are also opportunities to try out traditional activities, such as weaving or creating wearable art, and to watch music and dance performances in the museum's peaceful grounds.

OUTSIDE PHOENIX, ARIZONA

170 Soak up a meteor shower

Arizona's wide-open skies and lack of light pollution make it the perfect spot to see meteors disintegrate as they enter the atmosphere. Head there to see the annual Geminids shower—caused by the Apollo asteroid 3200 Phaethon—which occurs in December.

SAGUARO NATIONAL PARK, ARIZONA

171 Hunt for a gila monster

The gila monster is a lizard, measuring 2 ft (0.6 m) long and the largest native to the United States. It has dramatic orange-and-black colorings, but is tricky to spot since it spends almost all of its time in an underground burrow and can go for months between meals.

168 Giant succulents at the Desert Botanical Garden

APACHE COUNTY, ARIZONA

172 Listen to the sound of song in the wilderness

One of the most popular places to visit in the Navajo Nation is the Canyon de Chelly National Monument. Its numerous Native American resident families believe the distinctive Spider Rock is home to the Spider Grandmother. To really feel their history and cultural tradition, enjoy the panorama of this massive bowl to the backdrop of a Navajo singer and drummer striking up a haunting song about their homeland and its traditions.

TAOS, NEW MEXICO

173 See a 1,000-year-old dwelling

There aren't many 1,000-year-old structures in the United States, but the adobe dwellings in and around Taos in New Mexico date back just that long. This village (just outside modern Taos) is a living historic community made up of a Native American tribe of Puebloan people. Take a guided tour to fully experience the architectural and cultural wonders of a place that's remained largely unchanged since well before European settlement of the region.

172 Dramatic Apache County

174 Eske's Brewpub beer garden

176 Artworks on Canyon Road

TAOS, NEW MEXICO

174 Try a Taos Green Chile Beer

Eske's Brewpub, located in the artsy, meditation retreat town of Taos, makes a green chile–laced beer with freshly roasted Sandia chiles added to a blonde ale base beer. The roasty, vegetal, and spicy flavors come through, though they're restrained and balanced. It's a unique beer that reflects the local flavors of this scenic region.

SANTA FE, NEW MEXICO

175 Discover a totally different city

Known as the "City Different," Santa Fe is rich in history, with Hispanic, Anglo, and Native American influences apparent in the architecture, food, and art. The city is a center for arts, where you can wander along centuries-old, shady lanes to the plaza, to peruse silver and turquoise designs of Native American jewelers.

SANTA FE, NEW MEXICO

176 Attend an art class in Santa Fe

Santa Fe is one of the world's great art cities. It has more than 250 galleries—many centered around Canyon Road, east of Santa Fe Plaza—and a rolling program of festivals, including Seeds Santa Fe, which celebrates Indigenous art and culture every August. It's a fabulous place to embrace your inner artist and take some classes.

COLUMBUS, NEW MEXICO

177 Trek the Continental Divide trail

Do you believe that dehydration, lightning, falls, avalanches, hypothermia, bears, mountain lions, and blisters are all merely obstacles to be overcome? Then the Continental Trail might just be the trek to top your bucket list. An ambitious 3,100-mi (4,989-km) mission running from Canada to Mexico, this walk takes around six months to complete.

ROSWELL, NEW MEXICO

178 The truth may be out there, or it may be out here

Do you believe we're all alone in the universe or are you convinced we're being visited by alien races? If you're of the latter persuasion, or just curious, then Roswell should be on your radar. It was a nondescript town until 1947, when it became the sight of an alleged UFO crash and subsequent governmental cover-up. A UFO-loving subculture has evolved, and visitors can visit the International UFO Museum and Research Center when they're not training their telescopes on the night skies.

ALAMOGORDO, NEW MEXICO

179 Dance to a new dune

Sledding is all kinds of fun no matter how old you are. The only problem is that it requires a snowy climate and some obliging slopes. Snow and winter weather are in short supply in this part of the world, but the gypsum dunes of White Sands National Park offer a wonderful alternative. Buy a waxed, plastic snow saucer from the park store, and head to the dunes between mile markers four and six. Observe others or practice on shallow slopes first—sand in your mouth isn't as harmless as snow.

CARLSBAD CAVERNS NATIONAL PARK, NEW MEXICO

180 Watch bats swarm from a cave

Nothing can quite prepare you for the sight of half a million bats all exiting from the mouth of a cave for their evening feed. Enjoy the spectacle from a custom-built amphitheater at the mouth of the Carlsbad Caverns.

179 White Sands National Park

2

US MIDWEST

MEDORA, NORTH DAKOTA
181 See an ode to the Wild West

If you like the idealized, romantic version of the Wild West, with square dancing and lassoing and song, then the annual Medora Musical at Burning Hills Amphitheater is the show for you. Over 100,000 people come to see this celebratory performance every year. There's been a show at this open-air, purpose-built venue since 1958.

THEODORE ROOSEVELT NATIONAL PARK, NORTH DAKOTA
182 Spot badgers near a prairie town

Although Theodore Roosevelt was a prolific hunter, he was also a great conservationist, and he set about protecting more than 230 million ac (93 million ha) of public land as parks and reserves. Theodore Roosevelt National Park was established as a memorial after his death. Sit and watch huge towns of prairie dogs at dusk, and try to spot an American badger venturing out to hunt for its evening meal.

MINOT, NORTH DAKOTA

183 Uncover Nordic history

The Nordic countries are well represented in this region, with many locals tracing their roots back to Scandinavia. The Scandinavian Heritage Park is an outdoor museum that celebrates all of these cultures and includes a 240-year-old log house from Norway, a 27-ft-tall Swedish Dala horse, a Finnish sauna, a statue of Icelandic explorer Leif Erikson, and a Danish windmill.

LAKE METIGOSHE STATE PARK, NORTH DAKOTA

184 Discover a watery oasis in the Turtle Mountains

The Chippewa people called this lake "Metigoshe Washegum," meaning "clear water lake surrounded by oaks." It's an idyllic spot nestled among rolling hills and aspen forests. Those used to North Dakota's expansive prairie vistas will be surprised to find that woodlands and wetlands cover most of the park.

184 Lake Metigoshe at sunset

185 North Dakota Heritage Center and State Museum

BISMARK, NORTH DAKOTA

185 See the Smithsonian of the plains

The state's history is laid bare in a fascinating way at the North Dakota Heritage Center and State Museum, with exhibits dating back 600 million years. Geological time is illustrated, and there's even a dramatic fossilized T. rex and triceratops encounter. The earliest people and pioneers are also showcased, with everything from ancient crafts to a 1950s soda store.

FORT YATES, NORTH DAKOTA

186 Reflect at Standing Rock Sioux Reservation

This reservation has become an important civil rights location in recent times, with successful protests against polluting pipelines. Fort Yates is the headquarters of the Standing Rock Sioux Tribe. Its most important leader, Tatanka Iyotake (Sitting Bull) was shot to death over a minor incident in 1890 and his monument offers a humbling place to pay respects.

ROBINSON, NORTH DAKOTA

187 Stand at the center of North America

Since 1931, there's been some dispute as to the geographic center of North America. The town of Rugby was the first to make the claim, and it built a 15-ft (4.5-m) stone monument as declaration, but Robinson countered with supposedly more accurate measurements; the apparent center is marked here with a compass on the floor of Hanson's Bar.

190 Fireworks at a Pyrotechnics Guild International Convention

JAMESTOWN, NORTH DAKOTA

188 See a gigantic buffalo monument

If you're a buffalo fan, then this town is definitely the place to be. Not only is the National Buffalo Museum located here, but the region is also home to *Dakota Thunder*—an easy-to-spot buffalo sculpture measuring 25 ft (7.5 m) tall and a mighty 60 tons, making it the largest buffalo monument in the world. Afterward, head to Frontier Village to see live buffalo.

GRAND FORKS, NORTH DAKOTA

189 Take a drone for a spin

Drone technology has advanced rapidly in the last few years, and there's no better place to learn more than at the Grand Sky facility—an industrial park at the forefront of unmanned flight craft, dedicated to drones. Schedule a tour to discover what's happening on the cutting edge of technology, then take a drone for a spin around their specially constructed park.

WEST FARGO, NORTH DAKOTA

190 Have the most fun possible with fireworks

Since 1972, the world of fireworks has had its biggest US trade show at the annual Pyrotechnics Guild International Convention. Although focused very much on the industry, members of the public can also attend. Days consist of video presentations and seminars, but the evening shows light up the skies in ways that you've never seen before.

SOUTHWEST NORTH DAKOTA
191 Take in roadside art along the Enchanted Highway

There's a two-lane highway in North Dakota, running from Regent, heading north to Interstate 94. In 1989, local artist Gary Greff decided to create an attraction to revive the town's fortunes, and he began constructing huge metal sculptures, taking inspiration from local wildlife and historical figures, and positioning them at intervals along the highway. By 2006 he had created seven of these gigantic artworks from scrap metal, all celebrating aspects of the region, from Teddy Roosevelt looming over the hills to grasshoppers five times the size of a vehicle. Geese in flight and jumping deer also feature among the collection; Greff has even opened his own motel—the Enchanted Castle—if you're tempted to linger.

SPEARFISH, SOUTH DAKOTA
192 Hike a trail around Spearfish Canyon

Spectacular outlooks and beautiful waterfalls await hikers in this area of natural splendor. There are three trails of varying difficulty; the easiest is a short walk from Spearfish Canyon Lodge to Roughlock Falls. A bit more effort will take you to the 50-ft (15-m) drop of Spearfish Falls, while the steep 76 Trail delivers panoramic views of Spearfish Canyon.

191 Along the Enchanted Highway

192 Frozen falls in Spearfish Canyon

DEADWOOD, SOUTH DAKOTA
193 Relive *Deadwood* at the Bullock Hotel

The HBO show *Deadwood* deservedly has its fair share of fans, with its gritty, unflinching look at life in pioneer towns. Many of the characters were based on real-life individuals, such as Wild Bill Hickok and Calamity Jane. Deputy Seth Bullock was also an actual person, and he really built the Historic Bullock Hotel, way back in 1894.

DEADWOOD, SOUTH DAKOTA
194 Watch brave riders tame wild bulls

Every summer, during the last week of July, one of the country's best rodeos takes place. The Days of '76 Rodeo, now a week-long festival, dates to 1924 and pays tribute to the pioneers who poured into Deadwood in 1876, keen to find their fortune in gold. You can see some of the world's most skilled cowboys ride bulls and horses, watch parades, and explore the museum.

BLACK HILLS, SOUTH DAKOTA
195 Soak up the view from Black Elk Peak

The name of Black Elk Peak was granted to Harney Peak in 2016, to honor Black Elk, an important member of the Dakota Sioux tribe. The peak itself reaches just over 7,200 ft (2,195 m)—the highest point in South Dakota, and the highest point east of the Rockies. You can choose from a dozen ways to the top, where you'll encounter majestic views of the state.

195 Ascent to Black Elk Peak

KEYSTONE, SOUTH DAKOTA

196 Take a selfie with some famous faces

From 1927 to 1941, American sculptor Gutzon Borglum oversaw the carving of four colossal faces into the side of Mt. Rushmore. The faces of George Washington, Thomas Jefferson, Theodore Roosevelt, and Abraham Lincoln are world-famous, and people flock to see them. Position yourself as the fifth face and cement your own place in history.

CUSTER STATE PARK, SOUTH DAKOTA

197 Gaze at free-grazing bison

A herd of more than 1,000 bison enjoy roaming this 71,000-ac (28,733-ha) park, set among the bucolic Black Hills. You can gaze at these mighty beasts year-round, although in September there is a dramatic roundup and auction of hundreds of animals.

CUSTER, SOUTH DAKOTA
198 See the world's biggest rock carving

Although Mt. Rushmore is impressive, it pales in comparison with a project elsewhere in the Black Hills. The Crazy Horse Memorial, commemorating the Lakota warrior of that name, is an ongoing project that will result in a 87-ft (26.5-m) high head (the Mt. Rushmore faces measure 60 ft/18 m). For now, the face is visible, and there are models of the overall vision.

SOUTH DAKOTA
199 Explore the Native American Scenic Byway

This 350-mi (560-km) route crosses the reservations of four Lakota Sioux tribes and past where Sitting Bull lived and died. With prairies, rolling hills, and cliff-lined sections of the Missouri River, it offers great views and countless opportunities to spot wildlife—including on the Lewis and Clark National Historic Trail overlooking Lake Oahe; the great adventurers stopped fourteen times along this route.

WIND CAVE NATIONAL PARK, SOUTH DAKOTA
200 Ferret out a mustelid

There is only one species of ferret to be found in the United States, and you can see it in the Wind Cave National Park. It's the rather charming black-footed ferret—a speedy little hunter that feeds almost entirely on prairie dogs.

196 Mt. Rushmore's faces

WALL, SOUTH DAKOTA

201 Grab a doughnut from Wall Drug Store

There are apparently those who get these doughnuts shipped around the world—once you try one, it's easy to see why. They are crispy on the outside, superbly moist and cakey on the inside, and locals and visitors alike have been coming here since the late 1950s. It's an around-the-clock operation, and they never run out.

BADLANDS NATIONAL PARK, SOUTH DAKOTA

202 Pick a vantage point to view the Badlands

The eerily named Badlands rise up out of South Dakota's prairie, and the sharp pinnacles and deep canyons of striated rock never fail to capture the imagination. They're spectacular from ground level. Or if you can get higher—perhaps even by helicopter—you'll witness their true scale and majesty.

CLARK, SOUTH DAKOTA

203 Wrestle a stranger in some mashed potato

Potatoes rule the roost in this corner of the country, and every year in Clark on the first Saturday in August, there's a Potato Days festival. Recipes, parades, and tractor races are all on show, and you can even sign up for the mashed potato wrestling contest, or at least cheer on the contestants from the sidelines.

SIOUX FALLS, SOUTH DAKOTA

204 Admire the falls at Falls Park

This 123-ac (50-ha) city park is located just north of downtown, along the Big Sioux River—one of eighty parks in the city. As well as being home to some of the oldest buildings in Sioux Falls, the park shows off the beautiful falls themselves, with multiple viewing decks to choose from. There's also a 30-mi (48-km) Big Sioux River Recreation Trail to hike or bike along.

VERMILLION, SOUTH DAKOTA

205 Investigate a music museum with a difference

Don't expect the rock-star-sized egos of the Rock and Roll Hall of Fame. The National Music Museum is dedicated instead to the tools that made them famous. More than 15,000 instruments include everything from early grand pianos to unique guitars, which is why it's considered one of the premier museums of its kind.

THROUGHOUT SOUTH DAKOTA

206 Hunt down some local chislic

Declared the official state nosh in 2018, chislic is a regional dish of cubed red meat. It's traditionally made with lamb, though versions with game meats such as venison are also found. The name relates to the Turkish shish kebab and it's served hot, sprinkled with garlic salt, with soda crackers on the side. In Sioux Falls, it's lightly dusted with flour and fried.

202 Panoramic view of Dakota's Badlands

CHADRON, NEBRASKA

207 Hug a pine in America's biggest forest

Welcome to what is the largest man-made forest in North America—the Nebraska National Forest, which at one point was the largest in the world. Its 90,000 ac (36, 400 ha) allow for ATV riding, hunting, and hiking, and there are multiple campgrounds to choose from. The forest also has a high proportion of the noble ponderosa pine, which is very photogenic, as well as ripe for hugging.

CRAWFORD, NEBRASKA

208 Hitch a ride in a stagecoach

The Fort Robinson Museum is located in an outpost on the plains dating back to 1905. The museum illustrates the region's history, with Crazy Horse, the Cavalry, and World War II prisoners of war all forming part of the story, along with the K-9 corps, responsible for training dogs during wartime. You can also take a tour of the facility in an authentic stagecoach, as used in the earliest days of the fort.

HARRISON, NEBRASKA

209 Marvel at some giant toadstools

If you visit Toadstool Geological Park in Oglala National Grassland, you'll encounter what seems like a moonscape, populated with strange-looking rock formations, not dissimilar to giant fungi. Visitors can take a 1-mi (1.6-km) loop to view them and also spot fossils, many fine examples of which have been expertly excavated from the park.

BAYARD, NEBRASKA

210 See a rock soar to the heavens

The spire of Chimney Rock rises 325 ft (99 m) atop a conical base, overlooking the North Platte River. It was an important landmark for the pioneers on the Oregon Trail, confirming they were heading in the right direction. It was designated a National Historic Site in the 1950s, and a small museum helps interpret the importance of the rock.

210 Pioneer landmark Chimney Rock

ROYAL, NEBRASKA
211 Tour a prehistoric graveyard

Twelve million years ago, a volcanic eruption entombed a watering hole and all of the animals that frequented it. The fossil beds that resulted in the region (known as the Ashfall Fossil Beds) make up what's referred to as the "Pompeii of dinosaurs." Pay a visit to see some incredible displays of ancient rhino and archaeologists painstakingly excavating fossils.

GRAND ISLAND TO ALLIANCE, NEBRASKA
212 Tour a scenic byway

The gently rolling bucolic beauty of Nebraska is the backdrop to a 272-mi (438-km) journey between Grand Island and Alliance known as the Sandhills Journey Scenic Byway. The world-class natural beauty on the way includes undulating dunes, evocative grasslands, and striking blue lakes. By day you'll spot an abundance of wildlife, and by night, skies full of bright stars.

PLATTE RIVER VALLEY, NEBRASKA
213 Listen to sandhill cranes warble

The sight of huge flocks of sandhill cranes migrating in spring is stunning, but their loud, gurgling call is even better. A bottleneck in their travel patterns brings half a million birds to this stretch of the Platte River every year.

213 Flock of sandhill cranes

MONOWI, NEBRASKA
214 Visit a town with a population of one

Your own hometown may
be fairly small, but it's bound
to be much bigger than the
Nebraskan outpost of Monowi,
which officially has just a single
resident. As its sole citizen,
Elsie Eiler plays the roles of
mayor, town librarian, and
bartender, really putting the
"mono" in Monowi. Pass
through and say hello—
she'll likely be glad for
the company.

OMAHA, NEBRASKA
215 Shop the cobbled streets of Omaha

Omaha's Old Market
neighborhood features the
original brick-paved streets
that once resounded to the
noise of horse-drawn carriages
trundling along them at the
turn of the twentieth century.
Many buildings date back to
that time and beyond, and
this charming entertainment
and shopping district is on
the National Register of
Historic Places.

215 Old Market in downtown Omaha

INDIAN CAVE STATE PARK, NEBRASKA

216 Take a drive to escape the crowds

Tucked along the Missouri River, on the eastern edge of Nebraska, Indian Cave State Park is a pristine area of wilderness just far enough off the beaten path to keep foot traffic low. A road winds through the entire park with places to stop, providing access to the scenery without the hike.

VARIOUS SITES IN NEBRASKA

217 Witness tribal culture at a powwow

Understandably, most intertribal gatherings are solely for Native Americans, but some of the larger events open up to the public to celebrate an ancient culture and educate outsiders. Festivities can last over a weekend, with displays of traditional dancing, drumming, and singing in a family-friendly environment.

OAKLEY, KANSAS

218 Stand among "Nature's Stonehenge"

We're all familiar with the mysterious monoliths of England's Stonehenge. The stones at Monument Rocks are less mysterious but just as striking—towering chalk formations, remnants of the ancient Western Interior Seaway. They appear man-made, but are all natural, and also a National Natural Landmark.

218 Monument Rocks in Kansas

DODGE CITY, KANSAS
219 Relive the glory days in the Queen of the Cowtowns

Dodge City is undoubtedly one of the most legendary locations of the Old West, and the Boot Hill Museum (on the site of a cemetery of the same name) is dedicated to the cowboys and pioneers of its early years. The museum's 20,000 artifacts include some 200 original guns. You can also view lots of old-time structures and have the chance to order a sarsaparilla at the bar in your most cinematic manner.

MUSHROOM ROCK STATE PARK, KANSAS
220 Take shelter beneath a giant mushroom

The smallest national park in Kansas is home to one of the state's most striking natural wonders— a pair of rock formations dating back to the Cretaceous Period (over 45 million years ago) that resemble giant mushrooms. They are actually sandstone and sedimentary rock held together by natural cement. The largest is 27 ft (8 m) in diameter, meaning you can be photographed next to it pretending to be an elf.

219 Dodge City's Boot Hill Museum

220 Mushroom Rock State Park

WICHITA, KANSAS

221 Salute the Keeper of the Plains

At the confluence of the Arkansas and Little Arkansas Rivers stands a dramatic 44-ft (13.4-m) steel sculpture by the artist Blackbear Bosin. This giant Native American warrior was erected in 1974 to celebrate the US Bicentennial. Every night, people gather to watch the fifteen-minute "Ring of Fire," fueled by a ring of firepits around its base.

FLINT HILLS, KANSAS

222 Walk in grass that's taller than you are

The best place for tallgrass has to be Tallgrass Prairie National Preserve—11,000 ac (4,450 ha) that give an idea of how this part of America looked before it was plowed up for farming or built upon. Climb a hill to witness a sea of grass dancing in the wind. Or head into the grass to register just how tall it is, remembering it takes a season to grow and become "Tall in the Fall."

WAMEGO, KANSAS

223 Live out your Dorothy fantasies

Follow the yellow brick road to the OZ Museum, established in tribute to *The Wizard of Oz*. Famously, the movie was set in Kansas as well as Oz, and this museum has exhibits running from the earliest editions of L. Frank Baum's book to jeweled ruby slippers to rare artifacts from the movie production. Click your heels and peek behind the curtain.

TOPEKA, KANSAS

224 Discover Topeka's best vantage point

The six floors of the Kansas State Capitol are very impressive, as befits a state capitol that has stood since 1889. If you have a head for heights, climb the 296 steps to the top of the beautiful cupola. There are viewing platforms along the way, but the top is the highest point in town, affording wonderful views.

TOPEKA, KANSAS

225 Get perspective on civil rights

In the 1954 case of *Brown v. Board of Education of Topeka*, the Supreme Court ruled that racial segregation in public schools was unconstitutional. A National Historic Site to mark the event was erected in 1992, centered around Monroe Elementary School. Various exhibits give context to this key moment in civil rights history.

ATCHISON, KANSAS

226 Remember a pioneering aviator

Famed pilot and adventurer Amelia Earhart was born in Atchison, and it was here that her dreams of flying took shape. Her childhood home is now the Amelia Earhart Birthplace Museum, and self-guided tours give context to her upbringing, enhanced by artifacts and media from the time.

221 Keeper of the Plains

227 Children's Fountain, illuminated at night

228 A Boulevardia crowd

KANSAS CITY, KANSAS

227 Gush about your favorite of 200 fountains

When you think of a fountain-heavy city, you probably imagine Rome or Athens. Think again. Kansas City has 200 officially registered water features, with the oldest (Marlborough Plaza Fountain) dating to 1923. Another—Children's Fountain—was installed in 1995 to celebrate childhood, with its figures modeled on young local residents. Visit to choose your favorite.

KANSAS CITY, KANSAS

228 Go all weekend long at Boulevardia

The two-day Boulevardia festival is one of the best beer-focused events around. It features two days of craft beer, food, and live music with a makers' market, charity bike ride, and other family-friendly experiences. Boulevard Brewing brings it all together with a lineup of breweries from around the country. Local restaurants supply the food, and top musical acts headline.

BLACK KETTLE NATIONAL GRASSLANDS, OKLAHOMA

229 Be thankful for wild turkeys

Puffed up, male wild turkeys are among the most splendid birds around. They strut through woodlands, searching for acorns, gobbling in a fantastic manner. They travel in flocks, so if you see one, you'll likely see many more. The male is known as a "tom" or "gobbler" and his gobble is so loud it can be heard from a mile away. Although ground-nesting birds, they sleep in trees.

230 National Cowboy and Western Heritage Museum

OKLAHOMA CITY, OKLAHOMA
230 Give free rein to cowboy fantasies

It may sound frivolous, but the National Cowboy and Western Heritage Museum takes its subject seriously, with exhibits rooted in the reality of life in the Wild West. There's a wealth of fascinating Western and Native American artifacts and exhibitions that explore how cowboys lived. Photos and personal accounts get past the stereotypes, offering a fine tribute to an enduring period.

OKLAHOMA CITY, OKLAHOMA
231 Uncover an underground art hub

Beneath the streets of Oklahoma City, there's a hidden network of tunnels connecting parts of downtown. Opened in 1974, it's about a mile—or twenty blocks—long. The tunnels are color-coded, each corresponding to an art gallery, with striking displays of contemporary art for visitors to peruse. The challenge is to find the secret entrances to the tunnels—start in the basement of the Sheraton.

TULSA, OKLAHOMA
232 Take on a space shuttle

Tulsa has a proud history of aviation, and the Tulsa Air and Space Museum will get flight fans very excited. Visitors can inspect such rarities as a Grumman F-14 Tomcat and a Russian MiG-21, and explore a scale replica of Tulsa's original art deco airport. Budding astronauts will also relish the opportunity to operate a mockup of a space shuttle's robotic arm.

TULSA, OKLAHOMA
233 Try a beer Bomb!

Bomb! is an American-style imperial stout from Prairie Artisan Ales modeled off the dessert beer category. After brewing, it's aged for months with coffee, chocolate, vanilla beans, and ancho chile peppers, lending it an intoxicating but subtle kick. The peppers' heat complements the intense coffee and chocolate flavors for a balanced but boozy beer that's considered one of the best imperial stouts in the world.

BOONE, IOWA
234 Be powered by steam on the Boone and Scenic Valley Railroad

There's been a railway track at Boone since the 1890s, and a team of enthusiasts has ensured this legacy is preserved. Dozens of historic locomotives operate along the 11-mi (18-km) track, which takes in glorious views of the valley, especially from the Bass Point Creek High Bridge. Antique and seasonally dressed trains attract flocks of fans.

DES MOINES, IOWA
235 See sculptures made from butter

The Iowa State Fair, which has taken place every August since 1854, is famous for many things, not least its amazing scenes sculpted completely out of butter. Every year a different theme is chosen, and previous masterpieces have included Elvis and the cast of *Sesame Street*.

INDIANOLA, IOWA
236 Witness fleets of balloons take flight

The skies come alive as hundreds of hot-air balloons take part in the National Balloon Classic during the first week of August. All colors and shapes are on display, as are shows of skill by some of the world's best pilots. Sit back and watch the unfolding beauty of it all, or take to the skies yourself by buying a ride.

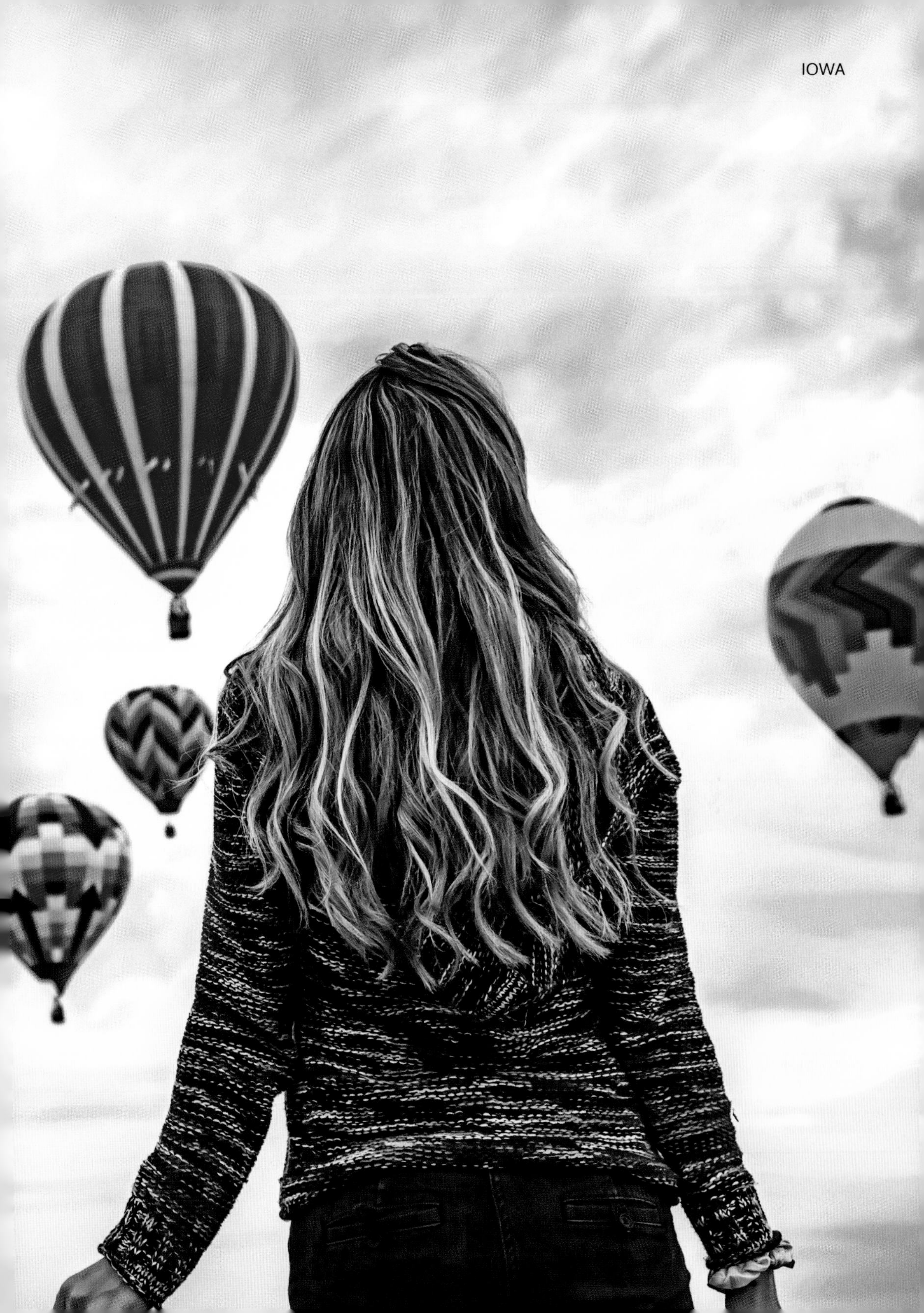

MADISON COUNTY, IOWA
237 Cross all the bridges of Madison County

The best-selling *Bridges of Madison County* book and subsequent movie made the covered bridges in this part of the world very famous. The ornate coverings were originally constructed simply to protect the roads, but they have become a huge tourist draw. There are six bridges to visit in total, and they are all easily seen in half a day by car. There are local guided tours, of course, or you can grab a leaflet from the tourist office, hop in your vehicle, and show yourself around.

COLUMBUS JUNCTION, IOWA
238 Swing across a romantic ravine

There's a ravine close to downtown that's locally known as Lover's Leap. In 1920, a couple of teenagers were crossing via some rickety wooden slats. The slats gave way and they fell eight stories but were miraculously unscathed. Two years later the bridge was rebuilt, and it stands to this day, albeit with fortifications over the years. You need something of a head for heights, and the bridge sways a bit, but you'll be able to enjoy gorgeous woodland views as you cross.

AMANA COLONIES, IOWA
239 See a different kind of American dream

In the mid-1800s, a group of seven villages sprang up just southwest of Cedar Rapids. The settlers were German immigrants who had escaped religious persecution in their homeland, and for the best part of a century in their Iowan home they were almost entirely self-sufficient. The villages now form a charming tourist destination that celebrates all things German, from rustic architecture to food, wine, and beer. There are also various themed festivals throughout the year.

238 Lover's Leap Swinging Bridge

240 Grant Wood's *American Gothic*

ELDON, IOWA

240 Stage your own Gothic masterpiece

In 1930, the artist Grant Wood toured this small Iowa town and spotted a white house with a large Gothic window. Wood quickly sketched the house, then returned home to Cedar Rapids to paint what would become one of the country's best-loved paintings: *American Gothic*. Visit this exact house and come away with your own interpretation of the famous scene.

MCGREGOR, IOWA

241 Undertake a spooky boat trip

Spook Cave owes its name to a time before it was discovered. Local residents used to hear strange noises coming from inside the hill, which they believed to be the groans of trapped spirits. In the 1950s, a large flooded cavern was discovered and the mystery explained. Spook Cave is now open for a half-mile boat tour that winds through its rocky formations.

KANSAS CITY, MISSOURI

242 Discover how people used to play

Before PlayStations and Wii Fit, children had to entertain themselves with analog toys and games. If you want to know more, the National Museum of Toys and Miniatures has a huge collection (over 72,000) of antiques, from elaborate Victorian dollhouses to all kinds of mechanical and musical playthings. The craftsmanship is remarkable and worth seeing in these days of mass production.

THE NATURAL BEAUTY OF MARK TWAIN NATIONAL FOREST

Luna moth

Table Rock Lake

Abandoned sawmill

KANSAS CITY, MISSOURI
243 Sample some barbecue at Arthur Bryant's

Many regions of the United States have their own take on barbecue and they naturally all believe that their version is the best! Missouri is no different, and Arthur Bryant's restaurant has a claim on being the country's most famous barbecue spot. Opened in 1908, it is now a regional institution, with its speciality being the "burnt ends" of slow-cooked beef brisket.

BRANSON, MISSOURI
244 Don your dancing shoes for a show like no other

Although it has a population of just 10,000, Branson boasts fifty music theaters, mostly on Highway 76. The tradition of country music shows here dates back to 1961 when the Baldknobbers Hillbilly Jamboree first played—and they're still playing. Shows happen day and night: some are long-running family acts featuring classic country songs, others are local bands from the area.

BRANSON, MISSOURI
245 Marvel at the world's largest *Titanic* replica

It's not often you'll find a half cruise ship resting up in the middle of a town. But it's not often you find a museum quite as dedicated to its subject as the Titanic Museum in Branson. Housed inside a half-size replica of the front half of the *Titanic*, it contains all manner of memorabilia.

BRANSON, MISSOURI
246 Feed a big cat obsession (ethically!)

There are several high-profile big cat sanctuaries in the United States, many with ethically dubious foundations. The National Tiger Sanctuary is a well-regarded nonprofit providing shelter for tigers, lions, mountain lions, and leopards. The focus is on the health and happiness of residents, so you can visit without reservation.

MARK TWAIN NATIONAL FOREST, MISSOURI
247 Be dazzled by a moth

With its fabulous lime-green color and flowing shape, the luna is a must-see of the moth world. It's also one of the biggest in North America, with a wingspan reaching 4½ in (11.5 cm). If you don't see one, there's still plenty to appreciate in this forest—once the victim of extensive logging and now preserved in its natural glory.

BONNE TERRE, MISSOURI
248 Dive in a network of caverns

Bonne Terre Mines regularly pop up in top-ten lists of adventurous things to do. They comprise the world's largest man-made underground caverns, with various levels of adventure available. The top levels are guided walking tours, but the real treasures are found along seventeen diving paths, dramatically illuminated with exciting structures.

249 Slide down a gigantic spiral slide

There are an undisclosed number of slides in St. Louis's City Museum and half the fun is trying to discover them all. The installations are built around the old spiral chutes of a former shoe warehouse, and they all differ in length and nature. There's a Ferris wheel version that's officially the tallest, but the longest slide stretches down through a whole ten thrilling stories.

250 Visit an original craft brewery

Schlafly Beer was founded by Thomas Schlafly in 1991 in a city dominated by Budweiser and Bud Light. The original lineup of beers consisted of Schlafly Pale Ale, Hefeweizen, and Oatmeal Stout, while experimental beers included the Ibex Cellar Series of barrel-aged saisons, sours, and high-gravity beers. The brewery now makes more than fifty beers annually and the tasting room is the best place to sample them. Book a tour of the brewery, which is housed in a restored wood and brick building that's listed on the National Historic Register.

249 City Museum's ten-story spiral slide

ST. LOUIS, MISSOURI
251 Paddle down the Mississippi

Channel your inner Mark Twain (who once worked as a steamboat pilot) as you cruise through Tom Sawyer country on a steamboat. In the 1930s, there were more than 1,200 steamboats on the Mississippi transporting cotton, rice, timber, and tobacco from fields to towns. Today they're more for pleasure than for work.

ST. LOUIS, MISSOURI
252 Ride to the top of the Gateway Arch

The 630-ft (190-m) steel arch in St. Louis is one of the country's most recognizable landmarks. Millions have looked out from the top of the structure since its completion in 1965, and the newly updated tram tour keeps that tradition alive. Interactive, preboarding exhibits bring the history to life.

KATY TRAIL, MISSOURI
253 Bike the longest "rail-to-trail" project

The 240-mi (390-km) Katy Trail is a segment of the Lewis and Clark Trail, located along the former corridor of the Missouri–Kansas–Texas Railroad. Nature and history buffs will enjoy the route, which loosely follows the Missouri River, past rolling farmland, scenic towns, wineries, and towering rock bluffs.

251/252 Paddle steamer passing St. Louis's Gateway Arch

255 Canoeing on the Ozarks waterways

VARIOUS SITES IN MISSOURI
254 Go underground at a show cave

The "Show-Me State" has almost 6,500 documented caves. The majority are not open for public exploration. However, some of the more accessible are known as "show caves," peppered around the Missouri park system. Try Meramec or Onondaga parks, both of which have guided tours of dramatic caverns, and the chance to sight bats and salamanders.

THE OZARKS, MISSOURI
255 Take to the water in the Ozarks

The Ozark National Scenic Riverways is America's first designated national park for the preservation of a wild river system. There's 80,000 ac (32,000 ha) to explore around two of the country's loveliest rivers (Current and Jacks Fork). Explore the waterways at your own pace, by canoe, kayak, or lying back on an inflatable tube, letting the current take you.

THE OZARKS, MISSOURI
256 Participate in a hillbilly fair

This part of the country has its own rural culture, and much of it is on display at traditional festivals such as the September Hillbilly Hullabaloo in the village of Laurie. Like any annual fair, there's music, food, and entertainment—expect to find tractor pulls, cornhole tournaments, and lots of moonshine among the general festivities.

257 High Falls in fall colors

GRAND PORTAGE, MINNESOTA

257 Admire Minnesota's highest waterfall

The dark basalt rocks that frame High Falls create a memorably dramatic backdrop to the state's tallest waterfall. The white waters fall some 120 ft (36 m) and make for a scenic deluge that lends itself to great photos. You can find the falls within the grounds of Grand Portage State Park, the only park in the nation managed in partnership with a local Native American band.

BOUNDARY WATERS, MINNESOTA

258 Steer into a mighty wilderness

Picture a lake of ice-still water, the trees and clouds reflecting off its surface, the silence broken only by the wolflike call of a loon. There are more than 1,000 lakes just like this in Minnesota's Boundary Waters, a wilderness area that stretches 150 mi (240 km) along the US/Canada border. Paddle by day and camp on shore by night, feasting on fish you've caught.

DULUTH, MINNESOTA

259 Watch ships pass under a bridge

Just beyond the shores of Lake Superior, the Duluth Ship Canal is an important working part of the city. The Aerial Lift Bridge across the canal is one of only two vertical lift bridges in the country (the other one is in Chicago). Walk across its 1,300-ft (400-m) span for great views, or watch ships sail under it as it rises to a height of 135 ft (40 m).

COOK COUNTY, MINNESOTA

260 Pick a season to enjoy the Gunflint Trail

Rent a snowmobile or flag down a dog-pulled sled and head out on the Gunflint Trail in winter. Moose and wolves are some of the larger residents that you might spot, alongside lynx, foxes, and rabbits. Stop and try ice fishing—there are plenty of outdoor options along the 57-mi (92-km) pathway. Or wait until the weather warms up and hit the trail on a bike.

CUYUNA LAKES, MINNESOTA

261 Pursue water sports in a mining range

Abandoned by open-pit mining companies over thirty-five years ago, this derelict area was rehabilited to build a recreation park. It features six natural and fifteen man-made lakes, all within a few square miles of each other. The boat and canoe rentals are the perfect way to explore, and fishing is an incredibly popular pursuit here, with trout and bass in abundance.

MINNEAPOLIS, MINNESOTA

262 Savor true peace and quiet

The anechoic chamber at Orfield Laboratories in Minneapolis absorbs 99.99 percent of sound, creating a silence that's so intense that visitors can actually start to experience visual and aural hallucinations. Reservations must be made around two weeks in advance.

MINNEAPOLIS, MINNESOTA

263 Devour a Juicy Lucy

The exact provenance of this decadent dish is up for discussion, but we do know that sometime in the 1950s, someone in Minneapolis (likely at the 5-8 Club or Matt's Bar) had a genius idea. A Juicy Lucy is a cheeseburger but with cheese cooked into the meat patty, meaning that the flavor (and piping-hot cheese) floods out as you cautiously bite into it.

ST. PAUL, MINNESOTA

264 Gaze up at St. Paul

One of the most distinctive cathedrals in the country, the Cathedral of St. Paul has loomed over the city from its location on Cathedral Hill since 1915. The jewel in its crown is the striking dome, which owes its dark exterior to its granite construction. The interior has warm colors and gold leaf, while twenty-four stained-glass windows create a dazzling effect.

CHANHASSEN, MINNESOTA

265 Make a Prince-themed pilgrimage

The state's most famous son, the musician formerly known as Prince, lived and worked at Paisley Park from 1987, producing some of the country's most memorable pop music. Containing studios and space for performances, the complex opened up to tours in 2016, and thousands of fans regularly pass through to pay respects.

260 Cycling the Gunflint Trail in summer

THROUGHOUT MINNESOTA

266 Tick off Minnesota's weird roadside attractions

There are roadside attractions all over the country, but Minnesota has an especially high concentration. A 400-mi (644-km) loop will take you past the world's largest crow, pelican, and loon, plus a huge otter, and a couple of giant Paul Bunyans. There's even a blue ox, a hairy mosquito, and a gigantic cherry in a spoon for good measure.

BAYFIELD, WISCONSIN

267 Visit a place where "water meets land and sky"

The Apostle Islands National Lakeshore offers a collection of twenty-one islands and 12 mi (19 km) of sensational natural coastline edging out into the waters of Lake Superior. Visitors can camp and hike; kayaking around the local sea caves takes in several historic lighthouses; and scuba divers can descend to several shipwrecks.

CHETEK, WISCONSIN

268 Cozy up at Canoe Bay

This secluded area of hardwood forest offers a series of cozy cottages on the edge of a cluster of lakes, which is just perfect for a romantic break for two. Enjoy a dramatic water view from a cantilevered private deck, or just curl up with a good book in a comfortable chair by the fire.

266 *Spoonbridge and Cherry*, Minneapolis Sculpture Garden

GREEN BAY, WISCONSIN

269 Join the cheeseheads for game day

Every city claims that its football team has the best fans, but the Green Bay Packers have an especially fervent following. Known as "cheeseheads" due to a historically insulting phrase, they brave harsh weather to cheer on the Packers, and many wear hats shaped like a block of cheese.

THROUGHOUT WISCONSIN

270 Look out for a national symbol

Since 1782, the bald eagle, with its soaring sense of freedom, has been the symbol of the United States, and even before that, it held spiritual significance for Native Americans, as it still does. It's a majestic bird, with a distinctive chocolate-brown body, bookended with a white head and a white tail.

270 The proudly
independent bald eagle

WASHINGTON ISLAND, WISCONSIN

271 Skip a stone on the world's best pebble beaches

Take a short ferry ride from the tip of the Door peninsula, out into the waters of Lake Michigan. You'll arrive at Washington Island with its quaint villages and lavender fields. The jewels here, though, are the gorgeous pebble beaches. Head to Schoolhouse Beach and walk on smooth limestones that glint in the sun.

OSHKOSH, WISCONSIN

272 Let your imagination take flight at the EAA Aviation Museum

Flight enthusiasts will be in heaven at this extensive museum, housing over 200 historic aircraft and some 20,000 artifacts. Highlights include a functional replica of the famous Wright Flyer, vintage aircraft, and even flying boats and cars. Warplanes and stunt aircraft are also featured, alongside the first private spacecraft.

WARRENS, WISCONSIN

273 See cranberries stretch to the horizon

The Southern states have their swamp tours, but in this part of the country there are 50 mi (80 km) of century-old cranberry marshes to explore. Visit in October for a tour of the Cranberry Highway, where you can pick fruit from the vines and enjoy many cranberry-based treats. There's even a museum with its own vintage ice-cream store, serving eleven cranberry-based flavors.

ELROY TO SPARTA, WISCONSIN

274 Trek the cool tunnels of the Elroy–Sparta State Trail

There are some 2,000 "rail-to-trail" projects in the United States, but this was the first, opening in 1967. Outdoor lovers flock to explore the 33-mi (53-km) route, which can be hiked, biked, or even seen by bobsled in winter. Outstanding natural beauty and three striking rock tunnels—the longest stretches 3,800 ft (1,160 m)—await, passing through wetlands, farmland, and prairies.

SPRING GREEN, WISCONSIN

275 Marvel at a 200-ft sea monster

The House on the Rock complex was built by one man over a couple of decades. It's a real-life fun house with surprises around every corner. Models of demons and strange animals abound, including a 200-ft (61-m) sea monster fighting a squid. Even the (sadly unrideable) World's Largest Indoor Carousel features 269 beasts.

SPRING GREEN, WISCONSIN

276 Appreciate the genius of Frank Lloyd Wright

Half a century after his death, Wright remains one of America's most influential architects. Taliesin was his home, studio, and school, important enough to have been designated a UNESCO World Heritage Site. Tour his home, and admire buildings dating from every decade of his career.

271 One of Washington Island's renowned pebble beaches

BARABOO, WISCONSIN

277 Survey the view from rock formations at Devil's Lake

This is hands-down one of the highlights of the Ice Age National Scenic Trail, which extends 1,200 mi (1,900 km) through the state, from the northwest corner to Lake Michigan. At Devil's Lake, dramatic 500-ft (150-m) quartzite bluffs overlook a stunning 360-ac (145-ha) lake in a pine-laden landscape. Postcard-perfect photos can be taken anywhere along the trails, and it's hard to imagine a more idyllic setting for picnics or taking a dip.

LAKE MENDOTA, WISCONSIN

278 Learn how the bufflehead got its name

Male bufflehead ducks are a striking black and white, while females are brown with a white patch on their cheeks. They dive under water to feed before bobbing back up. And that name? Apparently it's because their overlarge head resembles that of a buffalo!

277 Sunset view of Devil's Lake

MILWAUKEE, WISCONSIN
279 Bowl a strike at the nation's oldest alley

A popular spot since 1908, Holler House is regularly touted by lifestyle magazines as one of the best bars in America. It's an unusual place, apparently having received its name from the roar of the noise inside, and bedecked with more than 1,000 signed bras. It's also home to the oldest sanctioned bowling alley in the country—human beings are needed to reset the pins after each frame.

MILWAUKEE, WISCONSIN
280 Bask in beer heaven with the locals

Milwaukee isn't called "Brew City" for nothing. Ever since homesick German immigrants began importing and brewing beer here in the 1800s, the suds have come to define Milwaukee's character. The giant Miller Brewery has its home here (along with local greats Pabst, Schlitz, and Blatz), and you can tour everything from processing plants to the historic Pabst Mansion. Oktoberfest is quite something here, too.

ACROSS WISCONSIN
281 Uncover Wisconsin's ice age past

The Ice Age National Scenic Trail stretches from Wisconsin's northwest corner to Lake Michigan, passing through thirty of its seventy-two counties. Take a "mammoth" walk to uncover signs of life as it was 15,000 years ago, among topography left by glacial erosion. You'll encounter today's residents in the form of red foxes, white-tailed deer, and porcupines.

281 Trekking the Ice Age National Scenic Trail

283 Harley-Davidson Museum forecourt

284 Sunrise on Isle Royale

GREEN COUNTY, WISCONSIN
282 Eat all the cheese you can in a day

Cheese figures heavily in the culture of this region, and Green County is perhaps the cheesy epicenter of the scene. It's home to a dozen or so creameries, between them producing more than fifty varieties of cheese, from Limburger to Emmentaler. Take a tour and sample them all, or wait for September's Cheese Days festival (established in 1914) and taste them all in one day.

MILWAUKEE, WISCONSIN
283 Get revved up about Harleys

Of all the great American brands, Harley-Davidson is among the most evocative. The company has more than a century of motorcycle-making history in Milwaukee, and its museum attracts hundreds of thousands of enthusiasts every year. Interactive and antique exhibits include some 450 bikes, ten of which you can sit on for a photo, no matter how good your driving skills really are.

ISLE ROYALE, MICHIGAN
284 Hike Isle Royale

Isle Royale is a green strip in the blue of Lake Superior, located 15 mi (24 km) from the nearest land. The Greenstone Ridge Trail crosses the island east to west, through grassland, forest, and scrub. The weather is changeable, but the views across the lake, when they come, are worth it. In the 1940s, wolves crossed the frozen lake and now live here. They avoid people, but the moose they prey on are often sighted.

MICHIGAN STATE ROUTE 22, MICHIGAN
285 Trace the Lake Michigan coastline

This 117-mi (188-km) highway is regularly voted
one of the best scenic drives in the country, and
you'll soon discover why. It roughly follows the
coastline of Lake Michigan, weaving past inland
lakes, dunes, vineyards, and cute harbor towns.
There's outstanding scenery at stops, such as
Sleeping Bear Dunes National Lakeshore,
and wine tours in the Leelanau Peninsula.

MARQUETTE, MICHIGAN
286 Clamber over frozen waterfalls

The scenery around Marquette is spectacular in any
season, with rocky rivers and multiple waterfalls.
Come winter, when these waterfalls freeze over, it's
like another world. Stick ice cleats on your shoes
and feel the fun of walking under a frozen wall,
marveling at the many shades of blue in the ice.
To take the experience up a notch (literally!),
head to Munising for serious ice climbing.

285 Descending into Sleeping Bear Dunes National Lakeshore

MACKINAC ISLAND, MICHIGAN
287 Slow down on an island where motor vehicles are banned

Sitting on the waters of Lake Huron, between Michigan's Upper and Lower Peninsulas, Mackinac Island State Park is blessed with gorgeous trails, woods, and a striking area of limestone arch rock formations. More than 80 percent of the island is state parkland. Hop on the ferry and relax as you tour the island via bicycle, horse, or horse-drawn carriage. It's like stepping back in time to a less frantic world.

MARSHALL, MICHIGAN
288 See almost every trick that ever was

Founded in 1978, the American Museum of Magic was initially a display of the private collection of famed twentieth-century magician Harry Blackstone Sr. It quickly expanded and is now the largest museum of magic that is open to the general public. It lists over half a million artifacts, including legendary tricks such as the Milk Can and the Overboard Box used by Harry Houdini, as well as countless card tricks and illusions to bring the wonder of magic alive.

HELL, MICHIGAN
289 Prove that Hell exists on Earth

There probably aren't any jokes you can make that the residents of this town (about twenty minutes from Ann Arbor) haven't heard before. Several stories about how the town got its name persist, but whichever is true, there are plenty of funny photo opportunities. Every business has a sign bearing the name, and you can even get married in Hell at the local wedding chapel.

289 The "Gates of Hell," Michigan

CHICAGO: GATEWAY TO ROUTE 66

The Gemini Giant

Wall art, Route 66 Hall of Fame and Museum

Old Chain of Rocks Bridge

DEARBORN, MICHIGAN
290 Discover the age of invention

The Henry Ford Museum of American Innovation celebrates a golden age, when names like Edison and Ford were shaping the world. Inventions such as the motor car and light bulb took off in the nineteenth century, and visitors can relive those heady days. Ride in a Model T, step inside a replica of Edison's laboratory, and see world-class artisans display old-school skills.

DETROIT, MICHIGAN
291 Celebrate the music of Motown

In 1959, Berry Gordy Jr. founded Tamla Records. Just a year later, that company became the Motown Record Corporation, and the hits that it produced changed the musical landscape of America. Explore the history of Motown at its first headquarters, "Hitsville USA," which is now the Motown Museum. Various city tours also focus on this slice of musical history.

VARIOUS SITES IN MICHIGAN
292 Investigate the birth of the automobile

In 1896, Henry Ford test-drove his first automobile in Detroit. The city has since been a major part of car history, where some of the biggest manufacturers have set up shop. Explore top-notch facilities, including the Henry Ford Museum, the General Motors Heritage Center, and the Automotive Hall of Fame—all with cars not found elsewhere.

CHICAGO, ILLINOIS
293 Get your kicks on Route 66

The most written and sung about thoroughfare on Earth, Route 66 runs from Chicago to Santa Monica on the Pacific coast. Most travel it east to west, and although the 2,448-mi (3,940-km) drive can be completed faster, many recommend twelve days, including two rest days. From Chicago, farmland leads to St. Louis and the famous Old Chain of Rocks Bridge, which crosses the Mississippi (although vehicles now take the New Chain of Rocks Bridge). The rolling hills of the Ozarks follow, as the road winds down to Springfield, then to Oklahoma, where it turns dry and dusty. Toward New Mexico, the scenery becomes exotic, heavy with Native American and Spanish influences. Next comes Albuquerque, Holbrook, the Navajo Nation, the dramatic landscape of Arizona, then Vegas and its attendant pleasures. From there, it's a hop to the end of the road.

CHICAGO, ILLINOIS
294 Lose yourself in art

You can easily spend hours at the Art Institute of Chicago. It has works spanning the globe and the centuries. Famed as the first museum in the country to put a selection of modern art on permanent display, it also boasts a world-class selection of Impressionists and Postimpressionists, from Seurat to Van Gogh, plus many Monets—his first solo museum show in America was in Chicago.

295 Cruising Chicago by riverboat

CHICAGO, ILLINOIS

295 View skyscrapers from the water

Chicago is the spiritual home of the skyscraper. Its famous skyline has 1,384 high-rises now, and it's where the world's first was built in 1885. A river cruise is the best way to admire the architecture and trace its development from turn-of-the-century buildings to recent giants such as the Willis Tower (Sears Tower), the tallest in the world when it was built in 1974, and 2009's ninety-eight-story Trump Tower.

CHICAGO, ILLINOIS

296 Study at the Joe and Rika Mansueto Library

At first sight, it seems there's something essential missing here: books. Beneath the soaring elliptical glass ceiling, the 180-seat Grand Reading Room is part of a modern concept in book borrowing. Books are stored underground and retrieved using an automated request system and robotic cranes; you simply sit in peace beneath the vast glass-domed ceiling while you wait for delivery.

CHICAGO, ILLINOIS

297 Just once, smell a skunk

The name "Chicago" may come from the Native American word *shikako*, or "skunk place"—so where better to sniff out this stalwart of children's stories? Skunks spray a foul oil from their anal scent glands when they feel threatened.

CHICAGO, ILLINOIS

298 See your reflection in *Cloud Gate*

Providing an antidote to the soaring heights and hard lines of Chicago's skyscrapers is Anish Kapoor's *Cloud Gate*, situated in the AT&T Plaza in Millennium Park. Fondly known as "the Bean," the highly polished stainless steel sculpture was inspired by the form of liquid mercury. Its topside reflects the sky and the city's skyline, but walk underneath and a concave dip creates multiple warping reflections of visitors.

469 Cheering on the Cubs at Wrigley Field

CHICAGO, ILLINOIS
299 Catch a game at Wrigley Field

There's something typically Chicagoan about watching a game of baseball, and the historic Wrigley Field is the classic place to do just that. The stadium itself is over a hundred years old, and every game day, around 40,000 spectators come to cheer on the home side, the Chicago Cubs. It's a very special venue, so grab a hot dog and a beer and be part of a beloved city ritual for a day.

CHICAGO, ILLINOIS
300 Judge Chicago's pizza for yourself

Which city has the best pizza? It's a debate that will likely never be settled, but outside of New York, the most distinctive variety certainly has to be the Chicago deep dish. A high crust edge contains deep, sloppy amounts of cheese and tomato sauce, and locals love it. For a prime example, Lou Malnati's is a local chain that's been baking these delicious pies since the early 1970s.

OAK PARK, ILLINOIS
301 Visit Hemingway's childhood home

This unassuming suburb just west of downtown Chicago was where one of the country's most famous writers was born and raised. The house has been restored to its Victorian-era splendor, and since 2001 has been the home of the Ernest Hemingway Birthplace Museum. Artifacts, family photos, and details of Hemingway's early life will delight the fans who come to pay homage.

304 Lincoln's Springfield home

BROOKFIELD, ILLINOIS
302 Get your video game on

Video games have been a part of our culture for decades now, and the Galloping Ghost Arcade—the largest video arcade in the country—provides games from every era. Opening in 2010 with 130 games, it now boasts some 650 gaming units, all free to play once you pay a twenty-dollar entry fee. Classics such as Donkey Kong and Space Invaders mix with rarities and obscure games that you'll only find right here.

ALTON, ILLINOIS
303 Play a tune on a trumpet

Miles Davis was introduced to the trumpet at the age of thirteen and quickly developed a talent for it; little did he know then that he'd go on to dominate the jazz world. Take inspiration from the phenomenonally talented musician by picking up the instrument and learning a tune on it in Davis's birthplace of Alton—you'll discover that it's more about vibrating your lips than simply blowing into the mouthpiece.

SPRINGFIELD, ILLINOIS
304 Get acquainted with a president

Just before he became the sixteenth president of the United States in 1860, Abraham Lincoln resided here, living the regular life of a husband, father, and neighbor. It's the only home that Lincoln ever owned, and the house, as well as the four surrounding blocks, have been turned into a memorial illustrating his life at that time—a fascinating insight into one of America's most respected sons.

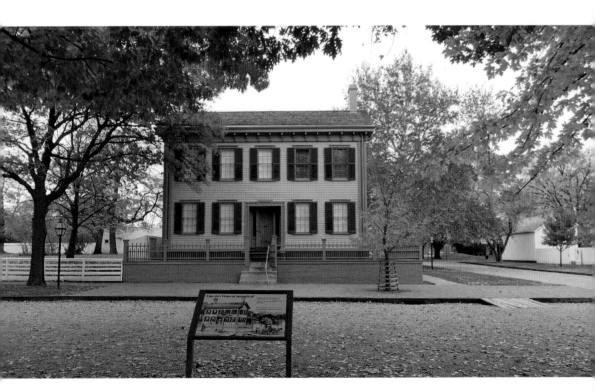

BELKNAP, ILLINOIS

305 Scuba around an underwater petting zoo

A spring-fed stone quarry is the unlikely venue for a wonderful underwater adventure at the Mermet Springs scuba diving facility. Qualified scuba divers can take to the waters and explore all sorts of strange relics—submerged planes, trains, and automobiles, and a cement "petting zoo." Meet animals ranging from lions to eels, and the star of the show, Bruce the Shark.

METROPOLIS, ILLINOIS

306 Celebrate your favorite superhero

During the second weekend in June, as many as 30,000 comic book and movie fans descend on this unusually named town for its annual Superman Celebration. Metropolis was, of course, the fictional home city of Superman, and the Man of Steel is still incredibly popular. The weekend sees fan films, street vendors, a carnival, a costume contest, and a Super Car Show, so bring your best cape.

ANGOLA, INDIANA

307 Accelerate down a toboggan run

You can experience one aspect of winter sports whether it snows or not at this refrigerated toboggan run. Located in Pokagon State Park, the run is a quarter of a mile long and replicates a real-life bobsled run in miniature. It's no less exhilarating, and it's an intense thirty seconds, with a 30-ft (9-m) tower, a total vertical drop of 90 ft (27 m), and all the dips and valleys that make the real thing so exciting.

INDIANA DUNES NATIONAL LAKESHORE, INDIANA

308 Test yourself on a dunescape

Along the southern edge of Lake Michigan, huge dunes rise from the shores, in places reaching a height of 200 ft (61 m). Hike up the park's three tallest dunes on a 1½-mi (2.4-km) trail that climbs the equivalent of 55 stories of a high-rise—although on a base of soft sand, it might feel more like 555. At the peaks, enjoy spectacular views of white beaches and the lake.

INDIANAPOLIS, INDIANA

309 Feel the excitement of the Indy 500

The suburb itself is called Speedway, so the fact that it's home to the Indianapolis Motor Speedway—one of the world's largest sporting venues— is no surprise. There have been races here since 1909, and the annual Indy 500 is by far the most famous. Over 250,000 people gather to watch this test of endurance as drivers complete around 200 laps of the historic course.

COLUMBUS, INDIANA

310 Discover a hub of modern architecture

Located 50 mi (80 km) south of Indianapolis, an unassuming town is a surprising architectural hub. In the 1950s, several modernist building projects started up; soon a high proportion of the public buildings—banks, churches, schools—were completed in this style. Some of the biggest names in modernism, including Richard Meier and Robert Venturi, have works here.

307 Perennial winter at the Pokagon toboggan run

MARBLEHEAD, OHIO

311 Picnic in the shade of a lighthouse

Since the late nineteenth century, visitors have flocked to this picture-perfect lakeside town. A state park has developed around the historic lighthouse, which is still operational. Picnic tables are dotted along the coastline, with stunning views of Lake Erie, Sandusky Bay, and Cedar Point. You might even spot the very rare lakeside daisy.

SANDUSKY, OHIO

312 Chase thrills all day at Cedar Point

There's been an amusement park here since 1870, making it the second oldest in the country behind Lake Compounce. The park is home to some seventy-one rides, including seventeen roller coasters—the second most in the world behind Six Flags Magic Mountain. Thrill seekers can choose from any of the six roller coasters that are at least 200 ft (61 m) high, or Maverick, with its 110-ft (29-m) drop.

312 Cedar Point's GateKeeper roller coaster

CLEVELAND, OHIO
313 Stage a pierogi crawl

With a strong and proud community from Poland and the Balkans, Cleveland has a wealth of culinary delights, the pierogi being one of the most essential. This potato dumpling has sweet and savory incarnations, and they're snack-sized, so a crawl to sample the best is completely acceptable. Head to the Tremont neighborhood and try Sokolowski's University Inn and Prosperity Social Club.

CLEVELAND, OHIO
314 Pay homage to your idols at the Rock and Roll Hall of Fame

In 1993, stars such as Pete Townshend, Chuck Berry, and Billy Joel were present as the ribbon was cut to open this monument to the world's best musical talent. There's an annual ceremony to induct new musicians, and the museum itself documents the entire history of rock and roll, with exhibits of musical instruments, memorabilia, and firsthand stories.

314 I. M. Pei's pyramid at the Rock and Roll Hall of Fame

KENT, OHIO

315 See some unusual black squirrels

At Kent State University in Ohio, the squirrels found around the campus are black—a genetic mutation of the usual gray specimen. It is believed that there used to be far more black squirrels in the wild when America was more densely forested. These squirrels, however, originated from a handful brought from Canada in the 1960s.

MILLERSBURG, OHIO

316 Sample the lifestyle of the Amish

Ohio's Amish Country is a fascinating community that's steeped in the past, where technology has not taken over an unchanging way of life. This historic village is listed on the National Register of Historic Places and has period architecture, especially Victorian. Visitors can also browse crafts such as metalwork, glassblowing, and lace making.

ZANESVILLE, OHIO

317 Cross a bridge to the same side of the river

One bridge crossing two rivers is a rare sight, but that's just what happens at the Zanesville Y-Bridge. This Y-shaped construction was built in 1902 and it crosses the confluence of the Licking and Muskingum Rivers, meaning you can technically "cross" the bridge and remain on the same bank. You can walk or drive across this architectural curiosity.

COLUMBUS, OHIO

318 Admire a Seurat in topiary form

A Sunday Afternoon on the Island of La Grande Jatte is a famous painting by French artist Georges Seurat—one that's entered the public consciousness and is frequently parodied. Perhaps the most interesting is the version located in the 7-ac (2.8-ha) Topiary Park of Columbus, where its scene has been brought to life in plant form, with life-size sculptures of hedges and shrubs depicting the various figures.

WEST LIBERTY, OHIO

319 Descend into colorful caverns

Thousands of years ago, an underground river shaped the ancient limestone in this region and created colorful cavernous rooms and passageways that are now known as the Ohio Caverns. Parts of this complex have been explored since the late nineteenth century, and the public can take safe, guided tours of the deepest cave in the state. Look out for one of the world's largest stalactites, the 5-ft (1.5-m) long Crystal King.

DAYTON, OHIO

320 Be impressed by the achievements of aviation

A truly world-class facility, the National Museum of the US Air Force is the oldest and largest military aviation museum in the world, with more than 360 aircraft and missiles on display. As well as rare and celebrated military aircraft, the museum has presidential planes and exhibits dedicated to the pioneers of flight, such as the Wright Brothers. A state-of-the-art 3-D movie theater brings some of the histories to life.

321 Vibrant exhibits at the American Sign Museum

CINCINNATI, OHIO

323 Catch a game by the oldest team

The Cincinnati Red Stockings may not be the most famous or successful baseball team in America, but in 1869 they were founded as the sport's first all-professional team. Now just known as the Cincinnati Reds, the team has moved around a lot over the years, but is now housed in the Great American Ball Park. The Reds last won the World Series in 1990, but fans are as enthused as ever.

CINCINNATI, OHIO

321 Bask in a neon glow

Neon signs are becoming something of a lost art, but remain an evocative part of Americana. The industry's history is over a hundred years old and enthusiastically celebrated at the American Sign Museum. It's a gaudy, flashing tribute with hundreds of signs across 20,000 sq ft (1,860 sq m), some signs dating back to the early 1900s—a treasure trove for those who love retro style and vintage Americana.

CINCINNATI, OHIO

322 Indulge your inner German

The river region around Cincinnati is steeped in German heritage, and nowhere in the country toasts all things Germanic quite like the city's Oktoberfest. Every fall, thousands submit themselves to polka music, lederhosen, culinary delicacies, and, of course, oceans of beer. Grab some sauerkraut and a brew and join in the fun, with drinking songs and wiener dog races.

PEEBLES, OHIO

324 Behold the mystery of an effigy mound

The early settlers of this region, who lived here from around 1000 BCE to 200 BCE, were big mound builders. You can see their work from Wisconsin down to Mississippi, though none are as striking as the Great Serpent Mound. This prehistoric effigy mound—1,300 ft (396 m) long and 3 ft (90 cm) high—depicts a giant snake devouring an egg (or the moon), and was designated a National Historic Landmark.

324 Ohio's seven-coiled Great Serpent Mound

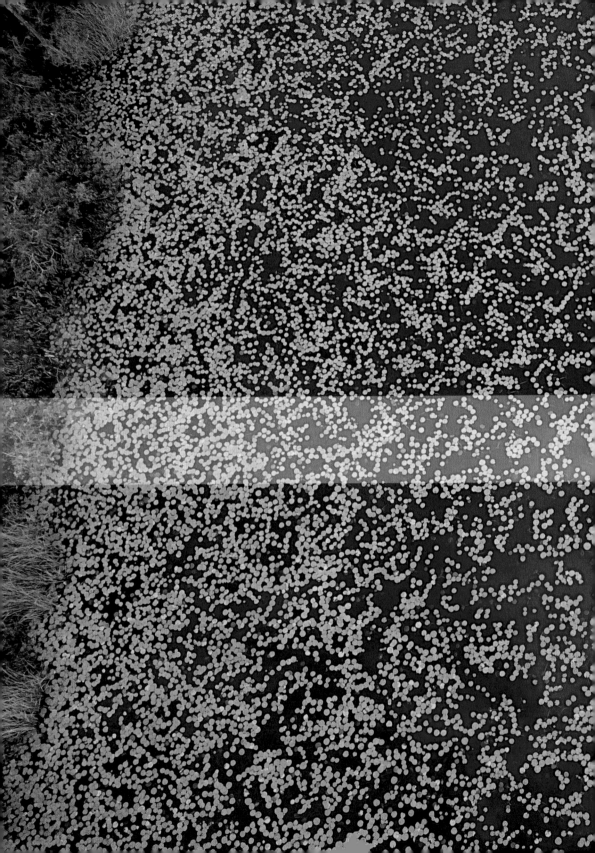

3

US SOUTH

TRANS PECOS WILDLIFE
DISTRICT, TEXAS

325 See deer and antelope play

If you're looking for that
special place where the deer
and pronghorn antelope play,
you might be lucky enough to
find them both here in a single
field—and you might then even
start to sing about it!

MARFA, TEXAS

326 Turn desert living into an art form

For a hundred years, Marfa was a
nondescript desert town. In 1971,
Minimalist artist Donald Judd
moved here and it became a
magnet for experimental artists.
Galleries and workshops opened
and Marfa grew in reputation
and size. Today it's a hub of
contemporary art, with festivals
and year-round tourism. Come
bask in the creativity and see
the Marfa Mystery Lights.

FORT WORTH, TEXAS

327 Join in an age-old Fort Worth tradition

There've been cattle auctions
and livestock trading in the Fort
Worth Stockyards, just outside
the central business district, since
1886. Every day, at 11.30 a.m.
and 4 p.m., a bygone era comes
to life as farmers herd livestock
through the streets. See a Texas
Longhorn cattle drive and actual
cowboys go about their business
in scenes reminiscent of the
Old West.

BIG BEND NATIONAL PARK, TEXAS

328 See Big Bend National Park

The night skies in Big Bend are
as dark as coal. Beneath them,
the sense of isolation is immense.
One of the park's treasures is
Gorman Falls. The climb down
is challenging and the rocks are
slippery, but there are ropes to
help. At the bottom, pitch a
tent and enjoy the cascading
water. There are also plenty
of suitable spots to launch a
kayak for a worm's-eye view
of the canyon.

SONORA, TEXAS

329 Cave into new levels of beauty

The landscape where Texas Hill
Country meets the Chihuahuan
Desert gets interesting when
you delve below the surface.
The Caverns of Sonora are widely
considered some of the most
beautiful show caves in the
world, full of twinkling, crystal
rock formations and dramatic
stalactites and stalagmites.
The highlight is the Butterfly,
a rare example of two fishtail
rock growths.

DALLAS, TEXAS

330 Admire the Dallas skyline

In 1978, a new tower known
locally as "the Ball" was unveiled,
part of a huge redevelopment
project in Dallas's Reunion
District. The tower is 561 ft
(171 m) high, and visitors
can ascend to the GeO-Deck
observation level and survey
the vast urban sprawl. There's a
restaurant in the tower, and you
can get a Tower after Hours
ticket to see the skyline and
its lights after dark.

328 Kayaking in Big Bend National Park

DALLAS, TEXAS
331 Tour the dark side of American history

Even if you weren't alive to remember where you were when John F. Kennedy was assassinated in 1963, it was such a seismic event that it retains its importance to this day. The Sixth Floor Museum examines his life and legacy, using films, photos, and interactive displays to examine the assassination and its context. A dark day, sensitively documented.

WILLOW CITY LOOP, TEXAS
332 Take a drive in bluebonnet season

The Texas bluebonnet is the official flower of the Lone Star State. After winter rains, these pretty wildflowers emerge in full force. They're best viewed on the scenic drive on the Willow City Loop, a narrow ranch road meandering 13 mi (20 km) through some of the oldest and most unique geology in central Texas.

AUSTIN, TEXAS
333 Dip into an ancient swimming hole

If you're bored with your local swimming pool, then here's somewhere with a backdrop straight out of *Jurassic Park*. Hamilton Pool Preserve is a natural pool that formed when the dome of an underground river collapsed thousands of years ago. It's now a state-run park, and the sparkling water is framed by dramatic limestone walls, with large stalactites along the ceiling.

332 Bluebonnet season in Texas

333 The ancient Hamilton Pool

AUSTIN, TEXAS

334 Get top views of Austin and beyond

Mt. Bonnell is considered the highest point in Austin at 775 ft (236 m). You'd be right in thinking that this doesn't require expedition-level skills to climb, and in fact a short, easily accessible hiking trail does the trick. The reward, though, outweighs the effort— a panoramic view of downtown and the 360 Bridge, perfect at any time of day but especially at dusk.

AUSTIN, TEXAS

335 Risk it for some brisket at a BBQ joint

In Texas, as in many places across the Southern states, they take the preparation of their meat very seriously indeed—barbecue especially— so for a restaurant to have gained respect and a loyal following, it has to be doing something special. The lines outside Franklin Barbecue speak for themselves. Arrive early, and dive into the menu of brisket, pulled pork, and more.

SAN ANTONIO, TEXAS

336 Stream your San Antonio pleasure options

One level down from the car-ridden thoroughfares of downtown, there's a shady park, the cooling San Antonio River, and a wealth of dining choices. The River Walk has evolved since the 1960s, and it's now a thriving center for art, retail, and culture. The pathways cover some 15 mi (24 km), and attract visitors at any time of day.

336 San Antonio's River Walk

SAN ANTONIO, TEXAS
337 Visit a place where a legend was born

If any place epitomizes the Texan ethos and old mythologies, it's the Alamo. The building is an eighteenth-century mission, and in 1836, a thirteen-day siege here pitted a small number of Texan soldiers against the Mexican Army. The Texans lost, but their fighting spirit became the stuff of legend. A museum now commemorates that battle and its place in history.

SAN ANTONIO, TEXAS
338 Enter a tree-climbing competition

Most people haven't climbed a tree since they were young, but there's no reason not to. If you've got what it takes, you can get competitive, too. In the Texas Tree Climbing Championship, competitors are scored for speed, accuracy, poise, and strength, all while safely attached to a rope— wearing a helmet, it should be added.

GALVESTON, TEXAS
339 Don't make Galveston your last resort

Texas isn't the first state that you think of when it comes to coastal destinations, but the resort city of Galveston is an overlooked gem. As well as terrific beaches, there are rides and entertainment along Galveston Island Historic Pleasure Pier, and at Moody Gardens, giant glass pyramids house animal residents. Galveston Island State Park also offers hiking trails and fishing holes.

339 Colonel Paddlewheel Boat, moored at Moody Gardens

HOUSTON, TEXAS
340 Relive the Space Race

NASA has long been a presence in Houston, and like its sister site in Florida, Space Center Houston has a wealth of treasures for space fanatics. The landmark attraction is *Independence*, the world's only space shuttle replica (shown here), and there are three flown spacecraft—from the Mercury 9, Gemini 5, and Apollo 17 missions—as well as moon rocks to see. Add "Mission Mars" and a host of other astral exhibits, and budding astronauts will be on cloud nine.

RIO GRANDE VALLEY, TEXAS
341 Watch an armadillo jump

Armadillos are mainly found in Central and South America, but the nine-banded armadillo has made such a success of life in the United States that it's now the state mammal for Texas. These cat-sized animals emerge at night to forage for insects, and when threatened can jump 3 to 4 ft (1 m) into the air to startle predators before retreating.

PADRE ISLAND NATIONAL SEASHORE, TEXAS
342 Give nature a helping hand

Several times every summer, the National Park Service oversees a process that gives Mother Nature a helping hand. The region is a hot spot for turtle nests, and Kemp's ridley sea turtle hatchlings need help making it into the sea. Visitors can watch this heartwarming tradition and lend moral support. The releases open to the public take place before 7 a.m. on Malaquite Beach, mid-June through August.

342 Turtle hatchling release at sunrise on Padre Island

344 Lafayette's Festival International de Louisiane

LAFAYETTE, LOUISIANA
343 Try a boudin in Cajun country

The Cajuns in this region have lived off the land for centuries, and some of their recipes have become local delicacies. One of the most popular is boudin—a sausage made from ground pork, rice, onions, and seasonings. Some of the best are found at various gas stations and delis, though most restaurants will have at least one option. Your best bet is to ask a local.

LAFAYETTE, LOUISIANA
344 Get hip to local music

They say everything is a gumbo down here, with influences from all over creating new forms, and music is no exception. Zydeco is a genre that evolved through French Creole speakers and blends blues, R&B, and Indigenous traditions. Every April, the city hosts the Festival International de Louisiane, where the region's (and by extension, the world's) best zydeco bands entertain the crowds.

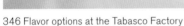

346 Flavor options at the Tabasco Factory

347 Louisiana's Old State Capitol interior

ACADIANA PARK NATURE
STATION, LOUISIANA

345 Choose the most owllike owl

For many, the barn owl
wins hands down at being the
most owllike owl, due to its
distinctive white rounded face,
and dark eyes. It's only its call
that disappoints—not a hoot but
a rasping scream. The Acadiana
nature center offers well over
a hundred other types of birds,
too, and around 8 mi (13 km) of
trails to explore.

AVERY ISLAND, LOUISIANA

346 Test your tolerance for heat

If you've ever put hot sauce on
your food, chances are you've
tasted Tabasco. Beyoncé keeps
some in her bag, allegedly. Its
factory sits on a scenic island off
the Louisiana coast, with lush
flora and beautiful oaks. You
can tour the factory and attached
Jungle Gardens and Bird City
wildfowl refuge, and of course
sample some of that famously
spicy sauce.

BATON ROUGE, LOUISIANA

347 Inspect the regal Old State Capitol

This striking Neo-Gothic
building overlooking the
Mississippi was built to look
and function as a medieval-style
castle. It's now referred to as the
Museum of Political History and
it's on the National Register of
Historic Places, with attractions
and exhibits showcasing the
building as an architectural
treasure, including some
beautiful stained-glass work.

349 Abita Mystery House

350 Whitney Plantation Museum

BATON ROUGE, LOUISIANA
348 Be a steam player

There's something so evocative about steamboats on the Mississippi, and thankfully this centuries-old experience is still available to visitors today. The *American Queen* is a six-deck re-creation of a classic Mississippi riverboat, and can accommodate more than 400 passengers. Join a cruise for a sedate jaunt up the river, complete with suitably traditional entertainment on board.

ABITA SPRINGS, LOUISIANA
349 Visit a curious mini world

Roadside attractions are a weirdly valuable piece of Americana, and this one is strange even by those standards. Artist John Preble has collected rocks, bottles, license plates, and general ephemera and created the UCM (you-see-'em) Museum, or Abita Mystery House. Enter through an old gas station and see mosaics, comb collections, antique arcade machines . . .

WALLACE, LOUISIANA
350 Don't overlook this daring museum

Plantations here mostly gloss over their dark origins, but the Whitney Plantation has an educational, ethical approach. It's a museum with an exclusive focus on the lives of enslaved people, doing admirable work to give context to its history. The French Creole raised-style main house dates to 1803, and around the grounds, exhibits lay bare life under slavery.

NEW ORLEANS, LOUISIANA
351 Let your hair down at Mardi Gras

A visit to New Orleans should be a bucket-list staple at any time of year, with bold and brassy architecture, innovative food, and music that's loud and never ending. Barely a week goes by without a party, but the city pulls out all the stops during the two weeks of Mardi Gras—a time for overindulging on food, wine, and song before Lent begins. There are two ways to enjoy it: Take in the drama from the balcony of a lodging house on the parade route, or down in the streets, among the jazz vibrations and smells of gumbo and jambalaya.

NEW ORLEANS, LOUISIANA
352 Hop between jazz clubs

Jazz has long been the musical lifeblood of New Orleans, and there's nowhere to experience its most authentic tunes like Frenchmen Street. Just a block from the historic French Quarter, the scene strikes up daily in the late afternoon. Bands playing ragtime, swing, and, of course, traditional Dixieland jazz let loose into the night at some of the Crescent City's oldest venues. Grab a cocktail and bounce between them—famous clubs such as the Spotted Cat, Snug Harbor, and the Blue Nile are all within a couple of blocks.

NEW ORLEANS, LOUISIANA
353 See a cemetery built on a swamp

The Crescent City is built on swampland for better or worse, but one of the side effects is that people must be buried in above-ground mausoleums. The city's cemeteries are an attraction in themselves, with elaborate marble resting places of several figures of note. Guided tours are compulsory, so sign up and explore the grounds, including the huge pyramid tomb that belongs to actor Nicolas Cage.

NEW ORLEANS, LOUISIANA
354 Spot the real Sunday best outfits

In New Orleans, Super Sunday isn't the day that the Super Bowl is played. In traditions that date back to the nineteenth century, it's the Sunday closest to St. Joseph's Day (March 19), when the mysterious Mardi Gras Indians stage their marches. Dressed in elaborate and colorful costumes, they playfully try to outdo each other with their "prettiness." Join the festivities early at A. L. Davis Park.

NEW ORLEANS, LOUISIANA
355 Tour NOLA in style

The original heart of New Orleans is famed for colonial-style buildings with ironwork balconies—mainly built by the Spanish after the original French buildings were destroyed by fire. The best way to see celebrated addresses like Bourbon Street and Jackson Square is in an open-sided vehicle so the sounds of the city don't pass you by. Hop in a mule-drawn carriage, to feel like a resident of yesteryear, or go twenty-first century in a pedicab.

THE SIGHTS AND SOUNDS OF NEW ORLEANS

Mardi Gras parade

Live jazz at the Spotted Cat

Pedicabs in the French Quarter

THROUGHOUT LOUISIANA
356 Relish the messiness of a crawfish boil

Most people call them crayfish, but down here they're crawfish, or even mudbugs—either way, they're delicious. The season runs from mid-January through early July, with peak months being March to May. Most bars run a boil. Spicy crawfish are dumped onto a table with fixings (corn cobs, garlic, potatoes, sausage) and then it's every person for themselves. Break off the shell, suck out the meat, repeat.

SOUTHWEST LOUISIANA
357 Boat into the bayou

Heading into the swamps down here is an adventurous undertaking, with many predators making a home for themselves in the murky depths. Take a guided tour, though, and an experienced guide will navigate through the wilderness and help you meet and photograph snakes and alligators in complete safety. It's hot and humid yet serene as you meander through the ancient forests.

EUREKA SPRINGS, ARKANSAS
358 Admire a half-sized tribute to Rio

The 125-ft (38-m) Christ the Redeemer in Rio is one of the world's most famous landmarks. Arkansas has its own version; at 66 ft (20 m), Christ of the Ozarks is around half the height but no less imposing. The statue overlooks the Victorian village of Eureka Springs, and even for non-Christians it's an impressive work of art. Neighboring Thorncrown Chapel is also a wonderful modernist building.

COSSATOT RIVER STATE PARK, ARKANSAS
359 Make a scenic stretch of river your latest crush

The name may translate as "skull crusher," but don't let that put you off. This river in the Ouachita National Forest attracts kayak and canoe fans of all levels, and while there are definitely some more technical rapids, there are also plenty of slower sections where beginners can paddle along and enjoy the scenery. Just be sure to get directions before you head out!

MOUNT IDA, ARKANSAS
360 Mine for your own treasures

If you're a fan of shiny stones, then you can try your hand at harvesting crystals at the Wegner Quartz Crystal Mines. The facility has a large, 40-ac (16-ha) open-pit surface mine where quartz crystals are at the surface just ready to be picked out, especially following a hard rainfall. You can keep all you can find, and although they're not valuable, they look great in homemade crafts—and they're free.

359 A tranquil bend on the Cossatot River

HOT SPRINGS NATIONAL PARK, ARKANSAS

361 Take the waters, inside and out

Hot Springs is a town so synonymous with thermal waters that it took the name. It features Bathhouse Row—a street with eight bathhouse buildings of beautiful architecture. Sadly, only two of them offer bathing experiences now, but there are many spring fountains where you can fill water bottles and drink the goodness instead.

CONWAY, ARKANSAS

362 Trade a road race for a toad race

There's a place called Toad Suck in Arkansas, its name's origins lost in the mists of time. In the 1980s, it hosted a music, arts, and food festival called Toad Suck Daze. The festival grew so big it had to relocate to downtown Conway, but its spirit remains intact. Every first weekend in May, thousands attend, the highlight being a race with the town's beloved toads.

LITTLE ROCK, ARKANSAS

363 Ask for the Bill at this tribute to Clinton

Little Rock might be largely bypassed these days if one of its residents hadn't become the most powerful person on earth. Former president Bill Clinton counts the place as his home, and as such, the William J. Clinton Presidential Library and Museum was constructed here— an expansive facility with lots of interesting American history and a pleasingly sleek design.

361 Public fountain in downtown Hot Springs

363 William J. Clinton Library and Museum

THROUGHOUT ARKANSAS

364 Fry some local snacks on for size

It's best to put your diet on hold when visiting Arkansas. It's not that healthy food isn't available (it probably is . . . somewhere); it's just that they do fried food so well. There are some compulsory items for a tasting menu: start with okra and green tomatoes, then move on to glorious fried hand pies, a local delicacy that is often sweet (apple and cherry) and sometimes savory.

TUPELO, MISSISSIPPI

365 Grace the land where the King was born

For many fans of Elvis, a trip to Graceland is a once-in-a-lifetime pilgrimage. Elvis wasn't from Memphis, though, and for the most serious fans, a stop in Tupelo, his birthplace, is a must-do. See his childhood home, his school, and the store that sold him his first guitar. If you're lucky, a couple of his former classmates will be there to regale you with stories.

OXFORD, MISSISSIPPI

366 Discover William Faulkner's private world

Rowan Oak was William Faulkner's home. It's a handsome house in the Greek Revival style, full of personal possessions. However, for fans of the Nobel Prize–winning author of *The Sound and the Fury*, it's a small room at the back of the house that's of most interest. Here, written on the walls, is Faulkner's plot outline for his celebrated novel *A Fable*.

366 Faulkner's home, Rowan Oak

INDIANOLA, MISSISSIPPI

367 Celebrate the king of the guitar

From humble beginnings, Riley B. King, or B.B. King, became an American legend, widely recognized as one of the most important guitarists of the twentieth century. He grew up around these parts, so it's fitting that a state-of-the-art museum in his memory (he died in 2015) was opened here in 2008. His life and music, as well as blues in general, are celebrated.

VICKSBURG, MISSISSIPPI

368 A civil place to learn about an uncivil war

In 1863, Vicksburg was where Ulysses S. Grant drove back Confederate forces, one of the most important events in the Civil War. The region is now dedicated to memorials and monuments and is a perfect place to learn about this awful conflict. Start at the Vicksburg Battlefield Museum, with its gigantic diorama of the Siege of Vicksburg.

GULF COAST, MISSISSIPPI

369 See a gulf paradise

A string of six islands offshore from Biloxi on Mississippi Gulf Coast offers visitors some beautiful beaches, swimming, hiking, and mellow vibes. There are also some fantastic wildlife-watching opportunities here. Look for pelicans gulping down fish, loggerhead turtles bobbing in the water, alligators hiding in the marshes, and nine-banded armadillos scurrying in the bush.

369 Welcoming pelicans at Gulfport Beach

BILOXI, MISSISSIPPI

370 Test your nerve with a game of blackjack

A quick stroll along Biloxi's Beach Boulevard will give you ample choices for a casino to play a few hands of blackjack. There are eight in town, so plenty of opportunity to find a game to suit your experience and budget. For novice gamblers, blackjack is a good place to start as the rules are simple (as long as you can add up to twenty-one). Set your budget in advance!

VARIOUS SITES IN MISSISSIPPI

371 Experience the authentic Delta blues

Juke joints are traditionally where African Americans went to listen to blues music. Often ramshackle places, they were common a century ago, but now only a handful remain. Red's Lounge in Clarksdale is a good starting point, or the Blue Front Café in Bentonia—both still host real Delta blues as regularly as they can. Other juke joints are disappearing fast, so visit soon.

NATCHEZ, MISSISSIPPI

372 Don't race the Trace

The 444-mi (715-km) Natchez Trace Parkway winds its way from Natchez up to Nashville, Tennessee, roughly following a 10,000-year-old travel corridor (the Old Natchez Trace) used by Native Americans, European settlers, and soldiers. You can drive it in two days, but the plethora of historical sites and wonderful scenery along the way mean that you'll want to opt for a much more leisurely pace.

371 Red's Lounge in Clarksdale

373 Find the best catfish in the Hospitality State

Catfish are so named because of the wonderful barbels that grow from their bottom lips, like cats' whiskers. However, in Mississippi that's of little interest. What you're after here is a quality batter on your fried catfish and tasty sides such as fried green tomatoes and hush puppies, all enjoyed in a convivial restaurant—which, to be fair, describes most eateries in the Hospitality State.

374 Follow the Mississippi Blues Trail

Some great things have come out of America, and blues music is one of them. It evolved out of the plantations in the Delta, and some of the movement's most famous musicians were born here and went on to become globally famous. The state has put together a trail of musical markers that take in important cultural sites, so follow it and get to know Robert Johnson, Skip James, and a dozen other legends.

375 Visit Helen Keller's childhood home

There can't be many well pumps as significant as the one at Ivy Green—childhood home of author and disability rights advocate Helen Keller, who was left blind and deaf after an illness at nineteen months. It was the link between feeling water from the pump and the tapping of the letters w-a-t-e-r by her teacher, Anne Sullivan, that led to Keller developing language.

374 Mural of blues greats in Leland

376 Wooded trail at Dismals Canyon

377 Talladega Superspeedway track

PHIL CAMPBELL, ALABAMA
376 Be enchanted by a rare phenomenon

The 85-ac (34-ha) Dismals Canyon was designated a National Natural Landmark in 1975. Although it's a scenic location to hike around in the daytime, with sunken forests, canyons, and waterfalls, it's only after dusk that it reveals its true beauty. This is when tiny bioluminescent creatures ("Dismalites") magically light up the woodlands.

TALLADEGA, ALABAMA
377 See a titan of the racing world

The Talladega Superspeedway, nicknamed "Dega," is a huge complex in size and reputation. With a track length of just over 2½ mi (4 km), it's the longest NASCAR oval and the home of the fastest laps in the sport. Several NASCAR and other motorsports events are held every year, so take your place with the crowds and watch some spectacular racing.

GUNTER HILL PARK, ALABAMA
378 Watch a flicker fly

Related to the woodpecker, the northern flicker is pretty enough when on the ground pecking for ants, its tawny plumage covered with neat black spots. But see one take to the skies, and you will be treated to a dazzling display from beneath its wings. Different flickers have different colors under their wings.

379 Woodland carvings on the Tinglewood Trail

MONTEVALLO, ALABAMA
379 Spot faces in the trees

The Tinglewood Trail sounds just like something out of a fantasy novel, and although it's only a short (half-mile) looped hike, magical elements are revealed to visitors along the way. The route is named for artist Tim Tingle, who has carved faces of people, animals, and fantastic creatures into the trees—it's as close to an enchanted forest as you'll get.

MONTGOMERY, ALABAMA
380 Pay respects to a monumental movement

Montgomery is key in the history of the civil rights movement. It was here that Rosa Parks took a seminal stand, where Martin Luther King Jr. spoke out in local churches, and where he and his family lived in the 1950s. The Rosa Parks Museum, the Dexter Parsonage Museum, and the National Memorial for Peace and Justice tell stories that all should hear.

TULIP TREE SPRINGS, ALABAMA
381 Steer clear of the bombardier

As beetles go, the bombardier looks much like many others. However, make the mistake of threatening it, and it'll release its bomb: a pungent chemical spray that can reach temperatures of 200°F (100°C) when fired from its abdomen! That's one way to see off your predators.

380 Monument to the victims of lynching, National Memorial for Peace and Justice

HIGHLIGHTS OF THE KENTUCKY DERBY

Thunder Over Louisville

Wild hats at the Derby

Preparation race for the Derby

MOBILE, ALABAMA
382 Play battleships for real on a 1930s vessel

After a long and distinguished life of service, the USS *Alabama*—built for the US Navy in the 1930s—is now a museum ship, saved from the breaker's yard and starting its new life in 1965. It's a major part of the Battleship Memorial Park, and together with half a dozen other ships, a rare chance to board a once-great military vessel.

GULF COAST, ALABAMA
383 Ring in a new year; wring out your clothes

People here love running into the sea on New Year's Day. At Flora-Bama there's the Flora-Bama Polar Bear Dip, where hundreds of costumed revelers dive into the Gulf of Mexico, or there's the Kiwanis Polar Bear Dip, where . . . hundreds of costumed revelers dive into the Gulf of Mexico. Take your pick, pick a costume, and take a dip.

LOUISVILLE, KENTUCKY
384 Cheer on your nag at the Kentucky Derby

The Churchill Downs Racetrack goes completely wild for the Derby, known as the "most exciting two minutes in sport" and the "run for the roses" (the winner is blanketed in the flowers). Follow tradition and drink a mint julep, wolf down a bowl of burgoo, and, of course, allow yourself a modest bet.

LOUISVILLE, KENTUCKY
385 Eat a Hot Brown

The horse racing and free-flowing bourbon that permeate these parts points to a decadent lifestyle, which makes even more sense when you consider what the local delicacy is. It's called the Hot Brown and it's roast turkey on toast, covered with a cheesy Mornay sauce, then topped with tomatoes and bacon. Loosen your belt and head for the Brown Hotel, where the dish was invented in the 1920s.

LOUISVILLE, KENTUCKY
386 Enjoy the world's biggest fireworks display

Thunder Over Louisville is the kickoff event of the Kentucky Derby. The pride that the city sets by this race is evident in the scale of the celebrations. Since the late 1990s the April night skies have become increasingly luminous as eight gigantic barges launch fireworks from both sides of the George Rogers Clark Memorial Bridge. Join a half-million spectators.

LOUISVILLE, KENTUCKY
387 Step up to the bat

The Louisville Slugger isn't a local snack but a type of baseball bat, originally made for players in the late nineteenth century. The first player ever to get the bat scored three runs on the first day of using it, and a legend was born. Louisville is a center of baseball culture, and the Louisville Slugger Museum and Factory has a wealth of exhibits, including interactive batting cages and the world's largest bat.

BARDSTOWN, KENTUCKY
388 Take a quiet pause

For more than 170 years, a community of Trappist monks has lived at the Abbey of Gethsemani outside Bardstown. They live in silence to allow the voice of God to flourish within them. It's a peaceful place to visit, emanating calm. Join the monks at prayer, partake in meditation, and leave clutching fruitcake and fudge made by the monks for their store.

LEXINGTON, KENTUCKY
389 Find that it's horses for courses in Kentucky

The Kentucky Horse Park is an extensive facility dedictated to the relationship between humans and horses. As well as watching live shows, visitors can visit the International Museum of the Horse, with its 60,000 sq ft (5,570 sq m) of exhibitions. If you're a serious enthusiast, there's even a campground so that you can extend your stay.

VARIOUS SITES IN KENTUCKY
390 Drink a toast to bourbon

There are thirty-seven bourbon distilleries in Kentucky—some over 200 years old, and some newcomers enjoying the increasing popularity of craft bourbon. Learn about America's only native spirit along the Kentucky Bourbon Trail. Take it even further with cocktail-making classes and staying in a bourbon-themed hotel.

390 On the Kentucky Bourbon Trail

CUMBERLAND FALLS, KENTUCKY
391 Witness a rare nighttime event

Cumberland Falls is a scenic delight, with water falling some 68 ft (21 m) into a gorge. It's also one of the few places in the world where you can regularly see a moonbow (also called a white rainbow or lunar rainbow). Aim to arrive on either end of the full moon and for two days or so, you can watch the moonlight refracted in the water.

MAMMOTH CAVE, KENTUCKY
392 See an underground record holder

The Mammoth Cave system was already one of the longest in the world, and in 1972 it was found to link with the Flint Ridge system, and now the Mammoth–Flint Ridge system is the world's longest. Join an evocative guided tour by paraffin lamp and see oddly named caverns including Grand Avenue, Frozen Niagara, and Fat Man's Misery.

PLEASANT HILL, KENTUCKY
393 Keep things simple

The Shakers of Pleasant Hill were a peace-loving, celibate religious group, committed to conservation, equality of race and gender, and the pursuit of simplicity. Their community lasted for around a century. Today, a visit to the village and surrounding area offers great insight into their world, complete with their farming techniques and simple artifacts.

393 The orderly world of Pleasant Hill

CORBIN, KENTUCKY
394 Investigate a culinary secret

Even global giants have to start somewhere. For Colonel Harland Sanders—of Kentucky Fried Chicken fame—that somewhere was the back of a small service station in Corbin that expanded into a restaurant across the road, the Sanders Café. It was here that he developed his secret recipe. The site is now a museum and café dedicated to the colonel and the early days of KFC.

MEMPHIS, TENNESSEE
395 Catch a duck parade in a hotel lobby

Every day at 11 a.m. and 5 p.m., a crowd of people gather in the lobby of the Peabody Hotel in downtown Memphis. They're there to witness a decades-old tradition, as a member of the staff leads a flock of ducks to the hotel fountain. Since the 1930s, these waterfowl have been treated as royalty, and you can line up and watch them waddle their way there and back.

MEMPHIS, TENNESSEE
396 Tune into a musical legacy

Graceland may be the most famous musical mansion in town, but Memphis also offers other unmissable musical pilgrimages. Stax was a famous record label and its state-of-the-art museum has memorabilia from stars such as Otis Redding and Isaac Hayes, while at Sun Studio you can step into the very room where Elvis and Johnny Cash recorded.

396 Sun Studio in Memphis

397 Graceland's TV room

398 Lorraine Motel, National Civil Rights Museum

MEMPHIS, TENNESSEE

397 See what it's like to live like a King

As soon as Graceland's gates open, you enter Elvis Presley's gaudy world. He bought the house in 1957, and some rooms, at the behest of Priscilla Presley, have been restored to their original appearance. The kitchen, where the notorious fried peanut butter and banana sandwiches were made, is a prelude to the pièce de résistance: the TV room, a riot of blue and yellow, with a mirrored ceiling and three TVs (to watch three football games at once). Elvis's tragic end is reflected in the Meditation Garden, where many tears have been shed by his graveside.

MEMPHIS, TENNESSEE

398 Reflect at a humbling institution

In 1968, Dr. Martin Luther King Jr. was assassinated at the Lorraine Motel. The news shook the world, and added to Memphis's importance as a city where the civil rights movement came into sharp focus. The site is now the home of the National Civil Rights Museum complex—a hugely important institution that records the history of the movement in the United States from the seventeenth century through to the present day.

NASHVILLE, TENNESSEE
399 Learn line dancing

"Step, behind, step, hitch . . . back the other way, and forward, hitch . . .". The beauty of line dancing is that the moves are never complicated and everybody is doing the same thing at the same time. Synonymous with country music, Nashville is *the* place to take lessons and perfect your Tush Push, Cupid Shuffle, and Watermelon Crawl. There's much joy to be found in dancing in unison with others.

NASHVILLE, TENNESSEE
400 Visit country music's hallowed ground

Music pulses through Nashville like blood through veins. You should hear live music in this city at least once. The acoustics at the Ryman Auditorium are legendary. Originally the Union Gospel Tabernacle, it was built to project booming evangelists' voices. It's where bluegrass was born, where the *Grand Ole Opry* was recorded, and where Johnny Cash met June Carter.

LYNCHBURG, TENNESSEE
401 Come and find out you don't know jack

This part of the world is awash with its favorite tipple—whiskey has been an important industry here since well before the Civil War. One rock and roll brand has become a global hit: Jack Daniel's. You can visit the facility where the famous whiskey is made. See behind the scenes, learn how the distilling process works, and sample the town's best-known export.

400 A benefit concert at the Ryman Auditorium

CHATTANOOGA, TENNESSEE

402 Investigate a prominent peak

At just over 2,300 ft (700 m), the mighty ridge of Lookout Mountain looms over downtown Chattanooga. It was the scene of the Battle of Lookout Mountain in 1863. Visit to explore Ruby Falls, the tallest cave waterfall open to the public in the United States, the ever-changing Rock City, and Incline Railway, one of the world's steepest passenger railways.

PIGEON FORGE, TENNESSEE

403 Go ditzy at Dollywood

Tennessee's most popular attraction is owned by the most famous Tennessean of them all— Dolly Parton's Dollywood, an adventure playground, is a fun, frivolous way to spend a day. Ride the thunderous roller coasters and revel in the famous Southern charm—and music.

402 The view from Lookout Mountain

404 Peaks of the Great Smoky Mountains

GREAT SMOKY MOUNTAINS NATIONAL PARK, TENNESSEE

404 Witness the world of fireflies

Seeing tiny lights flashing in a forest is magical—as if fairies are roving around with flashlights. It's no less magical when you discover it's the bioluminescence of fireflies creating patterns to attract a mate. One species can synchronize with each other to make a wonderful natural lightshow. By day, the park is no less magical, with forested mountains shot through with streams and waterfalls, and plenty more wildlife, including black bears, groundhogs, chipmunks, and hundreds of bird species. Of 150 hiking trails, several are self-guided nature trails, and all offer great views. There is also a treat for cyclists every Wednesday in summer when the Cades Cove Loop Road is closed to vehicle traffic.

DEALS GAP, TENNESSEE

405 Hang onto your hat on a twisting roadway

There's a winding stretch of Highway 129 beginning at Deals Gap on the Tennessee–North Carolina state line that's known as the Tail of the Dragon. With 318 curves in 11 mi (17 km), it draws thousands of motorcycle and driving fans a year. But take care—the curves need focus, and there are no gas stations.

ATLANTA, GEORGIA

406 Experience millions of gallons of water

There are some great aquariums in the United States, but Atlanta's Georgia Aquarium is one of the best. It was the largest in the world until 2012, and is home to thousands of animals, including whale sharks, beluga whales, and bottlenose dolphins. Brave visitors can participate in the Shark Cage Dive and come face-to-face with sharks from behind a cage.

ATLANTA, GEORGIA

407 Mind your manners at a refined tearoom

People talk a lot about Southern hospitality and the corners of refinement that you can encounter in the South. Mary Mac's Tea Room is one of these places. It's a 1940s tearoom, the last of sixteen that used to exist in Atlanta. The tearoom now serves up Southern comfort food classics like deviled eggs, all in a decidedly civilized, elegant atmosphere.

ATLANTA, GEORGIA

408 Cycle a rejuvenated freight corridor

When the popularity of transporting freight by rail shifted to transportion by truck, it left an abandoned ring of railroads around the city. Today, the Atlanta Beltline Project is turning this former railway corridor into popular urban trails and green spaces. Cycle along it to feel connected to the past and inspired by the future.

409 *Woolly Mammoth* for Atlanta Botanical Garden's *Imaginary Worlds* exhibit

ATLANTA, GEORGIA
409 Allow the plant world to inspire you

Atlanta Botanical Garden is all you'd expect, and more. It's a beautiful space, full of amazing plants, and it has rest areas where you can sit and contemplate. It also offers an imaginative events program to suit all ages and interests. Take a tai chi class surrounded by nature, join a toddler dance group inspired by the outdoors, or feed your mind learning about horticulture.

ATLANTA, GEORGIA
410 See a park dedicated to those with a dream

As a key figure in American history, it's only right that the memory and works of Martin Luther King Jr. are memorialized appropriately. The Martin Luther King Jr. National Historical Park includes a museum chronicling the civil rights movement, the childhood home of Dr. King, and the International Civil Rights Walk of Fame.

412 The Georgia Bulldogs human and canine mascots—Hairy Dawg and Uga

ATLANTA, GEORGIA
411 Get high on art

Fine art has had a following in Atlanta since the early twentieth century. The High Museum of Art can trace its origins back to 1905. It's now a huge facility that underwent a $124 million renovation in 2005. You can surround yourself with great names, from Renoir and Rodin to Matisse and Monet, while past exhibitions range from Cézanne to *The Rise of Sneaker Culture*.

ATHENS, GEORGIA
412 Catch a college football game

The University of Georgia's Sanford Stadium is one of the best for college football, with views over the hills and seating over 90,000. Georgia Bulldogs games are played "between the hedges" (privet hedges surround the field). Spot Uga, the English bulldog mascot, with his air-conditioned doghouse.

GEORGIA
413 Up the ante by traveling back in time

Between Athens and Macon, seven historic communities make up the 100-mi (160-km) Antebellum Trail (including Watkinsville, Madison, Eatonton, Milledgeville, and Gray/Old Clinton). Visit to see fascinating historic-house museums and battle sites along the route.

AUGUSTA, GEORGIA

414 Master your swing on a national course

To take a swing around the impeccably groomed, but fiendishly difficult, Augusta National Golf Club is the golfing dream. Home to the US Masters every year—the only major tournament held at the same location—each hole is named after a tree or shrub, and the flora and fauna around the course are a botanist's delight, so players can keep a smile on their faces, even if they're hitting a lot of balls into the water.

SAVANNAH, GEORGIA

415 Creep carefully among the Savannah tombstones

Captured in John Berendt's *Midnight in the Garden of Good and Evil*, Savannah has a unique and sometimes eerie atmosphere. Probably the most-photographed cemetery in the world is Bonaventure, where creative headstones abound—the cover of Berendt's book featured the Bird Girl statue, which once lay here but is now in the Telfair Museums. Colonial Park Cemetery is home to many of Savannah's oldest citizens, including plenty killed in duels, and it's a noteworthy stop on the city's popular ghost tours. The Laurel Grove Cemetery, meanwhile, is where 1,500 Confederate soldiers were laid to rest, and it's one of the oldest African American cemeteries still in use.

415 Tombstone in Bonaventure Cemetery

416 Forsyth Park's fountain

418 Okefenokee Swamp Park boardwalk

SAVANNAH, GEORGIA
416 Be there or be square in Savannah

Downtown Savannah was built around twenty-four squares (now twenty-two)—each slightly different but most very scenic, framed by historic homes and Spanish moss. Why not visit them all and track the city's evolution through their monuments? Some are said to be haunted, so you can also join an evening ghost tour.

BYRON AND FORT VALLEY, GEORGIA
417 Relish a peach

Georgia's pride produce is the peach, and every year there's a weeklong festival split between two towns that celebrates all things peachy. There are cooking presentations, music, kids' entertainment, and, of course, a hundred ways to sample peaches, from pies and jams to beers and cobblers. There's even a peach pie eating contest, if you're up to it.

WAYCROSS, GEORGIA
418 Go back millennia at Okefenokee

To experience the Okefenokee Swamp Park is to experience how this part of America would have been before European settlers arrived—a great tangle of trees rising out of swamp waters. Wander through on a boardwalk or take a boat along an original Native American waterway, looking out for egrets, herons, otters, and alligators.

419 Driftwood Beach on Jekyll Island

GOLDEN ISLES, GEORGIA
419 Visit the seaside wilds of Georgia

Georgia's coast is wonderfully wild and unique—fecund islands lapped by salt tides and peppered with marshes, estuaries, and miles of beach. Roaring rivers descend from the mountains, marshlands teem with fiddler crabs and swaying cordgrass, and the low whisper of the Atlantic is never far away. Four of the fifteen barrier islands are popular resort destinations; others are accessible only by boat and remain unspoiled natural escapes. But even the popular Jekyll Island, accessible by car, has its untouched secrets. Hidden down a palm-lined path is Driftwood Beach, where whole gray trees, preserved by salt air, rest on their sides like wild sculptures.

SEASIDE, FLORIDA
420 Question the nature of reality with a selfie

For most of its life, the beach community of Seaside was a little-known vacation spot on Florida's Emerald Coast. That all changed in 1998, when the movie *The Truman Show*, starring Jim Carrey and filmed at Seaside, became a worldwide hit. You can also visit nearby Santa Rosa Beach and capture a selfie outside the house he left every morning, located at 31 Natchez Street. We promise that the people you'll encounter there aren't actors.

422 Florida manatee coming up for breath

ST. AUGUSTINE, FLORIDA
421 Explore one of the oldest US neighborhoods

US history stretches to well before the first Europeans, but some settlements are still worth visiting. St. Augustine—founded in 1565—is the oldest continually inhabited European-founded town in the country. Survey five centuries of history, including the fort of Castillo de San Marcos, Fort Matanzas, and the Fort Mose Historic State Park.

THREE SISTERS SPRINGS, FLORIDA
422 Be soothed by the serene manatee

The manatee is undoubtedly one of the world's most lovable species. It's blubbery and peaceful, and has a very distinctive face. Large numbers of Florida manatees are present along the southeastern coasts of Florida all year, but in winter they seek out warmer waters, offering better viewing opportunities for nature lovers.

DAYTONA BEACH, FLORIDA
423 Get your heart racing at Daytona

Since 1959, Daytona Beach has been a hub for racing enthusiasts as the home of the Daytona 500, the most prestigious race in NASCAR. Thousands arrive to welcome the season, which usually commences in February. If you can't make it then, the Daytona International Speedway is open year-round, offering tours and exhibits.

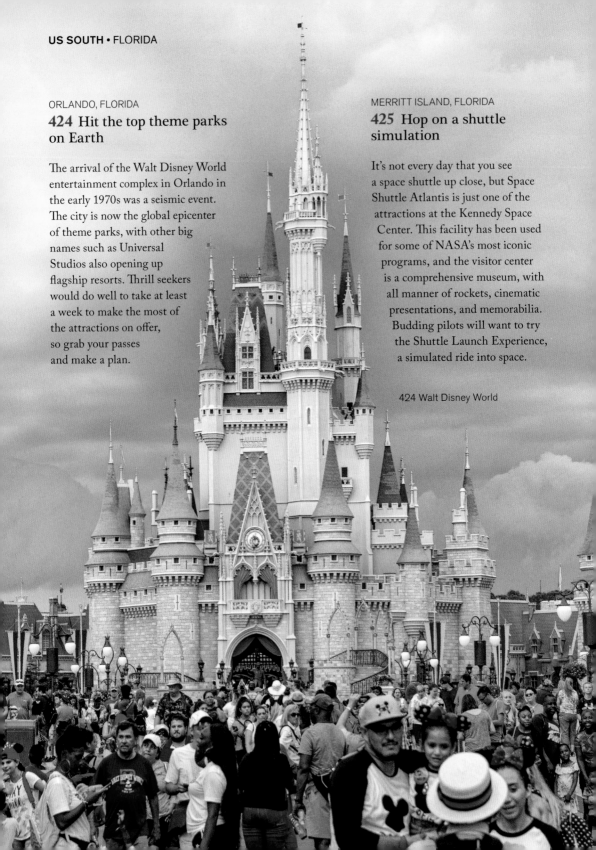

ORLANDO, FLORIDA

424 Hit the top theme parks on Earth

The arrival of the Walt Disney World entertainment complex in Orlando in the early 1970s was a seismic event. The city is now the global epicenter of theme parks, with other big names such as Universal Studios also opening up flagship resorts. Thrill seekers would do well to take at least a week to make the most of the attractions on offer, so grab your passes and make a plan.

MERRITT ISLAND, FLORIDA

425 Hop on a shuttle simulation

It's not every day that you see a space shuttle up close, but Space Shuttle Atlantis is just one of the attractions at the Kennedy Space Center. This facility has been used for some of NASA's most iconic programs, and the visitor center is a comprehensive museum, with all manner of rockets, cinematic presentations, and memorabilia. Budding pilots will want to try the Shuttle Launch Experience, a simulated ride into space.

424 Walt Disney World

WEEKI WACHEE, FLORIDA

426 Hear a siren's song in an underwater theater

There are real live mermaids to be spotted at Weeki Wachee Springs, an old-school roadside attraction outside Tampa. This was a glamorous resort in the 1950s and welcomed all the A-listers. The park retains its analog charms to this day, the main draw being the famous underwater theater, where the mermaids perform multiple shows a day to enrapt audiences.

TAMPA, FLORIDA

427 Soak up sun and beer

Held each March, Cigar City Brewing's Hunahpu's Day festival gathers hundreds of breweries from Florida and around the country to pour beer in Tampa. The occasion is the release of Hunahpu's Imperial Stout from Cigar City Brewing, made with chocolate and chili powder. Tickets to the festival, a beer lover's dream, include unlimited pours from every brewery, as well as bottles of the coveted stout.

ST. PETERSBURG, FLORIDA

428 See the surreal world of a visionary

In 1942, the Cleveland philanthropists Reynolds and Eleanor Morse attended a Salvador Dalí retrospective. It began a lifelong obsession that resulted in the $30 million Salvador Dalí Museum. The collection includes 1,500 artworks, making it home to more Dalí masterpieces than any other museum in the world. The architecture is appropriately surrealist, too.

428 Salvador Dalí Museum, St. Petersburg

430 White sands of Sanibel Island

BLUE HERON BRIDGE, FLORIDA

429 Go diving and spy a stargazer—under the sea

Despite the northern stargazer's name, you'll discover that it's in fact a fairly ugly fish whose features face upward rather than forward. This allows the fish to hide buried in the sand, waiting for prey, which it then pounces on when the prey passes overhead.

SANIBEL ISLAND, FLORIDA

430 Kick back on pristine sands

Off the west coast of Florida, Sanibel Island's beautiful white beaches are the main draw for visitors. Bowman's Beach is the island's most popular stretch for swimming, while Blind Pass Beach is a bit more off the beaten path and is a great place for shell spotters to collect conches and cockles, as well as the occasional shark's tooth.

431 Diving with lemon sharks in the shallows

JUPITER, FLORIDA

431 Discover not all sharks are gray

The lemon shark's yellowy brown to olive color helps camouflage it against the sand. Like all sharks, it uses electric impulses—and a keen sense of smell, which makes up for its poor eyesight—to track its prey. Because it favors shallow waters and hunts by day, divers have a good chance of spotting it at Jupiter. It's also not known to be aggressive toward humans.

COCONUT CREEK, FLORIDA

432 Witness a small miracle of nature

If you've never seen a butterfly emerging from a chrysalis, then why not cheat with a visit to Butterfly World in Florida's Coconut Creek? It's the largest butterfly park in the world, and home to thousands of live butterflies year-round.

MIAMI, FLORIDA

433 Dance all night

Miami Beach's nightlife is legendary. Its legion of clubs with their glowing neon exteriors and glitter ball interiors will keep you dancing until the sun comes up. The city offers clubs for all tastes: megaclubs with top DJs, local indie hangouts, or nightspots pumping out Latin rhythms.

MIAMI, FLORIDA

434 Take a boat ride around Biscayne Bay

Miami's skyscrapers rise from the blue waters of Biscayne Bay, extending along the coast. But a boat trip around the bay shows that this city is more than its downtown: There are beaches, deserted islands, homes of the stars, and abundant marine life. Where else could your tour guide move seamlessly from pointing out Gloria Estefan's home to spotting a manatee?

MIAMI, FLORIDA

435 See the art of a neighborhood makeover

Most cities have an arts district and in Miami that is Wynwood. Huge, vibrant murals have sprung up so that you can tour the streets in what has become an outdoor museum. Wynwood Walls showcases large-scale works by famous street artists, and warehouses here are now galleries and boutiques. Bring your camera and capture the most contemporary art.

MIAMI, FLORIDA

436 Hone the art of spotting future talent

Every September, the world's art community descends on the city, with Miami Beach turned into one big art installation at Art Basel Miami Beach. See the cutting edge of contemporary art at site-specific shows that are an extension of the famous Swiss festival, and buy something to take home. You may even pick a work by a future art world superstar.

435 Murals at Wynwood Walls

MIAMI, FLORIDA
437 Eat a frita

If it seems odd that eating a burger should be on your bucket list, then you haven't tried a frita. Originally a Cuban street food, it's now a staple of Little Havana in Miami. Picture a patty of spiced meat and onion, placed in a soft Cuban bun with a handful of shoestring fries and a squirt of ketchup. So simple, so good. You'll find them everywhere, but the ones at El Rey de las Fritas are award-winning.

MIAMI, FLORIDA
438 Dive into the oldest pool in town

In 1924, an old coral rock quarry was converted into a resort and pool. The Venetian Pool, as it came to be known, is now the only swimming pool on the National Register of Historic Places, and it was renovated in 1989 to restore the waterfall and grotto. It has a cool, vintage vibe that fans of Miami's retro chic will love, and it's very family-friendly.

MIAMI, FLORIDA
439 Admire the coastal chic of South Beach

Oozing 1930s glamour, South Beach has the highest concentration of art deco buildings in the world—many erected during a renaissance that revived Miami Beach in the 1940s. The Carlyle, Colony Theatre, and Miami Beach Post Office are just some of the examples, all made famous in various movies and photo collections over the years.

439 Art deco architecture in South Beach

440 Airboating into the Everglades

THE EVERGLADES, FLORIDA
440 Tell your gators from your crocs

The Everglades is an amazing subtropical wilderness and home to a huge amount of wildlife. It is also the only place where both alligators and crocodiles are found. If you have trouble telling them apart, remember that crocodiles have pointier, V-shaped snouts, while alligators' snouts are broad and U-shaped.

KEY LARGO, FLORIDA
441 Paddleboard through mangroves

It never gets too cold to paddleboard through the water trails and mangrove creeks of John Pennekamp Coral Reef State Park. Winter is when wildlife is at its best. In the trees and at the water's edge, look for ospreys, herons, egrets, cormorants, and pelicans. If you're lucky, you might spot a stingray or manatee below the water's surface. Traveling by paddleboard is so calm that you'll have the chance to see before you're seen.

MARATHON, FLORIDA

442 Come out of your shell at a turtle hospital

Sea turtles are among the most charismatic creatures in the ocean in this part of the world. They often have a hard time of things, though, and are prone to injury by predators or by humans being careless. The Turtle Hospital here rescues and rehabilitates injured turtles. Visit to see the work these heroes do behind the scenes, and learn more about these cute creatures.

KEY WEST, FLORIDA

443 Don't let the sun go down on your drink

If you don't have a specific celebration planned for your Key West vacation, no problem. You can just join the nightly Sunset Celebration that takes place at Mallory Square as locals and visitors alike raise their glasses to the setting sun. The city has turned it into a mini nightly arts festival, with music and street performers—a joyous tradition that brings everyone together for an hour.

443 Mallory Square's Sunset Celebration

DRY TORTUGAS NATIONAL PARK, FLORIDA

444 Explore a seabound fort

Reachable only by boat or seaplane, the Dry Tortugas is one of North America's most remote and least visited national parks. Your rewards for making the effort are snorkeling among sparkling coral reefs and an abandoned but beautifully preserved nineteenth-century fort to explore—Fort Jefferson.

BLUE RIDGE PARKWAY, NORTH CAROLINA

445 Meander along America's favorite drive

At 469 mi (755 km) long, the Blue Ridge Parkway is America's longest linear park. It links two national parks (Shenandoah and the Great Smoky Mountains), along the Blue Ridge mountain chain. Panoramic views await around every corner, so you'll want to make regular stops to take in the natural beauty.

ASHEVILLE, NORTH CAROLINA

446 Feel the chill on Cold Mountain

The Cold Mountain summit hike takes you on a strenuous 10.6-mi (17-km) round trip to the top of the mountain made famous by Charles Frazier's novel.

444 The moat at Fort Jefferson

ASHEVILLE, NORTH CAROLINA
447 See the estate of the nation

In 1895, work was completed on what remains America's largest private home. A sprawling, château-style mansion, Biltmore House was built for prominent industrialist George Washington Vanderbilt II. The estate itself is some 8,000 ac (3,240 ha), and you can wander the parklands and see parts of the home, with its French Renaissance architecture and decadent interiors. As close to royalty as the country gets.

ASHEVILLE, NORTH CAROLINA
448 Learn to pair beer and cheese

The Funkatorium is Wicked Weed Brewing's outpost for its funky and sour beer program— one of the country's few taprooms dedicated exclusively to these beers. Located in the South Slope neighborhood, it features dozens of sour ales on draft and in bottles, with small plates to pair with them (think cheese, charcuterie, and duck confit salad). A recent expansion includes an outdoor beer garden and a live music venue.

LAKE LURE, NORTH CAROLINA

449 Don't put baby in the corner

This part of the world isn't famous for much, but in 1987, *Dirty Dancing* was filmed in the region. It was such a sensation that every September, the town holds a festival that is attended by hundreds of fans. Dance performances, competitions, and *Dirty Dancing*–themed games are all on offer. Buy some fan art and, of course, settle in to watch this enduring classic.

CHIMNEY ROCK, NORTH CAROLINA

450 Get your steps in for the top views in the state

A huge American flag marks the top of Chimney Rock, a 315-ft (96-m) granite monolith overlooking the entire region. Those who want the exercise can ascend 499 steps to the top, but if you're feeling less energetic, there's a handy elevator. Either way, at the top you're rewarded with panoramic views of the Blue Ridge Escarpment.

CHARLOTTE, NORTH CAROLINA

451 Enjoy a raft of water activities in Charlotte

Around 12 million gallons of recirculating well water make up the challenging channels at the US National Whitewater Center. Visitors can test their extreme rafting skills and, if advanced enough, can take on Olympic-standard courses. Beginners are catered to as well, and you can also try ice skating, rock climbing, and mountain biking across 1,300 ac (526 ha).

DURHAM, NORTH CAROLINA

452 Admire one of the country's great gardens

Duke University has been a respected institution since the late nineteenth century. In the early twentieth century, the college decided to pay tribute to some of its benefactors and the Sarah P. Duke Gardens was created. Across 55 ac (22 ha), different botanical sections display plants from around the world. Stroll this pastoral idyll and stop to smell the roses.

RALEIGH, NORTH CAROLINA

453 Cut a rug to some bluegrass

The Appalachian region has many traditions, but the one that's made the most waves is probably bluegrass—a more analog version of country music, usually played on acoustic instruments, with roots in folk and blues. In September, the International Bluegrass Music Association stages IBMA World of Bluegrass, with toe-tapping bands from around the world.

KILL DEVIL HILLS, NORTH CAROLINA

454 Be on the Wright side of history

Legend has it that these hills were named after a local rum strong enough to "kill the devil." The area is famous for very different reasons, though. In 1903, the Wright Brothers took off here for four powered airplane flights in their Flyer. Pay your respects at the Wright Brothers National Memorial, a must-see for aviation fans.

450 Reaching the summit of Chimney Rock

OUTER BANKS, NORTH CAROLINA

455 Meet some pirate ship descendants

This collection of barrier islands has seen little development, and some beaches are only accessible by 4x4s. Join a tour at Corolla and you can meet some mysterious locals: wild Spanish Colonial mustangs, said to have descended from horses that arrived on pirate ships centuries ago. Although you can't approach them, you can appreciate their majesty from a distance.

CROATAN NATIONAL FOREST, NORTH CAROLINA

456 Be fascinated by a flytrap

The carnivorous Venus flytrap, well known throughout the world, originates in the coastal bogs of North and South Carolina. It's a small plant with a hinged "mouth" at the end of its stem. The mouth sits open, waiting to be triggered by a passing insect or spider. It then snaps closed, trapping the prey inside, ready to be digested.

WILMINGTON, NORTH CAROLINA

457 Go it alone on an undeveloped island

At just over 8 mi (13 km) long, Masonboro Island Reserve is the longest undeveloped island in the state. It can only be reached by boat or kayak, but visitors can enjoy a wealth of natural bounty, such as turtles, red foxes, diamondback terrapins, and dozens of bird species. There are no facilities, so camping is only for hard-core nature lovers, but the sense of isolation is palpable.

455 Spanish Colonial mustangs in the Outer Banks

CLEVELAND, SOUTH CAROLINA
458 Visit a chapel nicknamed "Pretty Place"

The Fred W. Symmes Chapel is part of YMCA Camp Greenville and a true hidden gem. This mountaintop chapel comes with a breathtaking view that inspires you to sit still in silence and simply be.

DORCHESTER COUNTY, SOUTH CAROLINA
459 Educate yourself on a historic estate

Middleton Place is a regal home built in the early eighteenth century with elaborate landscaped gardens to rival any in the country for beauty. It was only made possible with slave labor, though, and the estate now welcomes visitors to educate them on the reality of life in those times, with permanent exhibits detailing plantation life.

CHARLESTON, SOUTH CAROLINA
460 See how the other half once lived

While many historic homes here are private residences, some operate as museums and give an insight into Charleston's past. Wander into the Aiken-Rhett House, for example, a sprawling merchant's residence. Make time to stroll down Rainbow Row, too; this aptly named row of pastel dwellings is the longest cluster of Georgian row houses in the country.

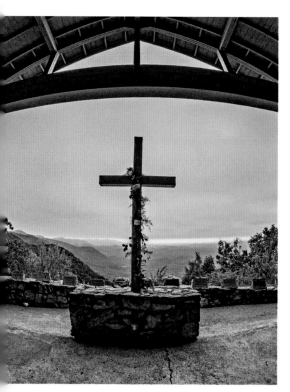

458 Fred W. Symmes Chapel

460 Charleston's Rainbow Row

CHARLESTON, SOUTH CAROLINA
461 Reflect at Fort Sumter

There's something about a sea fort that makes it easy to imagine yourself as a soldier. Fort Sumter is no exception. Intended as part of a plan for 200 such sites on the Atlantic and Gulf coasts, the Civil War came along and instead the fort became a garrison for Confederate troops. A two-year siege from the Union forces then left the three-story fort all but destroyed. It's a poignant place to remember America's past.

BOTANY BAY, SOUTH CAROLINA
462 Wander among zombie trees

South Carolina has some excellent beaches, and tourists come from all over to soak up the sun on their golden sands. Botany Bay is slightly different, though. This barrier island is wild and barren, save only for its "boneyard" trees, which were poisoned by seawater and turned white, like skeletons. They provide an apocalyptic, desolate backdrop that photographers love. Visitors are only allowed at low tide.

463 Empty sands on Hilton Head Island

HILTON HEAD ISLAND, SOUTH CAROLINA
463 Step onto the island beach of your dreams

The beach-to-town ratio on the island of Hilton Head favors seaside lovers, the destination boasting some 12 mi (19 km) of alluring coastline. Thousands of visitors head to these world-class sands, and you can find your own spot among the crowds. Coligny and Folly Field are lively and have excellent facilities, while Driessen and Mitchelville offer a more tranquil experience.

COASTAL SOUTH CAROLINA
464 Shuck it up at an oyster roast

Cities by the sea often have their own culinary traditions; some places have shrimp boils, while others serve up mountains of crayfish. In this state, you haven't experienced the local seafood until you've been to an oyster roast. Take your seat at a long table adorned with saltines, shell buckets, cocktail sauce, and lemon wedges, and wait for the chef to dump out the main course. It's every person for themselves.

467 Descending from the Endless Wall Trail into New River Gorge

469 Gauley River Recreational Area

SOUTH CAROLINA

465 Enjoy a resurgent Low Country culture

The Gullah are a community of African Americans in the Low Country of South Carolina and Georgia. They're known for preserving their cultural heritage, and you can discover more at several festivals. Head to the Gullah Celebration on Hilton Head Island in February, the Gullah Festival in Beaufort in May, and Heritage Days on St. Helena Island in November.

POINT PLEASANT, WEST VIRGINIA

466 Encounter West Virginia's mythical beast

There's a strange beast at large in this neck of the woods. Sightings of a winged monster with huge red eyes and the face of an insect date back to the 1960s, and in 1975, John Keel's book *The Mothman Prophecies* told of his investigations into those sightings. You can guarantee a meeting today—with the 12-ft (3.7-m) steel statue found in downtown Point Pleasant.

FAYETTEVILLE, WEST VIRGINIA

467 Hike an endless trail

There are many great hiking trails around this town, the pick of which is probably the Endless Wall Trail. This 3-mi (4.8-km) loop passes some of the region's outstanding views, the overlook at Diamond Point delivering particularly dramatic views of the New River below. You might also see some of the thousands of rock climbers, working their ways up the gorge's vertical sandstone walls.

470 BASE jumping off New River Gorge Bridge

CHARLESTON, WEST VIRGINIA

468 Hear rising talent at a live recording

For more than thirty years, *Mountain Stage* radio show with Larry Groce has been a live music mainstay. It's recorded live at the Culture Center Theater and syndicated to around 250 stations across the country. Counting Crows, R.E.M., and Norah Jones all played the show before they became famous, so book a ticket and you might spot some superstars of tomorrow.

SUMMERSVILLE, WEST VIRGINIA

469 Make an adrenaline-fueled descent

If you like your rafting extreme and your waters white, then the Gauley River National Recreation Area is for you. The river drops more than 650 ft (200 m) through miles of rugged terrain, with complex stretches of more than a hundred rapids across a steep gradient. The hardest parts require experience, but the Park Service can advise on gentler sections for beginners.

VICTOR, WEST VIRGINIA

470 Take it to the bridge for a party

When completed in 1977, the New River Gorge Bridge was the world's longest single-span arch bridge, as well as the highest with a regular roadway. It was a much-celebrated achievement, and the celebrations continue on Bridge Day. Join locals and visitors on the third Saturday of October as the bridge opens up for one big party, with rappelling, ascending, and BASE jumping.

CASS, WEST VIRGINIA

471 Get in training to see the splendor of Appalachian forests

Built in 1901 to serve loggers working at the local mill, the steam railway here still runs. Cass Scenic Railroad is a memorable route for lovers of trains and nature, climbing for 22 mi (35 km) through the Appalachian countryside, passing through changing tree lines on its way to Bald Knob. Hop onboard and watch the vistas float by.

CANAAN VALLEY, WEST VIRGINIA

472 See a chipmunk fill its cheeks

Explore the wooded areas here to discover how much sweeter these striped rodents are when their cheeks are stuffed with seeds, nuts, and berries (to be later stored in their burrows).

MOUNDSVILLE AND WESTON, WEST VIRGINIA

473 Go ghost hunting at two haunted facilities

The architectural features of the West Virginia Penitentiary and the Trans-Allegheny Lunatic Asylum lend themselves to spookiness. Both have dramatic Gothic features and macabre histories. Follow a guided ghost tour to see if you can spot any paranormal activity; both have rooms that once contained some of the region's most dangerous offenders.

BERKELEY SPRINGS, WEST VIRGINIA

474 Put the wash in Washington

The promotional material for this historic artifact is hard to argue with: "the only outdoor monument to presidential bathing"! A young George Washington lived and worked here as a surveyor's assistant, and, as was the custom at the time, often took a postwork bath in the open air. The "tubs" were holes dug into the ground and lined with stones.

DROOP MOUNTAIN, WEST VIRGINIA

475 Re-create history

Bring history to life by taking part in the reenactment of a Civil War battle. Choose to join the Union troops or the Confederates and get outfitted in all the gear before faithfully re-creating the Battle of Droop Mountain, one of the largest battles in the state (spoiler alert: the Union won). Every October, hundreds meet up to re-create the event, camp on the mountain, and enjoy a weekend planned with military precision.

GEORGE WASHINGTON AND JEFFERSON NATIONAL
FOREST, VIRGINIA

476 Scale the state's highest peak

At 5,700 ft (1,737 m), Mt. Rogers is Virginia's
highest point, and, being near the Appalachian
Trail, a popular diversion for hikers. It's set in a
national forest that's replete with vegetation, and
home to feral ponies. Take on the 9-mi (14.5-km)
loop and you'll be rewarded with stunning views
over thick spruce and fir forests.

LURAY, VIRGINIA

477 Be awed by a giant organ

The Luray Caverns was discovered in 1878
by a local tinsmith, and visitors may tour this
underground wonderland of rock formations.
In among the stalactites and stalagmites is the
world's largest musical instrument—the Great
Stalacpipe Organ. Composed of thirty-seven
stalactites over 3½ ac (1.4 ha), it produces gentle
musical tones and an otherworldly ambience.

STAUNTON, VIRGINIA

478 To be or not to be in a replica playhouse

There's nothing like seeing Shakespeare performed as it was meant to be, and the American Shakespeare Center has gone to some lengths to make that happen. The Blackfriars Playhouse is a faithful reproduction of the sixteenth-century London original. See any of the company's sixteen plays a year and you'll experience a fair facsimile of the time that those first crowds had.

SHENANDOAH NATIONAL PARK, VIRGINIA

479 Start a bird-watching hobby

The red body and bill of the male northern cardinal are easy to spot. These birds are a regular sight in this park, which makes it the ideal place to start a new hobby.

SHENANDOAH NATIONAL PARK, VIRGINIA

480 Survey the clouds

The historic 105-mi (169-km) Skyline Drive winds along the spine of Virginia's Blue Ridge Mountains. There are seventy-five overlooks along the way, offering stunning views of the Shenandoah Valley in the west and rolling Piedmont to the east. Nestled at Skyline Drive's highest elevation, Skyland has phenomenal views and rustic cabins that stretch along the crest.

480 Atop Old Rag Mountain, Shenandoah National Park

CHARLOTTESVILLE, VIRGINIA

481 Visit Thomas Jefferson's architectural masterpiece

Constructed between 1768 and 1809, Monticello is one of the finest examples of the early Classical Revival style in the country. Now a UNESCO World Heritage Site, the building and grounds are open to visitors, and you can see Jefferson's love of innovation and practicality shining through the design. The impressive gardens also demonstrate his love of botany and farming.

NATURAL BRIDGE, VIRGINIA

482 Take a natural bridge to Blue Ridge beauty

One of Mother Nature's most dramatic rock formations, Natural Bridge is a huge arch at the southern end of the Shenandoah Valley. It's a gateway to Cedar Creek Trail, and its beauty inspired the worship of the Monacan tribe. Young George Washington surveyed it, and Thomas Jefferson purchased it. Now it's a National Historic Landmark, and you too can gaze upon it in wonder.

FAIRFAX COUNTY, VIRGINIA

483 Delve into the life of America's first president

Mount Vernon is, most famously, the home of George Washington and his wife, Martha. As such, history abounds in the region. History buffs will love the Washingtons' Mount Vernon Estate, and as befits a former president, there's the Fred W. Smith National Library for the Study of George Washington. Nature fans are also catered to with the scenic George Washington Memorial Parkway.

WILLIAMSBURG, VIRGINIA

484 Step into history at a colonial enclave

In the late 1920s, Colonial Williamsburg was created as a way to celebrate early US history. It's now a huge living-history museum, with buildings from the seventeenth to nineteenth centuries. Costumed characters bring the place to life, using authentic historical language; it's as close to traveling back in time as it's possible to get. Stop by the tavern or admire the imperial Governor's Palace.

WILLIAMSBURG, VIRGINIA

485 Mend a broken heart with a bitter

Each January, Alewerks produces a special Bitter Valentine beer to mend broken hearts on the loneliest of holidays, Valentine's Day. With its orange hue and huge aromas of grapefruit, pine, and resin, this double IPA is one of the East Coast's best beers. Once available only in 625 ml (22 oz) bottles, it now comes in tallboy cans for greater consolation.

NORFOLK, VIRGINIA

486 Head to a vintage diner for a tradition that's cone but not forgotten

The eating of ice cream was made much more pleasurable and way less messy thanks to the invention of the waffle cone in the early 1900s by Abe Doumar. His waffle machine eventually became the basis for a family business known as Doumar's. It's still open today, so swing by for a cone from a true American original.

484 Horse-drawn carriage in Colonial Williamsburg

4

US NORTHEAST

487 Take shelter at the US National Arboretum

Sited 2 mi (3 km) from the Capitol, this living museum sprawls across hundreds of acres. The twenty-two sandstone Corinthian pillars that were once part of the Capitol give the National Capitol Columns monument an otherworldly feel, while the bonsai collection is strangely meditative and includes a tree that dates back more than 400 years.

488 Flight up your life

From the earliest contraptions designed by the Wright brothers to the future of interplanetary travel, humans have always been fascinated by flight. Washington's National Air and Space Museum is an unmissable, world-class museum with exhibits from every era of aviation. Stand alongside truly historic exhibits, including early planes and lunar command modules. There's even a model of Star Trek's starship *Enterprise*.

489 Paddle up to history

For a tourist-free view of the Jefferson Memorial, head to the Tidal Basin (pictured here with cherry trees in bloom), where you can rent a paddleboat for the afternoon. As you enjoy a leisurely paddle, there will be nothing but water between you and the monument.

WASHINGTON, DC

490 See DC in bloom

One of the most stunning exports from Japan is the
fabulous cherry blossom that appears in Washington,
DC, each March and April. The trees were a gift of
friendship from the City of Tokyo in 1912. Each year
when they bloom, Washington holds the National
Cherry Blossom Festival, incorporating art, kite flying,
picnics, and concerts.

491 Escape the political jungle

Mason's Island was once a badly maintained slice of farmland in the Potomac River. In the 1930s, it was transformed into Theodore Roosevelt Island, a living memorial to the twenty-sixth president of the United States. Roosevelt was a great outdoorsman and conservationist, and the forested landscaping, now replete with hiking trails, reflects his love of nature.

492 Write the novel you know is in you

Everyone has a novel in them. To provide the inspiration to complete the arduous journey from blank page to bookstore, arrange a visit to the Library of Congress in the US capital. The 38 million volumes in the world's largest library include 6,487 books that once belonged to Thomas Jefferson.

493 Educate yourself about a history that's still happening

Opened in 2016, the National Museum of African American History and Culture is the world's largest museum dedicated to the African American story. With 40,000 items in its collection, exhibits cover everything from the terrible days of slavery to the life of Muhammad Ali. You'll be humbled and inspired in ways you hadn't imagined.

494 Enjoy a wealth of art history

The National Gallery of Art is split into two buildings. The West Building is characterized by huge pillars and neoclassical grandeur; the East Building is a modernist, geometric design. This contrast hints at the scope of exhibits, from *Ginevra de' Benci* (the only Leonardo da Vinci painting in the Americas) to Jasper Johns, with thousands of key artworks in between.

495 Bird is the word at Kenilworth

There are plenty of tough old political birds in DC, but for actual feathered friends, head to Kenilworth Park and Aquatic Gardens. Some 250 species have been spotted in these peaceful parklands, not far from the city center. If you're lucky, you'll see bald eagles, woodpeckers, and a host of waterfowl. Beavers, deer, and foxes also vie for attention.

496 Play out your James Bond fantasies

Where there's political power, there's espionage. The world of spying might seem a glamorous playground of gadgets and missions, but the International Spy Museum reveals there's much more to it. Discover its complete history, from early Egyptian times through to the Cold War and today. You're even given your own cover identity upon arrival.

NATIONAL MUSEUM OF AFRICAN AMERICAN HISTORY AND CULTURE

Metallic shading screen inspired by southern ironwork

Contemplative Court

Interactive exhibit of the Greensboro Lunch Counter

WASHINGTON, DC
497 Reflect on some monumental history

The National Mall and surrounding area is synonymous with America's history. To visit it is to feel part of this history, from presidential inaugurations to Martin Luther King Jr.'s "I Have a Dream" speech, to protests about the Vietnam War and women's rights. It's a moving place, and the many memorials give tribute to the nation's past.

497 Maya Lin's Vietnam Veterans Memorial, Constitution Gardens

498 Lincoln Memorial by night

499 Selfies at the White House

WASHINGTON, DC

498 Admire the city's great memorials

The grandiose architecture of the nation's capital provides a setting like no other. Some suggest that it's best to catch the sunrise from the Lincoln Memorial and sunset at the Jefferson Memorial. But the opposite can be just as impressive. With imperial pillars and majestic monuments everywhere, you won't be short of things to admire.

WASHINGTON, DC

499 Picture yourself at the White House

You can't come to DC and not take a selfie in front of the world's most famous house. Gone are the days when you could wander around the grounds, but there are still plenty of photo opportunities. Book a tour to see beyond the neoclassical facade, or stand at the edge of the North Lawn and strike a pose. You might not see the president, but you'll at least feel presidential.

WASHINGTON, DC

500 Breathe in political power at the Capitol

The sense of history is tangible at this famous building, home to the House of Representatives and the Senate. This is where it happens—where America's elected officials conduct business, debate laws, and pass bills. Stand beneath the dome and see the beautiful murals and *The Apotheosis of Washington* fresco. It's a powerful place in every sense.

ANNAPOLIS, MARYLAND

501 See who's top gun as fighter jets dance in the skies

How does a country's navy display its pride and professionalism? One way is to have its best pilots form a flight demonstration squadron, and in the United States, that squadron is called the Blue Angels. Look for their special air shows and important events in the naval calendar, where you can see them performing choreographed maneuvers and dramatic stunts.

LAUREL, MARYLAND

502 See the prettiest moth in the United States

With its pink and cream markings, the candy-colored rosy maple moth is surely America's prettiest of all. Visit the Patuxent Research Refuge and judge for yourself.

BALTIMORE, MARYLAND

503 Tour in the only place acceptable to be Poe-faced

With even the local football team named after one of his poems ("The Raven"), the influence of American horror master Edgar Allan Poe is everywhere in this city. Pay your respects at his family home or, more appropriately, his grave, and raise your glass in the last bar that he frequented. Statues, libraries, and monuments abound.

BALTIMORE, MARYLAND

504 Experience truly visionary art

While away an afternoon exploring the ways that the human spirit finds a voice through art at the American Visionary Art Museum. The colorful, often eccentric art here is all by self-taught artists, resulting in some highly individualistic pieces, each with its own written story attached. The sculpture garden even features a 55-ft (17-m) tall wind-powered *Whirligig*.

BOONSBORO, MARYLAND

506 See a monument that was built in a day

Although its sister monument in DC steals all the attention, the Washington Monument State Park in Maryland is home to the original. In 1827, the citizens of Boonsboro took a day out of their lives and built a 40-ft (12-m) tower honoring George Washington, at the top of South Mountain. It's an easy hike to a little-known landmark that's also a great spot for bird-watching.

BALTIMORE, MARYLAND

505 Get tanked up and up close to aquarium residents

Baltimore's excellent National Aquarium has a popular Atlantic Coral Reef exhibit that visitors can explore as scuba divers. The tank is 13 ft (4 m) deep, with 335,000 gallons of salt water, and houses lots of tropical fish and a couple of small and very friendly sharks. Participants must be over eighteen, with Open Water Diver certification.

501 Blue Angels in formation

BLACKWATER, MARYLAND

507 Float through the "Everglades of the North"

You don't have to go to Florida to see sprawling, photogenic marshlands. In the Chesapeake Bay region, the rich tidal waters of the 27,000-ac (10,900-ha) Blackwater National Wildlife Refuge provide a habitat for ducks, waterfowl, and the largest breeding population of American bald eagles on the East Coast. Bask in the stunning scenery without running into gators.

DELMARVA PENINSULA, MARYLAND

508 Appreciate the majesty of wild horses

Local folklore tells that the wild horses of Assateague Island are descended from the survivors of a shipwreck, though no records confirm the tale. Encountering their wild strength and beauty on an uninhabited island, just 37 mi (6 km) long, commands respect and a sense of awe. It's advised to observe the feral horses from a safe distance.

COASTAL MARYLAND

509 Catch your own crab dinner

April 1 to December 15 is crabbing season in Maryland, allowing plenty of time to get in on the shellfish action. Boat charter companies run crabbing tours and rent equipment for catching your own blue crabs. Local fishermen can then advise you on how to dress, cook, and eat your catch, although there are plenty of restaurants as a safety option.

508 Assateague Island horses

511 Horseshoe crabs on Delaware's Slaughter Beach

512 Dogfish Head's Steampunk Treehouse

WILMINGTON, DELAWARE

510 Visit Versailles without a passport

The Nemours Mansion and Gardens offers a slice of Parisian opulence that doesn't require a flight to France. This 300-ac (120-ha) country estate includes a 105-room neoclassical mansion resembling a French château and glorious French-style gardens. It was built in 1910 by the industrialist Alfred du Pont as a gift for his wife. Fulfill your Marie Antoinette fantasies without leaving the country.

DELAWARE BAY, DELAWARE

511 Time it right to witness a natural wonder

It's a millennia-old spectacle: every spring, hundreds of thousands of horseshoe crabs lay eggs on the shores of Delaware Bay. Head here in May and June around the times of new and full moons, and arrive at the beach around 30 minutes before high tide. You should be able to witness countless crabs coming ashore, so dense that they appear as huge, brown paving stones. Truly awe-inspiring.

MILTON, DELAWARE

512 Explore the origins of extreme beer

The original American beer innovator is located in the small town of Milton. Sam Calagione's Dogfish Head Brewery is known for off-centered ales and extreme beers. Drop in for a tour and tasting to try the range. Classics include 60 Minute and 90 Minute IPAs (try 120 Minute if you dare!), while newer beers like SeaQuench Ale (brewed with black lime and sea salt) will have you wanting to return.

LEWES, DELAWARE
513 Hop aboard the Cape May–Lewes Ferry

This began life as a regular ferry route, allowing people and vehicles to cross from Delaware to New Jersey. Over time, its popularity has grown, and while it still serves its original purpose, it's also great just for the ride. Often this includes live music or brunch, and there are regular events such as onboard beer festivals, wine dinners, and firework cruises.

BETHANY BEACH, DELAWARE
514 Catch a movie on the beach

Bethany Beach is all about family fun. By day you have a huge sandy beach, great eateries, and all manner of events. Then, when the sun sets, you can head back for even more activities. On Thursdays there's a campfire, and on Mondays, you can grab some popcorn and a deck chair to catch a movie under the stars while feeling the sand between your toes.

LAUREL, DELAWARE
515 Glide through an ancient forest

It's not every day that you can explore a prehistoric landscape. Trap Pond State Park is an ancient wetland that is home to the country's northernmost forest of bald cypress trees, with evocative waterways that are ripe for exploration. Kayak, canoe, or join a pontoon tour. You'll spot herons, owls, and woodpeckers as you drift along, plus terrapins popping up to say hello.

515 Tranquil waters of Trap Pond State Park

PITTSBURGH, PENNSYLVANIA

516 Be inclined to take in two great views

When a city is blessed with not one but two funicular railways, it's only right that you should ride both. Opened in the 1870s to serve residents of Mt. Washington, they are two of the few remaining such services in the country. Both the Duquesne (doo-KANE) Incline and the Monongahela Incline ("Mon Incline") deliver great views of the city skyline.

MILL RUN, PENNSYLVANIA

517 Visit a masterpiece of modern architecture

Renowned American architect Frank Lloyd Wright designed Fallingwater as a holiday retreat for a private client. Built over a waterfall in the Pennsylvania mountains, it exemplifies his philosophy of harmoniously uniting art and nature. The house and the surrounding Bear Run Nature Reserve are open to the public, but you'll need to book in advance.

PUNXSUTAWNEY, PENNSYLVANIA

518 Watch a local celebrity hog attention

As depicted in the movie *Groundhog Day*, residents here have celebrated this festival since 1886. It happens on February 2, and crowds gather to see if the world's most famous groundhog, Punxsutawney Phil, shows his face and casts a shadow. The result predicts when spring will come, but either way, you can join the accompanying party, with music and food galore.

516 View from the Duquesne Incline

CENTRE HALL, PENNSYLVANIA

519 Tour a dark cavern by boat

There are nine show caves in the Pennsylvania region, but only one that you can explore entirely by water. At Penn's Cave and Wildlife Park, you join a tour that leads gently into the darkness on a flat-bottomed boat. Guides point out dramatic rock formations and stalactites, and explain the history of the caves and their historical importance to Native American people. It's a truly effortless adventure.

TIOGA STATE FOREST, PENNSYLVANIA

520 Gorge yourself on canyon views

Arizona's Grand Canyon is a top attraction, but have you heard of the Grand Canyon of Pennsylvania? Pine Creek Gorge cuts through the beautiful Tioga State Forest for 47 mi (75 km) at a depth of 1,450 ft (440 m). Its tree-clad walls stretch as far as the eye can see. Head to Leonard Harrison and Colton Point State Parks for the best observation points.

GETTYSBURG, PENNSYLVANIA

521 Transport yourself through a Civil War site

In 1863, a three-day battle here between Union and Confederate forces became a turning point for the Civil War. The 6,000 ac (2,400 ha) now contain more than 1,300 monuments and memorials, and it's one of the most important locations in American history. Joining a Segway tour is a good way to get around the huge site, or a horseback tour, for that added element of realism.

519 Penn's Cave boat tour

521 Gettysburg Segway tour

520 The waters of Pine Creek Gorge

HERSHEY, PENNSYLVANIA

522 Drink an elfish brew

Clocking in at 11 percent ABV, Tröegs Independent Brewing's Mad Elf is a winter warmer that always signals the start of the holiday season. Brewed with chocolate and Munich malts, German and Czech hops, and a spicy Belgian yeast strain, it's a cheerful holiday treat. If you're visiting the brewery, look for Wild Elf, a tart foeder-fermented version of Mad Elf spiked with Brettanomyces and sour cherries.

WAYNE, PENNSYLVANIA

523 Enjoy America's most romantic garden

Chanticleer Garden is one of the most relaxing gardens you'll ever encounter, located just thirty minutes outside Philadelphia. With only 35 ac (14 ha) open to the public, it's a world away from larger, busier gardens in the United States. Its Teacup Garden is a secluded courtyard that's bursting with seasonal colors—the perfect place to erect an artist's easel and let your creativity flow.

APPALACHIAN TRAIL, PENNSYLVANIA

524 Don't miss the miniscule underfoot

There are more than 12,000 different types of plant hopper—a prevalent group of insects that are invariably camouflaged to blend in with their environment. Some are a rich green color, while others are speckled like bark, with long, twiglike protuberances. There are thought to be well over 100 species in Pennsylvania, so see how many you can spot.

523 The Teacup Garden at Chanticleer Gardens

526 Philadelphia's LOVE Park

PENNSYLVANIA DUTCH
COUNTRY, PENNSYLVANIA

525 Investigate a simpler way of life

In the scenic Piedmont region of the Appalachians, there's a high concentration of Pennsylvania Dutch, Mennonites, and Amish communities. For centuries they've practiced a simple way of life, untouched by technology. They've opened up to tourism in recent years and you can peek in on their lifestyle, and purchase produce and crafts, all made by hand in a timeless fashion.

PHILADELPHIA, PENNSYLVANIA

526 Feel brotherly love in LOVE Park

Officially, the famous square in the heart of Philadelphia is the John F. Kennedy Plaza, but with Robert Indiana's iconic *LOVE* sculpture taking center stage, everyone simply refers to it as LOVE Park. Grab yourself a meal from the ever-changing array of food trucks and hang out on one of the lawns to watch the Philly world go by— a popular activity for nearby office workers and visitors.

PHILADELPHIA, PENNSYLVANIA

527 Steak your claim to a famous sandwich

In the 1930s, a Philadelphia hot dog vendor started selling steak sandwiches. They were such a hit that before long, a much-loved version with cheese had become a hot menu item. These days, the Philly cheesesteak is a ubiquitous sandwich in the city. Several outlets claim to have the best, but for authenticity head to Geno's Steaks or Pat's King of Steaks, twenty-four hours a day.

528 Steps of the Philadelphia Museum of Art

529 The Liberty Bell, Liberty Bell Center

PHILADELPHIA, PENNSYLVANIA

528 Rock your own tribute to a classic scene

In 1976, a little-known actor made a gritty movie about a journeyman boxer who gets a chance to fight for the world title. The actor was Sylvester Stallone, and the *Rocky* movies became a hugely successful franchise. In one famous scene, Rocky sprints up the seventy-two stone steps to the Philadelphia Museum of Art. Breathe in, then take your own shot.

PHILADELPHIA, PENNSYLVANIA

529 Ring in a new appreciation for history

Commissioned in 1752 and subject to a couple of recastings as bell makers refined the construction, the Liberty Bell has become a symbol of American independence. Now hanging in the Liberty Bell Center, the bell sports a large crack from wear and tear. It now sits quietly, proudly imperfect, and you can take your own photographic tribute.

PHILADELPHIA, PENNSYLVANIA

530 See the birthplace of a nation

There's likely no more important spot in America's history than the unassuming redbrick Independence Hall. It's here that both the Declaration of Independence and the US Constitution were debated and adopted, and it's now a UNESCO World Heritage Site. Take a tour and imagine the beginnings of a nation taking place within its hallowed walls.

531 Tubing on the Delaware

DELAWARE WATER GAP NATIONAL
RECREATION AREA, NEW JERSEY
531 Float down the Delaware River in a tube

There is an art to river tubing:
Lie back, relax, and watch the
riverbank drift by. If you haven't
been in a rubber ring since you
were a child, it's time to embrace
it all over again. It's a peaceful
way to spend an afternoon,
drifting in the current while
on the lookout for raccoons,
beavers, or otters, and bald
eagles gliding overhead.

FAR HILLS, NEW JERSEY
532 Have a day of botanical delights

New Jersey is the Garden State,
so you should expect great things
from its actual gardens. Gaze
upon the best of the best at the
Leonard J. Buck Garden, a
delightful, bucolic wonderland.
Built in the late 1930s, these
33 ac (13 ha) contain woodlands,
lawns, water features, and exotic
rock gardens, with coordinated
displays of colors and scents that
will please all your senses.

WEST ORANGE, NEW JERSEY
533 Discover the origin of light(bulbs)

Thomas Edison was such a
prolific inventor that he held
1,093 patents in the United
States. His home and laboratory
now form the Thomas Edison
National Historical Park.
The laboratory showcases his
collaborative style of invention,
while the house includes his
garage and potting shed—both
built in single poured concrete,
one of his many inventions.

534 Delaware and Raritan Canal Towpath

FRENCHTOWN TO NEW
BRUNSWICK, NEW JERSEY

534 Escape the urban clamor in New Jersey

You don't get many chances
to regress to the Victorian
age, when horse-drawn barges
forged along canals and modern
technology had not yet arrived.
The 77-mi (124-km) Delaware
and Raritan Canal State Park
Trail is a tranquil slice of those
times, and now a trail for hiking,
jogging, horseback riding, and
biking. Take a day and follow
its calm waters.

JERSEY CITY, NEW JERSEY

535 Orbit the stars at a gigantic planetarium

Only a select few get to travel
into space, and really, who has
time to train as an astronaut?
The next best thing could be a
visit to one of the world's biggest
planetarium—the Liberty
Science Center. A state-of-the-
art audiovisual display propels
you into orbit and dances around
the solar system and beyond, the
wonders of the universe before
you in incredible detail. Space
out in the best way possible.

PRINCETON, NEW JERSEY

536 Stroll around an Ivy League campus

If you want to be able to say
"I went to Princeton" without
being a straight A student,
then there's an easy loophole.
Simply visit the Princeton
campus (you can even buy a
university-branded bumper
sticker or polo shirt) and revel
in the glorious Gothic Revival
architecture of Blair Hall, East
Pyne, and the Graduate College.
Easier than a degree and way
less time-consuming.

STOCKTON, NEW JERSEY
537 Visit the state's last covered bridge

There were once around seventy-five covered bridges in New Jersey—some more ornamental than others, but all built with a purpose: to protect the wooden bridge beneath. Green Sergeant's Covered Bridge, crossing the Wickecheoke Creek, is the last surviving authentic example. It might have outlasted horse-drawn carriages, but you can still imagine their hooves echoing in the tunnel.

JACKSON, NEW JERSEY
538 Ride the world's tallest roller coaster

Do you have a head for heights? Not only is Kingda Ka at Six Flags Great Adventure amusement park the tallest roller coaster in the world (measuring more than 456 ft; 139 m high), it's also one of the longest and second-fastest, accelerating up to 128 mph (206 kph) in just 3.5 seconds. Only Formula Rossa, at Ferrari World in Abu Dhabi, is faster. Buckle up for the ride of your life!

VARIOUS SITES IN NEW JERSEY
539 Keep it in the family

The Sopranos is one of the most beloved TV shows, and fans have long obsessed over the locations used for each scene. Luckily it's possible to witness many of the places where Tony Soprano conducted his nefarious business. Organized tours include stops at the infamous Bada Bing club and Barone Sanitation. Or simply eat at the Tick Tock Diner or Holsten's Brookdale Confectionery, where the final scene was shot.

538 Kingda Ka roller coaster

ATLANTIC CITY, NEW JERSEY

540 Walk the Atlantic City boards

There's been a boardwalk here since the late nineteenth century, attracting tourists from around the world. The development thrives today and comes replete with ocean views, entertainment, and stores selling everything from designer labels to saltwater taffy. Breathe in the sea air and 150 years of tradition. Fans of *Boardwalk Empire* will particularly appreciate the backdrop.

OCEAN CITY, NEW JERSEY

541 Say hello to the summer months on Memorial Day

A few resorts on the Jersey Shore have a Memorial Day tradition that symbolically welcomes the beginning of the summer season. It's a happy occasion when the worst of the winter is over. Ocean City has its Unlock the Ocean ceremony, where an official turns a giant wooden key in the sand, and you can join hundreds of participants who dash into the sea, often in costume.

542 Pick a booth and sample classic American delights

New Jersey is many things, including diner capital of the world. At the last count, some 600 diners operated in the state, an all-American tradition that has to be sampled on any trip. It was one of the first places to embrace diner culture, with many establishments decades old—the Dumont Crystal Diner, for example, opened way back in 1925.

543 Get your motor running at a race from yesteryear

In the early days of racing, there were no standards or governing bodies; drivers just showed up with the fastest vehicle their team could make and the competition was on. The Race of Gentlemen harks back to those days. Visit this stretch of shoreline in early October and see dozens of pre-1935 cars and motorcycles race, complete with vintage clothing and a whiff of old-school adventure.

543 Wildwood's annual Race of Gentlemen

CAPE MAY, NEW JERSEY
544 See diamonds by day or night

Cape May has more than one glistening treasure to offer. The first are Cape May diamonds—not actual diamonds but quartz pebbles washed down from the Delaware River, tumbled into a polished smoothness on the way. Then by night, shift your gaze and your camera upward to admire clear views of the Milky Way. If you're lucky, you might just catch a shooting star.

NIAGARA FALLS, NEW YORK
545 See the falls from a helicopter

With its near-perfect horseshoe formation and thundering falls dropping up to 190 ft (58 m) in places, Niagara Falls is a wonder of nature, whatever angle you view it from. However, secure a bird's-eye view with a helicopter ride above the falls and you truly appreciate the scale and the power of the river—plus, you're in a helicopter, which is always an epic experience.

546 Lake view of Boldt Castle's Power House

547 View across the Adirondack Mountains

THOUSAND ISLANDS, NEW YORK

546 Play king or queen of a castle for a day

In the early twentieth century, two self-made millionaires had the same idea in the same place. George Boldt and Frederick Bourne built huge replica castles—German and Scottish styles, respectively—in this region: Boldt Castle and Singer Castle. Admire their refined sensibilities and grand architectural flourishes while wandering around these impressive structures.

ADIRONDACKS, NEW YORK

547 Pick one of forty-six peaks to climb

In the 1920s, a couple of mountaineers compiled a definitive list of all the peaks above 4,000 ft (1,220 m) in elevation in the Adirondacks. They counted forty-six mountains, all except three of them being in Essex County, south of Lake Placid. Some need commitment beyond a casual hike, but easier climbs like Big Slide and Cascade Mountains offer spectacular views.

FINGER LAKES, NEW YORK

548 Take the Seneca Lake Wine Trail

Wineries encircle most of the Finger Lakes, but the highest concentration is the thirty members of the Seneca Lake Wine Trail. Spend a day visiting tasting rooms, and don't miss the east side of Seneca Lake— nicknamed "the banana belt," due to the climate's proclivity to run a few degrees warmer than elsewhere in the region. Whether folklore or fact, the wine culture is undeniable.

551 Hunter Mountain's monumental zip line

COOPERSTOWN, NEW YORK
549 Swing for the fences

There have been professional
baseball leagues in the United
States since 1901, and the
Baseball Hall of Fame in
Cooperstown since 1939.
Established to encourage tourism
during the Great Depression,
this museum has welcomed
millions of fans, and has new
inductees every year. See
programs from every World
Series, and pay tribute to legends
like Babe Ruth and Hank Aaron.

MOHONK PRESERVE, NEW YORK
550 Enjoy "the Gunks" year-round

The Shawangunk Mountains
("the Gunks") offer such a variety
of hiking, climbing, and skiing
options that even the influx of
thousands of tourists every
weekend doesn't result in crowds.
The grand Mohonk Mountain
House has hosted winter guests
for almost a century. Or for a
slice of summer tranquility,
opt for the Jenny Lane Trail
or Lake Awosting.

CATSKILLS MOUNTAINS,
NEW YORK
551 Zip down a mountainside

For many, hiking around the
Catskills is rewarding enough.
But if you need an extra
adrenaline hit, head for the
Hunter Mountain zip line. At
600 ft (180 m) up and 4.6 mi
(7.4 km) long, it's the world's
second longest, reaching speeds
of 50 mph (80 kmh). It's the
most exciting way to descend,
and views are breathtaking.

553 Famous Katz's Delicatessen

554 Garden Court at the Frick Collection

HYDE PARK, NEW YORK

552 Get better aquainted with FDR

Springwood wasn't just the family home of America's longest-serving president, Franklin D. Roosevelt, it was also a working farm and an experimental forestry plantation. It was where FDR went to recharge his spirit, and visiting the 1,000-ac (400-ha) park gives great insight into the man, his passion for the environment, work ethic, and love of family.

MANHATTAN, NEW YORK CITY

553 Get your fill of fame

Manhattan can feel like a movie set, with its famous landmarks, and many of its eateries have actually been used as movie sets. Track down locations such as Katz's Delicatessen from *When Harry Met Sally* or Smith & Wollensky from *American Psycho*. Places such as the Loeb Boathouse in Central Park have been used multiple times, so pick your favorite A-list option for lunch.

MANHATTAN, NEW YORK CITY

554 Enjoy your art away from the crowds

The opulent eighteenth-century French-style mansion that was the home of steel magnate Henry Clay Frick is open to the public to view his impressive art collection. The Frick Collection is small and seldom crowded, and you can get up close to the artworks here, or enjoy the peace and tranquility of the interior court and reflecting pool.

MANHATTAN, NEW YORK CITY
555 Ride the ferry to Staten Island and back

There's been a ferry service between Manhattan and Staten Island since the early 1800s. For most people, it's a way to commute between the boroughs, but for visitors it's a free ticket to some of the best city views. Hop on and you'll be treated to unfettered panoramas of the Manhattan skyline and the Statue of Liberty. The service runs twenty-four hours a day, but it's best to avoid rush hour.

MANHATTAN, NEW YORK CITY
556 Feel the need for speed

Timothy "Speed" Levitch is a tour guide like no other. He came to fame with *The Cruise*, a documentary that recorded his bus tours. Hop on a bus and try and encounter the next Speed Levitch, or book a tour with the original. An erudite one-man show blending philosophy and trivia, tours explore the city hidden under our noses, covering such topics as the secret doors of Greenwich Village.

MANHATTAN, NEW YORK CITY
557 Appreciate art at the city's busiest station

In 1998, a restoration project cleaned the elaborate murals on the ceiling of Grand Central Station, previously covered by grime from decades of smoke. Look up now and you'll see a green-and-gold constellation looming over the main hall. While you're there, order a cocktail at the opulent Campbell Bar, with its own painted ceilings, grand fireplace, and leaded-glass window.

557 Historic interior of the Campbell Bar

555 Staten Island Ferry and the Statue of Liberty

558 Little Italy's Mulberry Street

562 Manhattan's High Line

MANHATTAN, NEW YORK CITY

558 Eat a lot in Little Italy

When Italians immigrated to the United States in the 1800s, many settled around Mulberry Street in Lower Manhattan. Little Italy is still the place to go for Italian food, with plenty of small family restaurants specializing in different regional cuisines. Visit in September when the Feast of San Gennaro fills the streets with festivities and a riot of red, white, and green.

MANHATTAN, NEW YORK CITY

559 Experience old-time Irish New York

McSorley's Old Ale House is NYC's oldest Irish tavern, dating to the mid-nineteenth century. (The exact year is disputed; the sign says "Established 1854," but records show it sat vacant until 1861.) Inside, not much has changed since then. It has just two beer selections: light or dark. Whichever you order, instead of a proper pint glass, it comes in two 8 oz (225 ml) beer mugs.

MANHATTAN, NEW YORK CITY

560 Catch a show on Broadway

There's always glamour in the air along theater land's most famous street, which remains the iconic place to catch a show. Whether you're a fan of drama, comedy, or showstopping musicals, with more than forty venues and 500-plus seats apiece, you'll find something catering to every theatrical taste imaginable.

563 Skating at Rockefeller Center

MANHATTAN, NEW YORK CITY

561 Laugh it up with world-famous comics

Even top comics need to road test material before they embark on national tours, and the NYC comedy clubs are where they try out new jokes. Head to the Comedy Cellar or Carolines and you may catch Dave Chappelle or Chris Rock trying out work in progress—usually unannounced, but you'll have a great night in any case, and the booked comics will be big names, too.

MANHATTAN, NEW YORK CITY

562 Walk the High Line

Amble along this elevated redeveloped section of disused New York Central Railroad for a leisurely and traffic-free way to get another perspective on the Big Apple. Opened in 2009, it's packed with pleasant foliage and provides unusual views of some of the city's favorite landmarks.

MANHATTAN, NEW YORK CITY

563 Glide around the Rockefeller Rink

The most recognizable skating rink in the world is wildly popular, and allows 150 skaters on the ice at one time. Get your skates on for an early session at 7 a.m., or wait until the Starlight Skate session from 10:30 p.m. to midnight.

MANHATTAN, NEW YORK CITY

564 Attend a Greenwich Village poetry reading

In its 1960s heyday, visitors apparently couldn't wait for a Jack Kerouac or a Bob Dylan to fill a smoky basement with revolutionary words. Open mic nights at venues like the White Horse Tavern and Café Wha? in the Village keep that tradition alive.

MANHATTAN, NEW YORK CITY

565 Hit the museums

Don't think of visiting NYC without seeing at least one of its world-class museums. Standouts include the Metropolitan Museum of Art (the Met), MoMA, the Whitney Museum of American Art, the Solomon R. Guggenheim Museum, and the American Museum of Natural History. Take at least a day for the bigger ones. There's an overwhelming amount to see, but that just means you have to come back.

MANHATTAN, NEW YORK CITY

566 Get in an Empire State of Mind

Despite the much taller rivals that have sprung up around the globe, the enchanting art deco Empire State Building remains the definitive skyscraper. Take a trip to its observation deck, which provides visitors with the best possible views of the Big Apple.

565 The Charles Engelhard Court at the Met

566 Empire State Building, seen from the Top of the Rock

MANHATTAN, NEW YORK CITY

**567 Take time to reflect
at the 9/11 Memorial**

The events of September 11, 2001, still
loom large in the public consciousness, and
as the last rubble from the Twin Towers was
cleared, a fitting monument was planned.
On September 12, 2011, the National
September 11 Memorial and Museum
was opened. Reflecting pools, trees, and a
museum now stand where the towers did;
it's humbling to pause and pay your respects.

MANHATTAN, NEW YORK CITY

568 Pen a line in a majestic library

The century-old Rose Main Reading Room in the New York Public Library is one of the city's most iconic locations. Light streams through the casement windows, illuminating the rows of weathered dark wood tables and brass lamps, where many well-known poets and authors have bent their heads to work.

MANHATTAN, NEW YORK CITY

569 Discover the pleasures of Central Park

Few city parks are as iconic as Central Park. This 843-ac (340-ha) space surrounded by skyscrapers, apartment blocks, and museums is a stalwart for almost every New York–based movie. Leafy avenues, lakes, and street performers mean that no one leaves without a memory.

MANHATTAN, NEW YORK CITY

570 Embark on a classic coast-to-coast

Immortalized in the 1981 Burt Reynolds comedy, the Cannonball Run is a classic car race, named in honor of driver Erwin "Cannonball" Baker. It runs from Manhattan's Red Ball Garage to California's Portofino Hotel in Redondo Beach. The record time for this journey of more than 2,800 mi (4,506 km) is twenty-five hours and thirty-nine minutes.

ELLIS ISLAND, NEW YORK CITY

571 Research your family tree

The first stop for the 12 million immigrants who arrived in New York between 1892 and 1954 was Ellis Island, and it's a great place to research a family tree. Head to the American Family Immigration History Center to scour its database of millions of arrival records, then visit the Wall of Honor, which is inscribed with the names of over 700,000 immigrants.

LIBERTY ISLAND, NEW YORK CITY

572 Ascend a symbol of independence

The Statue of Liberty was France's gift to the United States to celebrate the centennial of the signing of the Declaration of Independence. To see her presiding over the Hudson is to know you're in America, but peeking out through her crown at the jaw-dropping view is a very different experience. There is also the chance to see the beautiful interior craftwork.

THE BRONX, NEW YORK CITY

573 Hit the bleachers in the Bronx

Arguably America's most iconic sports franchise, the New York Yankees moved to a new Yankee Stadium in 2009. Built at great expense, amid much controversy, it is perhaps the most iconic sports stadium in the world. Catch a game at this sparkly facility, or experience the passionate atmosphere at Citi Field, where fierce rivals, the New York Mets, pitch and bat.

574 Yayoi Kusama's *Cosmic Nature* at the New York Botanical Garden

574 Meander through a verdant woodland

The New York Botanical Garden's spectacularly verdant 250 ac (101 ha) is a wonderland for everything that grows. It also contains one of the few remaining tracts of natural, uncut woodland in New York City. The garden offers a variety of classes in soul-nourishing subjects such as horticultural therapy, herbal medicine, and floral design.

575 Hit the shuffleboard decks at the Royal Palms

It's usually a pastime associated with Florida retirees, but the shuffleboard decks at the Royal Palms have been undergoing a renaissance. Ten bright blue courts await at this old-school venue, and a younger crowd is flocking to take up the game. It's more of a social scene with just a hint of competitiveness, and the game's so easy you can play after a few cocktails.

576 Pig out at Smorgasburg

People need to eat while they're shopping, and out of the renowned Brooklyn Flea came Smorgasburg, the foodie annex of the market. Since 2011, Smorgasburg has been a weekly open-air food fair, serving everything from Cantonese noodles to deconstructed candy bars. Save your appetite before you come, and revel in the culinary choices on display.

577 Brooklyn Flea, below the Manhattan Bridge

578 Prospect Park Carousel

BROOKLYN, NEW YORK CITY

577 Flea to Brooklyn for a bargain

Brooklyn Flea is such a good flea market that they hold it twice over every weekend at different locations. On Saturdays, head to Williamsburg; on Sundays it's in DUMBO (Down Under the Manhattan Bridge Overpass). If browsing vintage clothing and artisanal goods is your idea of a good time, you'll be in flea market heaven, with hundreds of stalls and vendors.

BROOKLYN, NEW YORK CITY

578 Get taken for a century-old ride

In 1912, Charles Carmel—one of the foremost carousel designers of the day—hand-carved fifty-three beautiful horses (plus assorted dragons, giraffes, and deer) for his latest design. Forty years later, this work of art arrived at Prospect Park. Renovated to its former glory in 2020, it's one of the city's best-kept secrets, so direct your attention away from Central Park and ride a slice of history in its Brooklyn sister park. There's also bird-watching, boating, skating, and sports available, but one of the true joys is to take that carousel ride, then set up for a picnic under a shady tree.

THE OLD-SCHOOL CHARMS OF CONEY ISLAND

Nathan's Famous

Mermaid Parade

Luna Park

BROOKLYN, NEW YORK CITY

579 Live the American Dream at Coney Island

Fancy some kitschy seaside fun? Visit "America's Playground," "Sodom by the Sea," and reputedly the only thing about the United States that interested Sigmund Freud. Coney Island's amusement park has been immortalized in books and movies, most set in its early twentieth-century heyday.

BROOKLYN, NEW YORK CITY

580 Stroll between two boroughs

Walking across the Brooklyn Bridge is a perfect New York City thing to do. It's just over a mile (1.6 km), so it's a good-length walk of thirty minutes or so, and you'll enjoy views of the city skyline that you can't see from anywhere else. You're also up close to a great feat of engineering, which you can appreciate the entire way across, before locating a coffee or beer on the other side.

580 Crossing the Brooklyn Bridge to Manhattan

BROOKLYN, NEW YORK CITY
581 Discover a former brewing capital

For nearly a century, Brooklyn was the country's brewing hub, with large-scale German-style breweries dotting the northern part of the borough. Many buildings that housed breweries are still standing, including the Nassau Brewing Company and Schaefer Brewing. An exhibit documenting Brooklyn's brewing past can be found in the tasting room at Williamsburg's Brooklyn Brewery.

QUEENS, NEW YORK CITY
582 Tower above the five boroughs

If you don't have the money for a helicopter, you can still see all boroughs at one time. The Panorama of the City of New York at the Queens Museum is an incredible scale model, and well worth a diversion from Manhattan. While you're in Queens, the Fantasy Forest Amusement Park, the Fountain of the Planets, and the Unisphere in Flushing Meadows Corona Park are all worth your time.

QUEENS, NEW YORK CITY
583 Celebrate the art of Noguchi

In a former photoengraving plant in Queens, a light-filled space has been transformed into the Noguchi Museum for the work of Isamu Noguchi, who designed it as an oasis in an industrial setting.

LONG ISLAND, NEW YORK
584 Swap ice tea for ice wine

New York is famous for many things, and wine isn't one of them. But head to the vineyards of Long Island and you can sample ice wine, a delicacy in the wine world that only grows in specific regions.

581 Brooklyn Brewery, Williamsburg

582 The Unisphere, Queens

586 Beach casting by Montauk Point Lighthouse

588 Saville Dam's Pump House

LONG ISLAND, NEW YORK

585 Head to the Hamptons

Want to experience summer like the wealthy do? Then head to Long Island, where a group of manicured villages and hamlets around Southampton and East Hampton constitute the Hamptons. This area contains the most expensive zip code in the country, and many of NYC's wealthy have summer homes here. Wander around Sag Harbor and wonder at how the other half live.

MONTAUK, NEW YORK

586 Enjoy the outdoor life in Montauk

Do what the locals do and hit the great outdoors with a trip to Montauk, Long Island. It's all about feeling the nature and enjoying the outdoors—not just the beaches but beach casting, horseback riding, bird-watching, surfing, and hiking, too. Breathe in the wildflowers on a walk out to the 200-year-old Montauk Point Lighthouse. And relax.

HARTFORD, CONNECTICUT

587 Re-create a Mark Twain adventure

Which big kid wouldn't want to tread where Tom 'n' Huck have? The best place to start an adventure is the unique Mark Twain House and Museum in Hartford, where the author spent his own formative years and which featured heavily in his writing.

BARKHAMSTED, CONNECTICUT

588 Take a selfie at a dam good-looking reservoir

The Hoover Dam gets all the attention, but the Saville Dam has it in the looks department, with regal-looking stone turrets and glorious views out across the Connecticut countryside.

OXFORD, CONNECTICUT
589 Explore eccentric wild ale

Founded in 2014 by Ben Neidhart, in connection with
its sister company international beer importer B United,
OEC (Ordinem Ecentrici Coctores) Brewing is one of
the few US breweries fully dedicated to sour beer
production. There is no flagship beer per se, but a
constantly rotating selection of ales aged in wood
barrels, concrete vessels, and stainless steel tanks. Visit
the tasting room or book a tour of the facility.

MILFORD, CONNECTICUT
590 Search for long-lost treasure

A sandbar leads to an unassuming 14-ac (5.6-ha) island,
home to a few seabirds and a thick copse of trees. Scenic
Charles Island is historically thrice-cursed, though the
second curse is the most famous, issued by Scottish
pirate Captain William Kidd as he lost his treasure
here. You can look for it, but beware the tides that
rush in and cut off the island from the mainland.

EAST HADDAM, CONNECTICUT
591 Discover secret passages in
a castle

Gillette Castle is everything a castle should be:
one man's eccentric home (in this case, actor, director,
and playwright William Gillette, best known as
Sherlock Holmes), full of secret passageways, and set in
amazing parkland with views over the Connecticut
River. It's a joy to explore—and to discover that Gillette
even designed the light switches himself.

591 Gillette Castle's riverside setting

NEW HAVEN, CONNECTICUT
592 Take an interest in Yale's architecture

There's been a university campus here since 1716, so it's no wonder that you can surround yourself in historical and architectural beauty with a visit to Yale. The looming Gothic masonry of Harkness Tower is a good place to start, with Sterling Memorial Library in the same vein and Connecticut Hall a grand example of Georgian style. Join a tour or guide yourself through a 300-year-old time capsule.

NEW HAVEN, CONNECTICUT
593 Eat a hamburger at its official birthplace

In 1895, a local blacksmith set up a food stand, and in 1900 he served some steak trimmings between two slices of toast to an impatient customer. This was, they claim, the birth of the hamburger. The restaurant, now called Louis' Lunch, still exists and still serves this sandwich in more or less the same way. Other places make the same claim, but snack on a burger here while you make up your own mind.

ROCKY NECK STATE PARK, CONNECTICUT
594 Spot a bobcat

There are as many as a million bobcats in the United States, yet they're only occasionally spotted during the day since they hunt at night, creeping up silently before pouncing on unsuspecting rabbits or squirrels. Bobcats are about twice the size of a domestic cat, although similar in color to many tabbies. They have distinctive tufted ears and a short "bobbed" tail—hence their name.

592 Yale University campus

596 Mystic's vintage vessels

MONTVILLE, CONNECTICUT
595 Burn rubber on a giant go-kart track

A road trip is an American tradition, but if you want to let loose behind the wheel, you need a special facility. SuperCharged is a 110,000-sq-ft (10,200-sq-m) multilevel track with go-karts that reach 45 mph (72 kmh)—the largest indoor track in the world. It's usually two separate tracks but on Thursdays, you can join a merged supertrack, taking twenty-eight karts.

MYSTIC, CONNECTICUT
596 Submerge yourself in maritime history

There are dozens of "living museums" these days, but one of the first dates back to the 1940s, when the acquisition of a whaling ship inspired this maritime time capsule. Mystic Seaport Museum is a working community of nineteenth-century boats and craftspeople. Come and see coopers and woodcarvers in authentic shops, and see dozens of historic vessels.

THROUGHOUT CONNECTICUT
597 Eat a lobster roll

Every region has its speciality sandwich and in this part of the country, it's a lobster roll. The original is said to have come from a restaurant called Perry's in Milford, in 1929. Now available everywhere in the state, the basic version is lobster meat served on a hot dog bun with butter or mayonnaise. Head to Lenny & Joe's Fish Tale or S&P Oyster Restaurant and Bar for some of the best.

PAWTUCKET, RHODE ISLAND
598 See the birthplace of a revolution

The year is 1793, and a small town has just made its first water-powered cotton mill operational. Before long, mills have spread across New England, making Pawtucket the birthplace of the American Industrial Revolution. Pay a visit to the Blackstone River Valley National Heritage Corridor and wonder at dozens of historic sites, managed by a series of Rhode Island visitors' centers.

PROVIDENCE, RHODE ISLAND
599 Watch an artist play with fire

In 1994, Providence artist Barnaby Evans created an exciting art installation to celebrate New Year's Eve. Called WaterFire, it used eleven braziers around Waterplace Park to create a fire sculpture. It was so well received that it now includes ninety-seven spectacular braziers and runs twice a month, May through November. Join tens of thousands of spectators to witness this fiery artwork.

PROVIDENCE, RHODE ISLAND
600 Eat at the country's oldest food truck

Food trucks may be the latest hip way to eat lunch, but the originals have been around a long time. Haven Brothers Diner was founded as a food truck in 1893 and it still operates to this day in its traditional spot next to City Hall. It's a simple menu of American classics: grilled cheese sandwiches, burgers, and chicken tenders, but insiders know to go for the signature Haven Dog with all the fixings.

599 A WaterFire performance in Providence

PROVIDENCE, RHODE ISLAND
601 Settle in with a book at the "Ath"

The Providence Athenaeum has literary history oozing out of its walls. It was a favorite haunt of horror aficionado H. P. Lovecraft, and Sarah Helen Whitman broke off her engagement to Edgar Allen Poe here. Behind the neoclassical columns, the stacks hide plenty of reading nooks, while the lower floor offers individually lit, comfortable leather seats.

PROVIDENCE, RHODE ISLAND
602 Have designs on a world-class institution

When the Rhode Island School of Design was founded in 1877, the campus included a museum to promote civic interaction. The school thrived and is now regarded as one of the best of its kind, and the RISD Museum is enjoying a similar trajectory. See exhibits of ancient, Asian, and contemporary art, alongside inspiring collections of costumes, textiles, and decorative arts.

NEWPORT, RHODE ISLAND
603 See the best of the best of the sailing world

There's a strong maritime tradition and history in Newport, so much so that the city's sometimes referred to as "the sailing capital of the world." It has played host to the world's top sailing competitions, and for many years hosted the prestigious America's Cup. Head here to watch annual 12 Metre sailing regattas and see the world's most skilled sailors out on the hallowed waters.

NEWPORT, RHODE ISLAND
604 Travel back three centuries for lunch

It's not every day that you eat in a place dating to the seventeenth century. Known as the "oldest operating restaurant in the US" and acknowledged as the world's tenth oldest, the White Horse Tavern has been serving guests since 1673. The architecture is Newport colonial, with clapboard walls, giant beams, and huge fireplaces—an evocative backdrop for a bowl of clam chowder.

603 Sailing in Newport

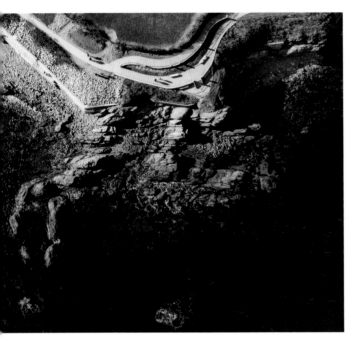

606 Newport's Cliff Walk

607 Entrance to the Breakers

NEWPORT, RHODE ISLAND
605 Rock out at the Newport Folk Festival

In the late 1950s, a folk music revival saw a small folk element added to the established Newport Jazz Festival. Since then it's grown to be a huge festival in its own right and the Newport Folk Festival has seen some legendary performances. In 1965, Bob Dylan was booed for playing an electric guitar, but he's been back many times since. The festival happens every July so come and enjoy the weather and some (mostly) acoustic music.

NEWPORT, RHODE ISLAND
606 Appreciate the Newport coastline

You will see some of the most breathtaking coastal scenery in New England from this 3.5-mi (6-km) path along the eastern shore of Newport. This National Recreation Trail also borders the back lawns of many of the seaside city's grand mansions, affording a chance to get a closer look at the elegant architecture.

NEWPORT, RHODE ISLAND
607 Take a break and tour a country mansion

Newport is home to a number of "summer cottages," which are actually huge, mansionlike homes for the wealthy. The most famous and grandest of them all is the Breakers, constructed by the Vanderbilt family in the late nineteenth century. It's a seventy-room palazzo in the Italian Renaissance style, designated a National Historic Landmark and now open for you to take a glimpse at the life of the elites.

POINT JUDITH POND,
RHODE ISLAND
608 Forage for dinner

The most popular seafood in
Rhode Island is the quahog,
otherwise known as hard-
shelled clam. Looking for clams
(clamming) is a popular pastime,
with places such as Point Judith
Pond among the better spots
during the season (September 15–
May 15). Delve into the mud
around an hour before low
tide and fill your basket with
shellfish, but check with guides
about how many you can take.

BLOCK ISLAND, RHODE ISLAND
609 Leave no trace on Block Island

The Mohegan Bluffs on Block
Island are named after a violent
sixteenth-century battle in
which the Manissean tribe forced
raiding Mohegans over the cliffs
to their death. Despite this
chilling past, the Bluffs are one
of many wild and beautiful spots
on this small island with big
conservation goals. To preserve
its natural beauty and thriving
wildlife, keep to the paths and
take all refuse away with you.

LEVERETT, MASSACHUSETTS
610 Find yourself at a peace pagoda

The New England Peace Pagoda
is a Buddhist monument that was
designed to inspire peace in its
visitors. Rest upon a bench beside
a pond filled with water lilies and
contemplate the beauty of nature.

609 Block Island

MANCHESTER-BY-THE-SEA,
MASSACHUSETTS

611 Hear the sound of "singing" sands

New England is replete with scenic beaches, and Singing Beach is among the most naturally blessed, with its clear waters and sandy coastline. This beach is more interactive than most, though. Its name comes from a strange natural phenomenon—the sands produce a high-pitched squeak, made by grains of sand rubbing together. It's not too melodic but definitely worth experiencing.

SALEM, MASSACHUSETTS

612 Check your resting witch face at a trial

This quaint city may have some photogenic historic architecture, but it has a famously macabre past. In 1692, the Salem witch trials found fourteen women guilty and executed them for satanic practices. It's a gruesome story, but one that's reenacted daily at several venues as local actors re-create the scenes and shed light on the events. Settle in for a trial like no other.

MINUTE MAN NATIONAL HISTORICAL
PARK, MASSACHUSETTS

613 See the legacy of war

New England is awash with history
relating to the American Revolution,
but at this park in 1775, the opening
battles of that famous war took place,
starting at Concord's North Bridge
(pictured). Take a guided tour and
see the battlefields, landscapes, and
historic structures that remain to this
day. The park's name comes from the
militia who were ready at a minute's
notice to fire on the British.

BOSTON, MASSACHUSETTS

614 Watch the city's most beloved sports team

They take their sports seriously in this city, and since 1912, Fenway Park has been home to the famous Boston Red Sox, making this the oldest active ballpark in Major League Baseball. It's relatively small for such a big team, but join legions of die-hard fans for a game during the season (April to October) and you'll be among some of the sport's most passionate supporters.

BOSTON, MASSACHUSETTS

615 Go where everybody knows your name

Dating to 1969, the Bull & Finch Pub was the inspiration for the TV show *Cheers*, which aired from 1982 to 1993. Over the years, it has become something of a tourist trap, but hard-core fans can still enjoy a pint among the memorabilia and trinkets commemorating the classic show. In 2002, the bar officially changed its name to Cheers Beacon Hill.

BOSTON, MASSACHUSETTS

616 View half a million pieces of art

When it opened on July 4, 1876, the centennial of the Declaration of Independence, Boston's Museum of Fine Arts housed 5,600 works of art. The collection swelled over the years, and the museum now holds close to 500,000 artworks and receives more than a million visitors a year. Wander through and see pieces ranging from prehistoric times through to the modern day.

614 Fans at Fenway Park

619 Boston Marathon's Scream Tunnel

BOSTON, MASSACHUSETTS
617 Celebrate the old country

Americans love St. Patrick's Day more than anyone else in the world, and with a historically huge Irish population, Boston probably has the biggest party come March 17. The pubs are alive with Irish menus, live music, and Irish dancing, and there are special events citywide. Don't show up without wearing at least a hint of green or you'll face friendly punishments.

BOSTON, MASSACHUSETTS
618 Work your way along the Freedom Trail

Boston is known as the birthplace of the American Revolution, and the city's Freedom Trail makes it easy to explore this history. A path laid in brick starts at Boston Common, where British soldiers once camped before going into battle. It passes by fourteen important sites before ending at the Bunker Hill Monument, the site of a major battle in 1775.

BOSTON, MASSACHUSETTS
619 Run a marathon

Boston Marathon is the oldest annual marathon in the world and perhaps the most prestigious—runners earn a spot by meeting a stringent qualifying time. The course is narrow for a city marathon, with notable sections including Wellesley College's Scream Tunnel at mile twelve (block your ears to the wall of sound the students create). For a race with serious bragging rights, it's hard to beat.

STELLWAGEN BANK NATIONAL MARINE
SANCTUARY, MASSACHUSETTS
620 Watch whales off an urban coast

You don't need an expensive cruise in a far-flung
place to go whale watching. Thanks to an
underwater plateau at the mouth of Massachusetts
Bay just outside Boston, anyone can access one
of the top ten whale watching spots in the world.
Species seen here include the acrobatic humpback
whale, minke whale, and pilot whale, as well as
other sea mammals such as dolphins and seals.

PLYMOUTH, MASSACHUSETTS
621 See a famous rock for yourself

Did the Puritans really, as the song says, get a
shock when they landed at Plymouth Rock? Judge
for yourself at Pilgrim Memorial State Park on
the shore of Plymouth Harbor, where a boulder
has been designated the exact landing spot of the
Mayflower in 1620. Whether or not this rock was
the first touched by the Pilgrims, it's an iconic
piece of the American story, and the history
still fascinates.

622 Facing east on the Cape Cod National Seashore

CAPE COD NATIONAL SEASHORE, MASSACHUSETTS
622 Put all of America behind you

The hook-shape peninsula off the coast of Massachusetts is a site of quaint villages, lighthouses, seafood shacks, and unspoiled Atlantic shoreline. The Cape Cod National Seashore stretches for 40 mi (64 km) around the Cape's outer curve and is a bounty of unspoiled beaches, salt marshes, dunes, and well-preserved forested trails. Head for Bound Brook Island—as remote a beach as you'll find here.

MARTHA'S VINEYARD, MASSACHUSETTS
623 Have a vine time at one of the country's most exclusive spots

This refined corner of New England became a hot ticket in the 1960s, when the glitterati and political classes started to frequent the island. Take a day trip to Vineyard Haven, with its Victorian boardwalk ambience, and Edgartown, awash with boutiques and historical maritime architecture. You may even spot a modern-day celebrity in line at the ice cream parlor.

BURLINGTON, VERMONT
624 Take in views while knocking back suds

With its wealth of world-class brewers, it's no surprise that the Vermont Brewers Festival is one of the premier beer festivals in the world. It's also one of the most picturesque, held by Lake Champlain overlooking the Adirondack Mountains. The Vermont Brewers Association invites nearly fifty breweries from Vermont and surrounding states to participate. It's typically held on the third weekend of July, and has been going for more than twenty-five years. Visit for experiential tastings and pairing classes, live music, food, and craft vendors.

MT. PHILO STATE PARK, VERMONT
625 Hear a woodpecker peck

The hammering of the pileated woodpecker is a sure way to identify this bird. Mt. Philo State Park is also popular for viewing raptors and fall migrations.

626 Swimming in Dorset Quarry

626 Swim in a marble quarry

In 1785, America's first marble quarry opened, and its bountiful stone supplied some of the most famous buildings in the region, including the New York Public Library and Brown University Library. The quarry was subsequently abandoned, but lives on as a popular swimming spot. Jump from sheer marble walls into the clear waters, and look out for small sculptures carved into the walls.

627 Take a road less traveled

You probably at least know the lines "Two roads diverged in a wood, and I—/I took the one less traveled by,/And that has made all the difference." They're from Robert Frost's most famous poem, "The Road Not Taken," and you can find your own road to take on the Robert Frost Interpretive Trail. Wander a mile loop among bucolic woodlands, and see several of his poems mounted in nature.

628 See where the ice cream magic happens

There can't be too many people who don't like ice cream, and one of the most famous brands is made by the bohemian, hippie-tinged Ben & Jerry. If you're a fan of Chunky Monkey, Cherry Garcia, or Phish Food, then you can take a Wonka-esque tour of the place where ice cream dreams are made.

629 Pay homage to canines at the Dog Chapel

"Welcome all creeds, all breeds, no dogmas allowed," states the sign outside the small chapel celebrating the spiritual bond between dog and man. The chapel is the pet project of folk artist Stephen Huneck, who was inspired to build the canine sanctuary on his mountaintop farm after a near-death experience.

630 Village hop in Vermont

Vermont is full of quaint villages, linked by a network of highways and byways—the perfect opportunity for a tour by cycle. Opt for relaxing country roads with minimal traffic, or hop on a mountain bike and tackle challenging routes along logging trails, steep woodland paths, and gravel tracks. And a visit in fall offers the bonus of stunning foliage.

631 Snow time like winter for Nordic sports

It's winter and you want to have fun in the snow but don't want to commit to a resort? Southern Vermont offers a suitably Nordic environment and a wealth of casual ways to engage with it. The most fun is probably snow tubing in Grafton—hurtling down slopes on a large rubber ring. You don't need any expensive equipment.

THROUGHOUT VERMONT

632 Watch the state's famous syrup being sugared

At the end of winter in Vermont, small farm buildings that have lain dormant come to life, the plumes of steam coming from them telling everyone that the maple syrup season is upon us, in a process known as maple sugaring. Most producers offer a behind-the-scenes tour before you buy their product, and if you're particularly keen, there's the New England Maple Museum in Pittsford.

THROUGHOUT VERMONT

633 Say cheese 150 times

Outside of Wisconsin, Vermont is probably the country's most famous cheese producer, and there are some forty-five top-rated cheesemakers operating across the state. To make life easier for cheese chasers, there's a recognized Vermont Cheese Trail that promises 150 varieties of cheese along the way. Sadly the beer and wine pairings may impair your progress, but we advise leaning into the challenge.

MT. WASHINGTON/WHITE MOUNTAINS, NEW HAMPSHIRE

634 Fall for fall colors at their peak

Deciduous trees changing color is something so commonplace that we don't always take the time to admire the beauty it brings to the landscape. New Hampshire, with its rolling hills and many lakes, offers dramatically beautiful fall scenery every year. Get up high on the Mt. Washington Auto Road in the White Mountains for views over miles of orange-hued trees. Look for a place to take the perfect photo of trees reflected in water in the Lakes Region—Squam Lake offers outstanding views—or enjoy being on foot among the vibrant shades by hiking on Mt. Kearsarge.

LINCOLN, NEW HAMPSHIRE

635 Avoid a Scot-free life at a Highland Games

If you want to see burly men in kilts compete with each other to see who can toss huge logs the farthest, then you're in luck. No Caledonian pilgrimages are necessary as this New Hampshire town hosts its very own Highland Games every September. As well as the famous caber toss, there is a full celebration of Gaelic culture, with dancing, bagpipe and drum groups, and tartan as far as the eye can see.

NORTH CONWAY, NEW HAMPSHIRE

636 Test out the Conway Scenic Railroad

Travel on the Crawford Notch route for a five-and-a-half-hour vintage-train journey through some of the most dramatic natural scenery on the Eastern Seaboard. The railroad was created over 140 years ago—a feat for its time. You'll find a cozy pub in North Conway at the end of the round trip.

634 Artist's Bluff in the White Mountains National Forest

NORTH WOODSTOCK, NEW HAMPSHIRE
637 Visit a truly white castle

Every winter in this town, the country's best
ice artists convene to create huge structures
using specially shaped icicles. They're part of the
spectacular Ice Castles attraction, and the results
draw thousands of spectators. The castles include
dramatic LED-lit sculptures, frozen thrones,
tunnels, and fountains, and even towers, some
of which reach truly astonishing heights.
Bundle up and admire these icy works of art.

CHARLESTOWN, NEW HAMPSHIRE
638 Take to the skies in any way you choose

Commercial flying has had much of the fun taken
out of it these days, with cramped seats and frequent
delays. There's a place to rediscover the adventure
of taking to the skies, though. Morningside Flight
Park is one of the most complete flight parks in the
country, with options to hang glide, paraglide, and
zip-line through the air, all with expert instruction
and guidance. Take flight without the baggage.

637 North Woodstock's Ice Castles

640 Hiking the bald-topped Mt. Monadnock

CANTERBURY, NEW HAMPSHIRE
639 Pray in wilderness

A series of visions led Reverend Steve Blackmer to establish a "church" in 106 ac (43 ha) of forest, bringing the spirit of nature back to religious practice. Church of the Woods is a place where people of all faiths can celebrate the natural world as the bearer of the sacred. Visitors are welcome to meditate, walk in the woods, or simply sit quietly on a fallen tree.

DUBLIN, NEW HAMPSHIRE
640 Peak at the world's second most scaled slope

Mt. Monadnock is said to be the world's second most climbed peak after Japan's Mt. Fuji. You can join the 125,000 or so annual hikers attracted by its accessibility. The peak is just over 3,000 ft (914 m) and trails with differing levels of difficulty lead to the top. Once there, you're higher than anywhere in view, so you'll feel on top of the world.

PORTSMOUTH, NEW HAMPSHIRE
641 See how people lived half a millennium ago

It's almost 500 years since European settlers populated Portsmouth. Strawbery Banke Museum is the oldest European-settled neighborhood in the state, named for the fruit spotted as the first immigrants arrived. It's now an impressive outdoor museum, with thirty-seven restored buildings dating as far back as the seventeenth century.

SALEM, NEW HAMPSHIRE

642 See America's Stonehenge

Historians have long theorized about how ancient slabs of rock came to form the world-famous Stonehenge. America, too, has a smaller but still mysterious arrangement without a definitive origin story. The archaeological site at Mystery Hill has pre-Colombian stone formations including sacrificial slabs and hints at primitive stone-on-stone techniques for its construction.

THROUGHOUT NEW HAMPSHIRE

643 Like them apples

Visiting New England in the fall is always a good idea given the colorful show that nature puts on. There's a secondary, connected reason, though, and that's to make the most of the orchards. Visitors are encouraged, and they can pick their own apples and stone fruits, and enjoy perfect apple cider, as well as everything else that the state has to offer at this abundant time of year.

THROUGHOUT MAINE

644 Have a berry fun time picking your own blue harvest

If apples aren't your thing, then a fashionable superfood might be. Maine is awash with blueberry farms, and like other fruit producers in the region, many allow the public to get their hands sticky picking fruit. The season is slightly earlier in the year, though, so visit in late summer. Jams, pies, and other blueberry items are also widely available.

MOOSEHEAD LAKE, MAINE

645 Meet deer friends on a lake safari

Moosehead Lake didn't get its name randomly. There are loose moose about this region, and the best way to spot them is from a kayak safari. Maine moose in the North Maine Woods outnumber people three to one, so you should easily spot these majestic beasts. You can even glide right up close to them.

646 Tackling the slopes of Mt. Katahdin

BAXTER STATE PARK, MAINE
646 See a mountain and conquer it

Mt. Katahdin, the northern terminus of the
Appalachian Trail, is a mountain that cries out
to be climbed. It rises majestically from the lakes
and forests around it and can be seen for miles.
There are nine different routes to the summit, an
impressive 5,267 ft (1,605 m) up. None are easy—
one involves the well-named Knife Edge route—
but all offer fantastic views as you go and when
you reach the top.

ACADIA NATIONAL PARK, MAINE
647 Toast the sunset in Bar Harbor

Acadia National Park offers some of the most beautiful shorelines of New England, with granite cliffs and rugged bays. The sunsets over the bay are legendary, and from June to October, a cruise provides a chance to admire them from the water. Or remain in the historic harbor and feast on local seafood in the rosy glow.

PORTLAND, MAINE
648 Sample Maine from a lobster boat

Lobster has been fished off Maine since the 1600s and is one of the state's most successful industries. Join a lobster boat as it heads out to check its traps, and help to haul them in. As well as learning more than you thought possible about lobsters and lobster fishing, you can often buy the fresh catch, and take it home for your dinner.

PORTLAND, MAINE
649 Discover the other Portland

Portland, Oregon, is where to go for fusion food pop-ups and hipster clothing. Portland, Maine, is where to come for an incredibly well-preserved historic district. The town has a proud history of agriculture, craftsmanship, and maritime activity. Don't miss Portland Head Light—the state's oldest lighthouse (1791).

647 Dockside lobsters at Bar Harbor

PORTLAND, MAINE

650 Walk among half a dozen breweries

Allagash Brewing is located at 50 Industrial Way in Portland, but just steps away are several other smaller niche breweries that have incubated in this part of town. Current tenants include Bissell Brothers, Rising Tide Brewing, Foundation Brewing, Austin Street Brewery, and Battery Steele Brewing. On weekends, beer lovers can mosey between tasting rooms, without ever walking more than 300 ft (91.5 m). It's a magical slice of craft beer heaven in one of the most exciting drinking cities in the United States.

COASTAL MAINE

651 Take up a fishy hobby for the weekend

Maine has fish, and plenty of them. While some people like to hoist a sail, a more tranquil way to fish is to plant waders on the floor of a river. Maine has some of the world's best and most scenic fly-fishing spots, and there are plenty of guides to show you their favorite fishing holes. Head for the Crooked River or the Presumpscot River.

CAMDEN, MAINE

652 See the glorious Maine coast as they did in the past

Luxury yachts are all well and good, but treat yourself to an authentic sailing experience. Maine's maritime past means that there are numerous historic windjammers and schooners that take parties out to sea. You can even sail in the *Lewis R. French*, a National Historic Landmark and the country's oldest commercial sailing vessel.

5

CANADA

DAWSON CITY, YUKON

653 Cheer on the Yukon Quest dogsledding races

This is considered the toughest dogsled race in the world—even more challenging than Alaska's Iditarod. Contested every February since 1984, it follows the Klondike Gold Rush route, and Dawson City is the midpoint. Dogs and drivers arrive exhausted and ready for a rest having run 200 mi (320 km), the greatest distance between checkpoints of any sled competition.

DAWSON CITY, YUKON

654 Drink a cocktail garnished with a mummified toe

Here's a former frontier city that boomed as a base for prospectors during the Klondike Gold Rush of the nineteenth century. Several historic buildings have been preserved, and there's a small museum that tells the town's story. Stop off for a Sourtoe Cocktail at the Downtown Hotel. It comes with a genuine mummified toe at the bottom of it and you'll be gifted a certificate of authenticity.

KLONDIKE HIGHWAY, YUKON

655 Take a gold-standard road trip

Synonymous with the Klondike Gold Rush from 1896, this highway offers an exceptional 445-mi (715-km) trip from Alaska to Canada's Yukon. It runs alongside blue lakes and pristine rivers, over mountain passes, and through evocatively named landscapes like the Tormented Valley. Spare a thought for the prospectors who carried their provisions for a year across this terrain. By the time many arrived, the gold had all gone.

ST. ELIAS MOUNTAINS, YUKON

656 Explore the extremes of Kluane National Park and Reserve

Extreme is the word. This park is home to seventeen of Canada's twenty highest peaks, including Mt. Logan (19,551 ft; 5,959 m). It also contains the country's largest ice field and its most diverse population of grizzlies. Adventurous types can hike along alpine passes, or raft past glaciers on the Alsek River. Kathleen Lake is more accessible and enjoyed year-round by casual visitors.

656 Icy expanses of Kluane National Park and Reserve

657 SS *Klondike*, on the banks of the Yukon

658 Hiking in Tombstone Territorial Park

WHITEHORSE, YUKON

657 Relive the past on a visit to the SS *Klondike*

This proud, pristine-looking ship is a National Historic Site. It dates back to the late 1930s, and it ran the freight route between Whitehorse and Dawson City. This beauty was the largest of the fleet, and it has been meticulously restored to its original finery. You can take a self-guided tour to learn about its history and even play a traditional game of quoits.

TOMBSTONE TERRITORIAL PARK, YUKON

658 Spot bears, moose, and 150 kinds of bird

Known as Canada's Patagonia, the mountains here provide a breathtakingly dramatic backdrop and typify a rugged, otherworldly beauty. The wildlife is abundant, too. Visit in late August, when the hiking trails are framed by vibrant, autumnal reds and oranges, and look out for black and grizzly bears, caribou, and moose, as well as a plethora of bird species.

ACROSS YUKON

659 Follow a trail back through the Gold Rush era

The Trans Canada Trail passes through all of Canada's provinces, but Yukon is considered the jewel. It's a road of diverse scenery, and some of the most evocative sights surround the old stagecoach pathways that brought prospectors to towns such as Dawson City.

CAMPBELL RIVER, BRITISH COLUMBIA

660 Get a fish-eye view of a salmon run

It's one thing to see a river teeming with thousands of salmon heading back to breed at the site of their birth, but imagine donning a snorkel and experiencing the journey with them. The crystal clear water of the Campbell River makes for ideal viewing.

ACROSS BRITISH COLUMBIA

661 Hike through abandoned railway tunnels

The Kettle Valley Railway opened as part of the Canadian Pacific Railway in 1915, with the last train running in 1989. Now established as the Kettle Valley Rail Trail, visitors can hike, bike, or drive the 400-mi (650-km) recreational trail. Myra Canyon is perhaps the most scenic stretch.

HAIDA NATION, BRITISH COLUMBIA

662 Say hi to Haida Gwaii

This remote archipelago is the ancestral home of the Haida people. Few tourists venture out here; those who do are rewarded by traditional Haida hospitality and the serenity and cultural wealth of their laid-back communities. Find abandoned villages to the south and beaches flanked by rain forest to the east.

662 Haida Gwaii's famous Balance Rock

HOPE, BRITISH COLUMBIA
663 Look out for Sasquatch

The bucolic, forested area of Sasquatch
Caves, just outside Hope, has historically
recorded several sightings of the mythical
mammal Bigfoot, or Sasquatch. The
province itself has had over 200 incidents.
Proof remains elusive, but hikers will
nevertheless enjoy this network of trails.
There are several great vantage points and
dramatic caves to explore. Caving gear is
necessary for the deeper chambers.

JOHNSTONE STRAIT, BRITISH COLUMBIA
664 Kayak with killer whales

Watching orcas in their natural environment is an
exhilarating enough experience, but to do it from a kayak in
Johnstone Strait is one of life's must-have adventures. This
narrow channel between Vancouver Island and mainland
Canada is home to the Northern Resident community of
killer whales. As a result, sightings are highly likely, and
there's a great deal of knowledge about their behavior,
such as the way offspring stay with their mother throughout
their adult lives. These whales also display a very particular
behavior—beach rubbing. They come close to shore and
swim alongside it, rubbing their bellies on the pebbles.
Scientists think it's purely for a pleasurable massage.

664 Orcas in Johnstone Strait

REVELSTOKE, BRITISH COLUMBIA
665 Be enchanted by 350 forest figures

Since the 1950s, artists Doris and Ernest Needham have decorated 8 ac (3 ha) of forest—the Enchanted Forest—with sculpted tributes to the fairy folk, constructing everything from gingerbread houses to functioning waterways; visitors can spot figurines of magical inhabitants from dragons to dwarves and fairies. The forest also boasts some 800-year-old cedars and the tallest tree house in BC.

MAQUINNA MARINE PROVINCIAL PARK, BRITISH COLUMBIA
666 Catch a zodiac to Hot Springs Cove

A trip to this cove on Vancouver Island almost offers too much for just one day. First there's a boat trip with the chance of spotting whales, then an atmospheric walk through a rain forest to geothermal pools that bubble up through rocks before cascading down to the sea. Sitting in their heated waters with views of the Pacific is divine.

SMITHERS, BRITISH COLUMBIA

667 Hold your breath watching goats

As mountain goats leap from one tiny foothold to the next on near-vertical cliffs, it is almost impossible not to hold your breath. Although they might not look athletic, they are very narrow-shouldered, which is what helps them stick so closely to cliff walls.

PARKSVILLE, BRITISH COLUMBIA

668 Construct an epic sandcastle

Every summer, the most stunning display of sandcastles appears on the beach here—part of the annual Parksville Beach Festival competition. But "sandcastles" doesn't begin to do justice to these magnificent works of art, constructed by artists from all over the globe.

PORT RENFREW, BRITISH COLUMBIA

669 See Canada's "gnarliest" tree

Avatar Grove near Port Renfrew is a spectacular area of protected old-growth forest in the Pacheedaht First Nation territory. Take the boardwalk through huge firs and cedars to "Canada's gnarliest tree"; with its tangle of roots and multitude of lumps and bumps, it's a natural work of art.

PRINCESS ROYAL ISLAND, BRITISH COLUMBIA

670 Be mesmerized by a spirit bear

This rare subspecies of black bear, thought sacred by the Indigenous people, has a gene predisposing it to white fur. Spirit bears catch more salmon in daylight, when their color makes them harder to spot from below the water.

QUALICUM BEACH, BRITISH COLUMBIA

671 Sleep in a forest canopy sphere

This sleepy coastal town on Vancouver Island is a 45-minute drive north of Nanaimo and enjoys a Mediterranean climate. The surrounding forest is home to some unusual accommodations in the form of the Free Spirit Spheres. Suspended from trees and built to sway with the surroundings, the spheres are made with locally sourced wood and fiberglass. Each houses three people, and includes power supplies, bedrooms, and living areas (bathroom and dining facilities are separate). They're among the most original tree houses in the country, bringing a sense of whimsy to woodland living.

RICHMOND, BRITISH COLUMBIA

672 Meet over 500 cats

The RAPS Cat Sanctuary is the largest in North America. Visitors are allowed to come and visit the felines, lovingly taken care of until they find their forever homes.

VANVOUVER ISLAND, BRITISH COLUMBIA

673 Have a mindful moment on a beach walk

The scale of nature on Vancouver Island is so awe-inspiring that it's easy to overlook the smaller marvels. Slow down and potter along the beaches of Cox Bay, MacKenzie Beach, or Long Beach. What treasures will you find among the driftwood? What creatures might you spot in the tide pools? Hours can go by as you lose yourself in the smaller side of nature.

671 Alternative accommodation in a Free Spirit Sphere

PACIFIC RIM NATIONAL PARK RESERVE,
BRITISH COLUMBIA
674 Pick your favorite island trail

The Pacific Rim National Park Reserve covers
200 sq mi (500 sq km) on the scenic West Coast of
Vancouver Island. The area is steeped in the native
Nuu-chah-nulth culture and has three regions:
the West Coast Trail, Broken Group Islands,
and Long Beach, each with several hiking trails.
Wander through forests or along the coastline,
stopping for hot springs or whale watching.

TOFINO, BRITISH COLUMBIA
675 Attend surf school in Tofino

It might be colder than the Caribbean, but Tofino
is the surf capital of Canada. Although the coast
can be wild and windy, coastal havens and warmer
summer months attract surfers of all levels. Cox
Bay, Chesterman Beach, Long Beach, and Rosie's
Bay all have their charms, the last requiring a little
expertise. Long Beach and Cox Bay have room
for beginners, and surf schools are peppered
around the area.

675 Surfing at sunset at Cox Bay

677 Crossing the Capilano Suspension Bridge

UCLUELET, BRITISH COLUMBIA
676 Bathe in an ancient cedar forest

In Japan, *shinrin-yoku* ("forest bathing") is an intrinsic part of preventative health care. Regular walks in nature focusing on its sights, smells, and sounds are proved to lower blood pressure and reduce stress; one study has shown they can even help fight cancer. Wander around the Ancient Cedars Loop Trail, touch the trees, hear the wind in the canopy, and soak up the restorative powers of these mighty giants.

VANCOUVER, BRITISH COLUMBIA
677 Test your nerves crossing a gorge

Suspension bridges shout of our all-conquering nature: "I will cross this gorge, as if I were born to fly." The Capilano Suspension Bridge is a true sensation, 230 ft (70 m) high, two-people wide, and 450 ft (140 m) long. Set foot on it and you'll feel like you're stepping into thin air.

VANCOUVER, BRITISH COLUMBIA
678 Satisfy seafood cravings with an oyster bar crawl

Vancouver's oceanside location means that seafood is king when it comes to eating out. There are dozens of options, and oyster fans will do well to plan their route if they want to sample the bivalve highlights of the area's cuisine. Locals will have their own opinions on the best spots, but Rodney's Oyster House, Blue Water Cafe, and Fanny Bay Oyster Bar regularly top most lists.

VANCOUVER, BRITISH COLUMBIA
679 Drive the Sea to Sky Highway to Pemberton

The 75-mi (120-km) section of Highway 99 from Horseshoe Bay to Pemberton should take a couple of hours by car. But the gorgeous scenery means you'll want to set aside much longer for what is one of the world's great drives. The views from Porteau Cove across Howe Sound with the mountains in the background are worth the trip alone. Shannon Falls, third highest in the province, is another highlight.

682 Stanley Park in the fall

VANCOUVER, BRITISH COLUMBIA

680 Get caffeinated at Cold Brew Fest

There's a special affinity for all things coffee-related here, and caffeinated culture is celebrated with aplomb every August at the world's biggest cold brew festival. Visitors can taste rare brews, study the production process, and indulge themselves in a multitude of coffee-infused delights including cold-brew ales and irresistible confections. Don't plan on sleeping until very late that night.

VANCOUVER, BRITISH COLUMBIA

681 Understand the meaning of totem poles

There are lots of places in the Pacific Northwest where you can see fantastic totem poles created by the area's First Nations. However, to truly understand the significance of these iconic monuments, head to Vancouver's Museum of Anthropology, which has more than 300 examples to inspire you. Learn about the histories they reveal, the families they represent, and the purposes they serve.

VANCOUVER, BRITISH COLUMBIA

682 See a city bathed in fall colors

Stanley Park is a stunning, semiwild city park that sprawls over 1,000 ac (405 ha). Its famous Seawall skirts its edges, following the coastline. Nestled between the pretty rose garden and the forest is the Shakespeare Garden. This quiet space pays homage to the Bard through the secluded arboretum of more than forty-five trees mentioned in his works, accompanied by relevant quotes.

683 Top views from the Vancouver Lookout

VANCOUVER, BRITISH COLUMBIA

683 Contemplate the best views in town

Nothing gives a better perspective of a city than seeing it from above. Take the glass elevator up thirty stories to the Vancouver Lookout for panoramic views of the city and beyond. Part of the 1970s Harbour Centre, the viewing deck sits like a flying saucer on the top of the tower, emanating a sci-fi feel. It's not the highest viewing platform in the world but definitely one of the coolest.

VANCOUVER, BRITISH COLUMBIA

684 Visit Granville Island Public Market

When in Vancouver, make sure to take a tugboat across False Creek from Yaletown to this bijou island, the highlight of which is the daily fresh food market—established in 1979 for producers to sell their wares direct. They say everything here is fresh from the ocean, field, or oven, and it really is a foodie's treasure trove, with artisanal bakeries, gourmet coffee spots, fresh pasta, meats, and cheeses.

BRENTWOOD BAY,
BRITISH COLUMBIA

685 Inhale the scents of Butchart Gardens

Back in 1912, when her husband's limestone quarry at Brentwood Bay was exhausted of limestone, Jennie Butchart had the vision to turn the ravaged rocks into a sunken garden. Her family has built on this vision ever since, creating the delight that is Butchart Gardens, with more than 900 plant varieties, providing color and scent year-round.

VICTORIA, BRITISH COLUMBIA

686 Explore Victoria's Inner Harbour

There's been a functional harbor here since the early nineteenth century, and the beautiful Victorian buildings have welcomed countless vessels over the years. The Inner Harbour forms an oceanside promenade, with historic architecture framing an idyllic marina. Live entertainment and festivals enliven the place in summer, and visitors can take a tour on the water year-round.

WHISTLER, BRITISH COLUMBIA

687 Go mountain biking at a downhill park

The slopes of Whistler aren't a sporting playground only when they're covered in snow—from June to October they're a mountain biker's paradise. At Whistler Mountain Bike Park, put your bike on the ski lift, then choose your route down through meadows, rocky gullies, and forest paths. At 4,900 vertical feet (1,500 m), the route back to base is an adrenaline rush for both experts and beginners.

WHISTLER, BRITISH COLUMBIA

688 Book a heli-yoga package in the Rockies

BC has a typically West Coast approach to all things health-conscious. This is perhaps to do with the climate and the abundance of nature, and there's nothing like getting out into the wilderness to reconnect as you exercise. Some companies will fly you into the Rockies for an unforgettable yoga session, surrounded by mountains and lakes while you practice your sun salutations.

689 Whistler's ski slopes

WHISTLER, BRITISH COLUMBIA

689 Hit world-class slopes in Whistler

The mountains of Whistler and Blackcomb provide the backdrop to the largest ski resort in North America, with slopes for skiers and snowboarders of all levels. Snow lovers have flocked to Whistler Blackcomb resort since the mid-1960s and its slopes hosted the Alpine skiing events of the 2010 Winter Olympics. Take the Peak 2 Peak gondola for unforgettable views of Fitzsimmons Creek.

YOHO NATIONAL PARK, BRITISH COLUMBIA

690 Hike an iconic trail

All the hiking routes in this park are spectacular, leading to glacial lakes, tumbling waterfalls, and stunning mountain views. But to really make the most of the park, head above the tree line on the circular 8-mi (13-km) Iceline Trail. It takes some hard legwork to get there, but from this high up you can look down on glaciers winding through valleys, and out across peak after peak of the Rockies.

KEELE RIVER, NORTHWEST TERRITORIES

691 Paddle down the Keele River

Canoes are one of the oldest known forms of travel, and an emblem of Canadian and First Nation heritage. Paddling down a river and pulling ashore to camp for the night feels like an adventure, and it links us to how the country was originally developed. Follow the turquoise waters of the Keele through the Mackenzie Mountains, fishing for your dinner as you go.

693 Northern lights, seen from Yellowknife

NAHANNI NATIONAL PARK RESERVE,
NORTHWEST TERRITORIES

692 Visit the first natural location named a World Heritage Site

"One of the most spectacular wild rivers in North America, with deep canyons, huge waterfalls, and spectacular karst terrain." These aren't the words of the Canadian tourist board, but UNESCO World Heritage, listing the South Nahanni River as one of the reasons this wild and beautiful national park was one of the first natural areas to make it onto its list. The landscape is as stunning as it is interesting to geologists.

YELLOWKNIFE, NORTHWEST TERRITORIES

693 Use insider info to catch the northern lights

Seeing the northern lights is up there on every bucket list: the ethereal atmosphere, the skies dancing in color. Sadly, though, there's always the risk of a no-show. So how do you up your chances? At Yellowknife, the city is not only blessed with weeks of clear skies and surrounded by a plateau that enables you to see for miles, it also runs a special project monitoring space weather and signals via local lighthouses when impressive aurora borealis are due.

YELLOWKNIFE BAY,
NORTHWEST TERRITORIES

694 Mark the end of winter at a jamboree

Named after a humble piece of thermal underwear, the Long John Jamboree celebrates making it through the winter. Join locals on the ice of the bay, grab a drink from the Brr Garden, and marvel at the skills of ice sculptors.

BANFF NATIONAL PARK, ALBERTA

695 Trek across Canada's oldest national park

Banff National Park boasts some 250 hiking trails across more than a million acres (400,000 ha) of breathtaking scenery. Try the Lake Agnes, Tunnel Mountain, or Parker Ridge trails and spot bears, elk, bighorn sheep, and perhaps even cougars.

BANFF NATIONAL PARK, ALBERTA

696 Stare in wonder at Moraine Lake

The still, clear, turquoise waters of Moraine Lake reflecting the towering scenery of Banff National Park make it one of those scenes you could contemplate for hours. Don't miss this special view of Earth's natural beauty.

696 Moraine Lake's vivid hues

BANFF, ALBERTA

697 Enjoy hot springs on a cool day

Banff was established to attract tourists to the Rockies. However, the chance discovery of hot springs meant tourism boomed far beyond the original plans as pleasure-seeking Victorians flocked to "take the waters." At its peak, there were nine hot springs in town, but today only the outdoor Banff Upper Hot Springs remains. Lower yourself into the warm waters while air temperatures freeze your breath.

BANFF, ALBERTA

698 Ascend a mountain in eight minutes

It takes eight minutes to climb Sulphur Mountain—if you take the Banff Gondola. Climbing to an altitude of 7,486 ft (2,281 m), the four-person cabins take in memorably sweeping views of the Rockies. There's an equally impressive gondola experience in nearby Lake Louise, as well as similar structures at Sunshine Village and Mt. Norquay.

700 Venturing onto the Columbia Icefield Skywalk

BANFF, ALBERTA

699 Learn from the Whyte Museum

The Canadian Rockies have a proud historical and cultural heritage. Preservation continues in no small part due to this museum, opened in 1968. Its collections contain artifacts and exhibits that tell the collected stories of the people that shaped this region—Aboriginal people, explorers, artists, and skiers alike. There's also an art collection and six historic Heritage Homes.

BANFF, ALBERTA

700 Hover on a glass-bottomed cliff walkway

Just over 900 ft (280 m) up, suspended dramatically from a cliff edge in Jasper National Park, is the glass-bottomed Columbia Icefield Skywalk. It's not for the faint of heart, but those with no fear of heights can walk out across its radius and see for themselves the awe-inspiring power of the glaciers that carved out these ice-capped mountains and valleys.

THE CALGARY STAMPEDE: "THE GREATEST OUTDOOR SHOW ON EARTH"

Midway attraction

Dancing in Fluor Rope Square

A Canadian Cowgirl participating in the Stampede

IMPROVEMENT DISTRICT NO. 9, BANFF, ALBERTA

701 Scuba dive into an underwater ghost town

Lake Minnewanka stretches across 13 serene mi (21 km) in Banff National Park. Until 1941, you would find here Minnewanka Landing, a small but thriving village with hotels and restaurants. The area was then purposely flooded to construct a hydroelectric plant. The cold waters preserved the buildings, and with scuba gear, visitors can dive to see the eerie remains of what once was.

CALGARY, ALBERTA

702 Gain new insights at the National Music Centre

The collection here began with the installation of a pipe organ in 1987. The venue expanded quickly and now five floors celebrate and explain the history of music in Canada. Visitors can see recording studios, interactive instruments, and exhibits such as a piano used by Elton John. The neighboring King Edward Hotel is the facility's de facto live music venue.

CALGARY, ALBERTA

703 Join a stampede in Calgary

Arrive in Calgary during the Calgary Stampede and you'd be forgiven for thinking you'd landed in the Wild West. The ten-day festival celebrates every manner of Western entertainment: rodeo, bull riding, horse skills, chuckwagon racing— reminiscent of something Julius Caesar might have overseen—and, of course, twenty-four-hour country music parties. Don a Stetson, grab a whistle, feast on pancakes, and join the fun.

CALGARY, ALBERTA

704 Tick off all the cow sculptures in town

Calgary has a cowboy-tinged history, which is why it's also known as Cowtown or Stampede City. In honor of this legacy, in 2000 the city was peppered with more than a hundred life-size fiberglass cow sculptures—each one colorfully customized—as part of the installation *Udderly Art*. Several cows can now be seen at the Udderly Art Legacy Pasture.

DRUMHELLER, ALBERTA

705 Get acquainted with dinosaurs

With some 800 fossils of varying sizes on display, the Royal Tyrrell Museum of Palaeontology houses one of the world's largest dinosaur collections. Head to the huge Dinosaur Hall to fulfill your Jurassic Park fantasies and cozy up to thirty mounted skeletons, including impressive examples of triceratops and a near-complete T.rex.

COCHRANE, ALBERTA

706 Howl at the moon at a wolfdog sanctuary

The Yamnuska Wolfdog Sanctuary in Cochrane is committed to the preservation and well-being of wolfdogs, and offers tours for dog lovers to meet these majestic beasts and learn about them. The animals live in spacious enclosures, and seeing them up close is something very special.

708 Sunrise over Writing-on-Stone Provincial Park

709 Antlered moose

EDMONTON RIVER, ALBERTA

707 Help investigate a butterfly's travels

The painted lady is a salmon-pink butterfly with wonderfully complex black-and-white markings. Occasionally its numbers soar, and there is a mass migration to Alberta. Scientists are keen to know more and have urged the public to report sightings.

MILK RIVER, ALBERTA

708 See drawings that are 3,000 years old

For 10,000 years, the Blackfoot Indigenous people have lived in this region. Now a UNESCO World Heritage Site, Writing-on-Stone Provincial Park is home to a nature reserve and a large collection of petroglyphs (rock carvings) and pictographs (rock paintings).

JASPER NATIONAL PARK, ALBERTA

709 Spot a moose with antlers

You can see moose here year-round, but if you want to see males with antlers, you'll need to time your visit. They grow antlers in April, in time for the mating season, then lose them in winter. Moose are the largest members of the deer family and can grow as big as horses.

710 Waterton-Glacier International Peace Park

710 Shake hands across a border of peace

The world's first international peace park is a beautiful wilderness of lakes and mountains that represents the harmony of nations. It was formed when the United States and Canada merged two national parks into one. Shake hands across the border in a sign of goodwill.

711 Join a bison rewilding campaign

In the nineteenth century, the plains bison of Canada were almost wiped out, upsetting the ecosystem forever. However, a single herd was saved and moved to Elk Island National Park, to reestablish them in the wild. From there, a tiny herd was brought to Waterton Lakes in the 1950s. Since then, Waterton Lakes National Park has maintained a herd of plains bisons on its bison paddock.

ICEFIELDS PARKWAY, ALBERTA
712 Cycle the Canadian Rockies

The 143-mi (230-km) ride along Icefields Parkway, from Jasper in the north to Lake Louise in the south, is considered one of the world's most beautiful cycle journeys. Cyclists who set off on the four- to five-day ride through the untouched wilderness in the UNESCO-listed Canadian Rocky Mountains Park are rewarded with unspoiled views of ancient ice fields, glaciers, waterfalls cascading from rock spires, snow-covered peaks of the Rockies, and azure-blue lakes in sweeping valleys. The abundant wildlife is equally spectacular: grizzly and black bears, elks, golden eagles, moose, and wolves. You can enjoy well-earned breaks at one of many creekside campsites, complete with a permit for making a warming fire and a bear-proof locker!

THROUGHOUT SASKATCHEWAN

713 See a snowy owl in winter

This most beautiful of owls—which is either completely white feathered (males) or dappled white and black—only travels south of the Arctic during the winter. Perhaps as a result of the twenty-four-hour daylight of the Arctic summer, this owl is not nocturnal, so can be spotted hunting at any time.

714 Starry skies at the Grasslands National Park

GRASSLANDS NATIONAL PARK,
SASKATCHEWAN
714 Spot rare species on the prairies

This national park represents one of Canada's few remaining areas of prairie grassland. There are several trails to choose from, from family-friendly strolls to tougher routes for experienced hikers. Visitors might spot some rare wildlife, from plains bison to black-footed ferrets. You can also camp under the prairie skies, or stay at a historic ranch and take a wagon ride or practice your lasso skills.

LITTLE MANITOU LAKE,
SASKATCHEWAN
715 Float in the "Dead Sea of Canada"

The salinity of Little Manitou Lake is five times that of the nearest ocean. Even though that equals just half the salt content of Israel's Dead Sea, the buoyancy levels here are still remarkable. Fed by mineral-rich underground springs, its supposed curative properties also make it the perfect spot for a health-giving dip, as Indigenous people have known for thousands of years.

MOOSE JAW, SASKATCHEWAN
716 See the world's largest moose

You're unlikely to meet a bigger symbol of Canada than Mac the Moose, which stands 32 ft (10m) tall. This steel-and-concrete giant has lived in Moose Jaw since 1984, and on the grounds of the town's visitors' center (off the Trans-Canada Highway) since 2004. Although it was challenged by another moose sculpture in Norway in 2015, the addition of new antlers in 2019 cemented Mac's position as the biggest in the world.

719 Exploring Saskatchewan ranch country

THROUGHOUT SASKATCHEWAN

717 Order a bag of spudnuts

One of the region's summer traditions, spudnuts aren't a trendy new hybrid like your cronuts. Spudnuts have actually been consumed by locals here for more than a hundred years and, as the name suggests, they are doughnuts made with mashed potato, or potato flour in place of regular wheat flour. They are typically sweet, and the potato makes for a fluffy snack that's the perfect mix of comfort foods.

SOUTHWEST SASKATCHEWAN

718 Ride an ATV across sand dunes

Around 12 mi (20 km) south of the town of Sceptre are the Great Sandhills—an area of active, desertlike sand dunes. You could imagine that you are in the Gobi Desert, the sandy, rippled dunes stretching out as far as the eye can see. Mule deer and antelope can be spotted wandering the plains, and you can also join guided tours on all-terrain vehicles to explore this fascinating landscape further.

SOUTHWEST SASKATCHEWAN

719 Embrace your inner cowboy or cowgirl

Southwest Saskatchewan is ranch country. As you drive along the Saskatchewan River valley, the scenery begins to look like something straight out of a Wild West movie; you might even see the odd wandering coyote. Some of the working ranches here have opened up their businesses to include hospitality, so visitors can now stay, saddle up, and live out the dream of being in their very own Western.

ELLESMERE ISLAND, NUNAVUT

720 Test yourself in a far northern wilderness

Quttinirpaaq National Park is located in the northeastern corner of Ellesmere Island and is the world's second most northerly national park. Ellesmere Island itself lies within the Arctic Archipelago and as such is a beautifully unspoiled but challenging destination. Chartered expeditions are the best option, with adventurous groups being able to see Arctic hares and wolves, as well as the vast expanse of this extreme landscape.

BAFFIN ISLAND, NUNAVUT

721 Visit the world's largest lake on an island

Canada holds some interesting island- and lake-related world records. Ontario has the largest lake on an island in a lake (Lake Manitou) and the largest island in a lake on an island in a lake (Treasure Island in Lake Mindemoya, on Manitoulin Island). From Nunavut, you can join tours to see the world's largest lake on an island, Nettilling Lake on Baffin Island, spotting seals, polar bears, and the world's largest goose colony.

KINNGAIT, NUNAVUT

722 Get acquainted with Inuit art

Kinngait (Inuktitut for "where the hills are") is a small community at the tip of Baffin Island, but a huge center for Inuit art. Characterized by bold, stylized representations of inhabitants, wildlife, and landscape, work by many local artists can be seen in the National Gallery of Canada in Ottawa. Watch the next generation of artists at work in cooperative studios, and join a workshop if you're lucky.

DEVON ISLAND, NUNAVUT

723 Explore "Mars" or its earthly equivalent at Haughton Impact Crater

Around 39 million years ago, a meteor measuring a mile long (1.6 km) hit what is now Devon Island. The landscape here is the closest thing to Mars on Earth. Seeing it from the air is possible, with commercial flights from Montreal to Cornwallis Island and then a Twin Otter plane charter that can fly you over this incredible site.

BAFFIN ISLAND, NUNAVUT

724 Feel like an early explorer

For centuries the Northwest Passage was the explorers' ultimate challenge: navigating from the Atlantic to the Pacific and the bounties of the East. Roald Amundsen finally found a route—but it took him three years. Today, you can follow his route on a much shorter cruise, passing the obstacles he overcame, through incredible Arctic scenery.

BAFFIN ISLAND, NUNAVUT

725 Delight in Arctic wildlife

Visit the Arctic in spring and see wildlife as you've never seen it before. Polar bears emerge from hibernation, often with cubs in tow, to prowl across the ice, hunting for food. Narwhals, with their unicorn-like horn, migrate along the floe edge of Baffin Island, while inland you can spot Arctic hares, Arctic foxes, lemmings, and caribou.

BAFFIN ISLAND, NUNAVUT
726 Salute the world's tallest straight vertical peak

Mt. Thor has a look that's as intimidating as its name. Located in Auyuittuq National Park, its elevation is 5,495 ft (1,675 m), with a straight vertical drop of an astonishing 4,100 ft (1,250 m). This is more than double the height of Toronto's CN Tower. Climbing this beast is obviously only for the most technically skilled and courageous climbers, but guided hiking tours of the park operate out of Iqaluit.

IQALUIT, NUNAVUT
727 Admire an igloo-shaped cathedral in Iqaluit

Iqaluit is the capital of the Nunavut territory, with a population of almost 8,000. Many of the local population are Anglicans and their place of worship is one of the region's most recognizable buildings. St. Jude's Cathedral is a replica of an original building from 1970, destroyed by arsonists in 2005. This unforgettable igloo-shaped structure forms a curious dome topped with a cross, and it holds around 400 people.

726 Viewing Mt. Thor across the Akshayuk Pass

729 Encountering a polar bear on a Tundra Buggy tour

730 Little Limestone Lake

CHURCHILL, MANITOBA

728 Study climate change at the Arctic's edge

To know what the actual effects of climate change are involves a huge range of monitoring and studying. Join a volunteer expedition organized by the Churchill Northern Studies Centre that counts animals or studies plant growth in order to be an active part of the solution rather than a passive part of the problem.

CHURCHILL, MANITOBA

729 See polar bears on a Tundra Buggy tour

Imagine a viewing deck on wheels, then imagine those wheels are monster-truck in size and you'll know what a Tundra Buggy is all about. Designed to cross the Arctic tundra, this minibus on steroids takes you into the heart of polar bear country. You'll have smoother, warmer rides in your life, but this is one you'll never forget.

THOMPSON, MANITOBA

730 Observe a lake that changes color

By the side of the highway outside Thompson, there's a lake that's constantly changing color. Known as Little Limestone Lake, the water has a high concentration of marl, a carbonate-rich mud that reacts to changes in temperature. In the morning, the lake is a brilliant turquoise, then changes to vibrant blue as the day progresses.

SOUTHERN MANITOBA
731 See a burrowing owl make its home

The burrowing owl doesn't dig its own burrow but moves into those left by ground squirrels, badgers, and foxes. Look out for parents on guard outside a burrow's entrance.

GIMLI, MANITOBA
732 Discover your inner Viking

Join hundreds of visitors at the Icelandic Festival of Manitoba in August—an annual tradition dating back over 130 years. Grab a helmet, eat some dried fish, and down a shot of Brennivín.

NARCISSE, MANITOBA
733 See a hundred snakes writhe as one

At the end of spring, red-sided garter snakes emerge from hibernating in their dens to mate. Alarmingly, one female is likely to be engulfed by up to a hundred males!

731 Burrowing owls standing guard

ROSSER, MANITOBA

734 Catch a ride on the
Prairie Dog Central Railway

Time travel is almost possible on this
heritage steam train service, opened in
1970. This four-hour journey is a must
for lovers of vintage travel. The carriages
are around a hundred years old, but they
still seem luxurious, with oak paneling
and gas lamps. It's hard to imagine a
more civilized way to see the lovely
Manitoban countryside.

HUDSON BAY, MANITOBA

735 Be captivated by beluga whales

Most belugas live around Arctic waters, migrating south when the weather gets colder. The largest population arrives in Hudson Bay once the ice breaks up, which gives visitors the opportunity to see tens of thousands of these wonderful white giants. They're very vocal, making a range of clicks, whistles, and chirps.

WINNIPEG, MANITOBA

736 Sweat it out in a sweat lodge

Participating in a sweat lodge is far from indulging in the latest self-care trend; it's taking part in an ancient Indigenous ceremony dating back thousands of years. The session lasts two to three hours, and uses heated stones and a mixture of grasses and herbs. Workshops are available to help interpret this mysterious practice.

735 Beluga whales and calves

WINNIPEG, MANITOBA
737 Gain new understanding at the Canadian Museum for Human Rights

This important museum is located on sacred ancestral lands in the Red River Valley. Through its exhibits, which mix art and reportage, the museum is dedicated to exploring the diversity of human rights, including First Nation and Indigenous peoples in Canada as well as across the world.

ALGONQUIN PROVINCIAL PARK, ONTARIO
739 Hear a loon's wail

Loons' cries echo eerily across the lakes of this park, sounding more like the wail of a wolf than a bird. They use four distinct calls to communicate.

WINNIPEG, MANITOBA
738 Decipher the Legislature Building symbols

When British architect Frank Worthington Simon designed this building over a hundred years ago, he unwittingly created a place straight from Dan Brown's *Da Vinci Code* saga. As well as classic Beaux Arts architecture, the interior has a host of mysterious hieroglyphics and numerology symbols.

BANCROFT, ONTARIO
740 Learn how to identify a wapiti

Wapiti is another name for elk (*Cervus canadensis*)—American elk, at least. In Europe, "elk" is the name given to the animal that Americans call a moose (*Alces alces*). *Wapiti* is the original Cree and Shawnee name for this huge deer, which helps clear up all the confusion in one fell swoop. It refers to the "one with a white rump."

CALEDON, ONTARIO
741 Investigate red rolling hills

If you were standing on the Cheltenham Badlands 400 million years ago, you'd be standing on the bed of an ancient sea. Today the landscape is one of the country's most striking, with windswept hills and gullies formed from bright red and brown clay, streaked with green. It's like looking out across an alien planet, making it a great location for artistic photography.

EGANVILLE, ONTARIO
742 Venture into ancient caves

Next to the Bonnechere River, south of Ottawa, is a wooden shack—the entrance to Bonnechere Caves, a cave system that draws thousands of visitors every year. Groups are taken down into huge limestone caverns that formed 450 million years ago. You'll learn all about their formation, children will love looking for fossils, and you can even dine underground.

741 Red hills of the Cheltenham Badlands

MADAWASKA RIVER, ONTARIO

743 Take to a canoe on the Madawaska

For the Indigenous people of Canada, the canoe was critical to almost every facet of life and the principal means of transportation. Flatwater canoeing is restful and a great way to get in touch with nature. The motions of the water lead your thoughts to wander as you float along the glasslike surface of the river. It's no wonder the pastime is still so popular. Seek out some of the quieter stretches along the river, which make ideal spots for beginners.

BOREAL FORESTS, ONTARIO

744 Tell caribous apart

The female caribou is the only deer species that grows antlers like the male. The antlers of the males are bigger, but they are shed in winter after mating; female caribou, however, keep their smaller antlers until spring.

743 Waters of the Madawaska River in fall

HUNTSVILLE, ONTARIO

745 Ice skate through a forest

If you're heading to Arrowhead Provincial Park
during the winter months, take a pair of skates because
it offers some of the most evocative trails in the country.
Gliding through the beauty of the Muskoka forest is an
unforgettable experience—even more so as the daylight
fades, when the trail is lit by hundreds of atmospheric
tiki torches.

HAMILTON, ONTARIO
746 See 130 waterfalls in a single town

The nearby town of Niagara receives most of the global attention for its waterfalls, and while those falls are undoubtedly spectacular, the lesser-known town of Hamilton is also a must for waterfall fans. The town boasts over 130 of them, with very strict criteria for what constitutes an individual fall—it must have a vertical drop of at least 10 ft (3 m), the crest width must be at least 3 ft (90 cm), and the waterfall must be natural, not man-made. You can see plenty of them on the Chedoke Radial Trail. The most scenic is considered to be Webster's Falls, while the tallest is Tews Falls, at just a few feet less than Niagara Falls.

OTTAWA, ONTARIO
747 Skate on the world's biggest rink of all

Winters can be extremely tough in Ottawa, but there's at least one aspect that locals look forward to. From January through to March, weather permitting, the Rideau Canal freezes and transforms into a giant skateway. Skaters can glide along the length of the canal—it stretches for some 5 mi (8 km), forming the world's largest rink. Skating is free and the skateway is open twenty-four hours a day, seven days a week. When you've had your fill, warm up at the concession stands selling hot chocolate and BeaverTails (see opposite).

746 Inspecting a frozen waterfall in Hamilton

747 Rideau Canal in winter

OTTAWA, ONTARIO

748 See the nation's capital from a boat

During the warmer months, the Rideau Canal offers prime sightseeing opportunities, and you can take to the waters on a boat tour to get a fresh perspective on the capital. There's history aplenty as the canal dates back to the early nineteenth century, and the route from Dow's Lake to the Ottawa River takes in Parliament Hill and other landmarks.

OTTAWA, ONTARIO

749 Spend the night in a cell

Built in 1862, the Nicholas Street Gaol was the city's main jail for over a century, and was witness to all manner of gruesome public hangings and the like. It closed in 1972, and was purchased by a hostel company, which transformed it into the Ottawa Jail Hostel. Sleep in your own cell, and ignore the ghosts that are said to roam the corridors.

OTTAWA, ONTARIO

750 Eat a BeaverTail at its birthplace

In 1978, Grant and Pam Hooker started to sell their family fried-dough recipe at pop-up locations and fairs. Such was the demand that, in 1980, they opened a brick-and-mortar business and began selling their creation—BeaverTails—at their eponymous shop in ByWard Market. Fried dough, sugar, and cinnamon form the base, with sweet or savory toppings to taste.

750 BeaverTails, ByWard Market

OTTAWA, ONTARIO
751 See another side of Canada

Canadians are usually known for their polite passivity, but there's a strong military history in Canada, and Candian troops have provided invaluable support to Allied forces across the world over numerous campaigns. The Canadian War Museum houses artifacts from fighter planes to uniforms, showing off some fascinating Canadian military technology and explaining Canada's role across a wealth of overseas missions.

OTTAWA, ONTARIO
752 Get caught up in pomp and pagentry

Each summer morning, a military band and pipers march from Cartier Square Drill Hall, leading a troop of Ceremonial Guards in red jackets and busby hats. This is the Changing of the Guard, when a new set of guards takes over from that of the previous day and hands over the key to the guard room at Rideau Hall—the official residence in Ottawa of Canada's Governor General and monarch (Queen Elizabeth II).

FRYING PAN ISLAND, ONTARIO
753 Catch a plane (or boat) for fish and chips

Your fish and chips need to be pretty exceptional if you expect diners to take a plane or boat ride to reach your restaurant, but it's certainly not a problem for Henry's Fish Restaurant on Frying Pan Island. You can charter a boat or take one of the restaurant's water taxis, or opt for their Fly and Dine option out of Parry Sound Harbour.

THUNDER BAY, ONTARIO
754 Sail the world's biggest lake

At twice the size of Switzerland, Lake Superior can take quite some exploring. Start with a sailing trip from Thunder Bay and head to one of the lake's many features, such as Sleeping Giant, so called because the land formation looks like, well . . . a sleeping giant.

FATHOM FIVE NATIONAL MARINE PARK, ONTARIO
755 See how Flowerpot Island got its name

This island is less than a square mile (2.6 sq km), but it has a much larger reputation, thanks to two rock formations that resemble—you guessed it—flowerpots, formed from oceanic erosion. These sea stacks look somewhat precarious (a third once stood here, but collapsed in 1903), but they stand proudly for hikers and boaters to marvel at.

TORONTO, ONTARIO
756 Go star spotting at the TIFF

With almost half a million people attending annually, the Toronto International Film Festival is a major date on the movie industry's calendar. It's one of the biggest film festivals open to the public, and most people regard it as being second only to Cannes. Purchase a ticket in early September, dust off your finery, and rub elbows with the A-list.

755 The sea stacks of Flowerpot Island

THE CULTURAL HUB OF TORONTO'S DISTILLERY HISTORIC DISTRICT

A Soulpepper Theatre production

Annual Christmas Market

Restored Victorian industrial architecture

TORONTO, ONTARIO
757 Plan your escape from a real-life castle

There's a dramatic-looking Gothic Revival mansion in midtown Toronto called Casa Loma. It was completed in 1914, and in 1941 it was an undercover research center for antisubmarine detection technology. If that sounds intriguing, delight in the fact that you can now visit the castle. You can even make your visit more exciting by experiencing one of its three escape rooms.

TORONTO, ONTARIO
758 Experience the world's best ice fishing

If you spy a hut out in the middle of a frozen lake in Canada, chances are that someone inside it is enjoying the proud Candian tradition of ice fishing. A pole, a hole in the ice, and a plentiful supply of snacks and drinks are all you need. Lake Simcoe offers one of the most popular locations to sink a line and try for trout, perch, and pike.

TORONTO, ONTARIO
759 Wander the streets of the Distillery Historic District

In the 1830s, the distillers Gooderham and Worts were based here, producing some 2 million gallons of whiskey per year; 150 years later, the area was derelict, but in the 1990s, serious redevelopment took place, and in the early 2000s, the Distillery Historic District was reborn as a major arts, culture, and entertainment complex. The nineteenth-century buildings create an evocative scene, and hip artisanal restaurants and galleries were set up alongside theaters and boutiques. The area is worth visiting to see the well-preserved architecture alone. Corporate chains are banned, so there's an authentic feel to the place, with independent coffee shops instead of the usual big brands. One of the hearts of the complex is the Soulpepper Theatre Company, which provides a diverse year-round program of performances. Many of the restaurants offer outdoor dining in the warm months, so it's always a lively place to spend a day. And you might also recognize some of the locations from popular movies such as *X-Men*.

TORONTO, ONTARIO
760 Indulge your foodie side at St. Lawrence Market

There's been a permanent market here since the 1820s, and nowadays some 150 vendors set up shop across three buildings. Start your day with a peameal bacon sandwich from the Carousel Bakery, then flit among the stalls, each more tempting than the last. Fresh bread and pastries, cheeses, meats, and produce are available five days a week.

TORONTO, ONTARIO
761 Catch the Toronto Pride Parade

Toronto's Pride Parade comes at the end of Pride Toronto festival, which itself is the culmination of Pride Month. As you'd expect, it's a big, bright, brash affair that takes over much of the town center. Church Street is turned into one big festival site with beer tents, live music, and stalls. It's come a long way since the first gatherings in 1971, when people got together for a "Gay Day Picnic."

TORONTO, ONTARIO

762 Lose yourself in the Art Gallery of Ontario

Established in 1900, this museum is one of the biggest and most respected in North America. The permanent collection contains almost 100,000 works, and it enjoys stunning architecture thanks to Toronto-born legend Frank Gehry. The collection of Indigenous and historic Canadian art is impressive, and there are big hitters aplenty, from Rubens to Henry Moore.

TORONTO, ONTARIO

763 Ride to the top of the CN Tower

The CN Tower doesn't just grace Toronto's skyline, it defines it. Its elegant shape tapers to a point 1,815 ft (553 m) up in the air, dwarfing the skyscrapers around it. For the most thrilling experience, try the EdgeWalk, which involves walking hands-free (but harnessed) around a 5-ft (1.5-m) ledge that encircles the tower's main pod, 116 stories up. Test your vertigo as you survey sidewalk life below.

TORONTO, ONTARIO

764 Wander along Woodbine Beach

Woodbine Beach has a decidedly laid-back atmosphere. It's a rugged stretch of beachfront where you can watch kiteboarders and surfers, or join them. It gets busy in summer but it's not difficult to find a quiet spot— just keep walking eastward.

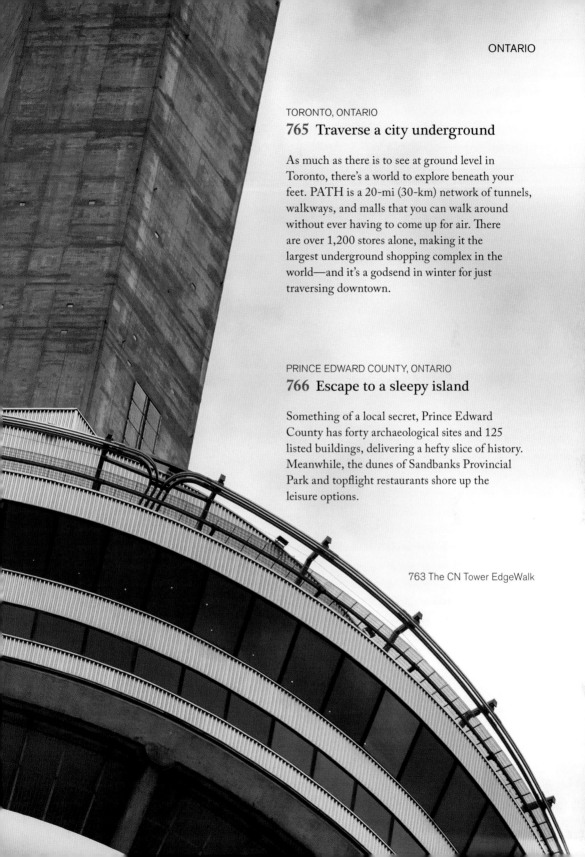

TORONTO, ONTARIO
765 Traverse a city underground

As much as there is to see at ground level in Toronto, there's a world to explore beneath your feet. PATH is a 20-mi (30-km) network of tunnels, walkways, and malls that you can walk around without ever having to come up for air. There are over 1,200 stores alone, making it the largest underground shopping complex in the world—and it's a godsend in winter for just traversing downtown.

PRINCE EDWARD COUNTY, ONTARIO
766 Escape to a sleepy island

Something of a local secret, Prince Edward County has forty archaeological sites and 125 listed buildings, delivering a hefty slice of history. Meanwhile, the dunes of Sandbanks Provincial Park and topflight restaurants shore up the leisure options.

763 The CN Tower EdgeWalk

STRATFORD, ONTARIO

767 Watch a wealth of boards treading at Stratford

As the name suggests, the Stratford Festival (which runs from April to October in the city of the same name) is a celebration of the best of the Bard. Although famed for its stagings of the plays of William Shakespeare, the program includes a diversity of theatrical talent and productions.

NIAGARA FALLS, ONTARIO

768 Take a Hornblower cruise into Niagara Falls

The falls at Niagara Falls are among the most recognizable natural wonders in the world. Seeing them from any of the vantage points around the Canadian and American sides puts their immense power and size into perspective. Take things further and dowse yourself in the mists on a boat tour into the falls themselves. Hornblower boats get as close as it's safe to get—a truly awe-inspiring experience.

768 Hornblower catamaran at Niagara's Horseshoe Falls

770 Niagara-on-the-Lake, against the backdrop of Lake Ontario

NIAGARA FALLS, ONTARIO
769 Overdose on kitsch in Niagara Falls

A feeling of retro, vintage kitsch has grown up around Niagara Falls. Clifton Hill's Street of Fun is the epicenter, with neon-tinged gift stores, wax museums, haunted houses, and video arcades. Check out Ripley's Believe It Or Not, the Niagara SkyWheel Ferris wheel, and Dinosaur Adventure Golf, which happens to be Canada's largest mini-golf course.

NIAGARA-ON-THE-LAKE, ONTARIO
770 Explore the Wineries of Niagara-on-the-Lake

This area is one of Canada's top food-and-wine destinations, wth some of the oldest vineyards in the country. More than twenty wineries promote themselves collectively as Wineries of Niagara-on-the-Lake. There's a huge variety, from famous names to boutique biodynamic estates, all within minutes of one another. Use the dedicated website to plan a day's itinerary.

GULF OF ST. LAWRENCE, QUEBEC
771 See one of nature's show-offs

Male hooded seals have a great party trick. Visit the Gulf of St. Lawrence to watch them inflating their nostril cavity into a big pink balloon that they use to ward off other males and attract a mate.

LAKE MISTASSINI, QUEBEC
772 Look out for goldeneyes

One of the inhabitants of Lake Mistassini, the common goldeneye (named for its yellow eyes), will test your patience. These birds often dive for food as a flock, leaving a temporarily empty patch of water.

773 Pingualit Crater's blue depths

KATIVIK, QUEBEC
773 Witness the purity of the Pingualit Crater

The almost perfectly circular lake that fills the Pingualuit Crater is said to be the purest freshwater lake on Earth. To reach it is a nine-day trek from Kangiqsujuaq village, through the vast boreal landscape of the Ungava Peninsula. On the way, you may spot roaming caribou, as well as Inuit people hunting and fox trapping.

MAGDALEN ISLANDS, QUEBEC
774 Photograph red rocks and blue waters

There's a timelessness to this archipelago in the middle of the Gulf of St. Lawrence, and few signs of modern life. Its most famous features are the striking red sandstone cliffs. The rest of the vista includes dunes, lagoons, and windswept beaches. Boat and kayak tours are the perfect way to see the islands—have your camera ready to capture incredible natural landscapes.

MONTREAL, QUEBEC
775 Feel dwarfed by the twenty-story biosphere

Its more famous American cousin resides at Florida's Epcot, but the gigantic Montreal geodesic dome is just as impressive. It was designed by Buckminster Fuller for the US Pavilion at the Expo 67 World's Fair. The original was damaged by fire in 1976, but the dome was renovated and reopened in 1995, save for five months in 1998 after a terrible ice storm. It now houses an environmental museum with interactive exhibits related to climate change, eco-technology, and sustainability.

775 The Biosphere, in Parc Jean-Drapeau

MONTREAL, QUEBEC
776 See Montreal from Mt. Royal

Mt. Royal is a small mountain in Montreal that gave its name to the city it towers over. It's the central feature of the Parc du Mont-Royal, and the 761-ft (232-m) elevation shouldn't prove too much effort for even a casual hiker. There are (steepish) steps that you can take to the summit, where you'll be rewarded with panoramic views over this beautiful city. Another draw is the variety of wildlife found around the peak—look out for raccoons, foxes, and marmots. The park is even home to a toboggan run and a sculpture garden.

MONTREAL, QUEBEC
777 Share a national sporting passion

Ice hockey or the maple leaf? It's hard to know which is more Canadian. The game's spiritual home is Montreal, and specifically the Bell Centre—home to the Montreal Canadiens (nicknamed "the Habs"). Catch a game and feel the fans' passion for the sport. The sport's reputation for on-rink fighting is part of the culture of the game and allowed within the rules. As comic Rodney Dangerfield once quipped, "I went to a fight the other night, and a hockey game broke out."

776 Vistas from Parc du Mont-Royal

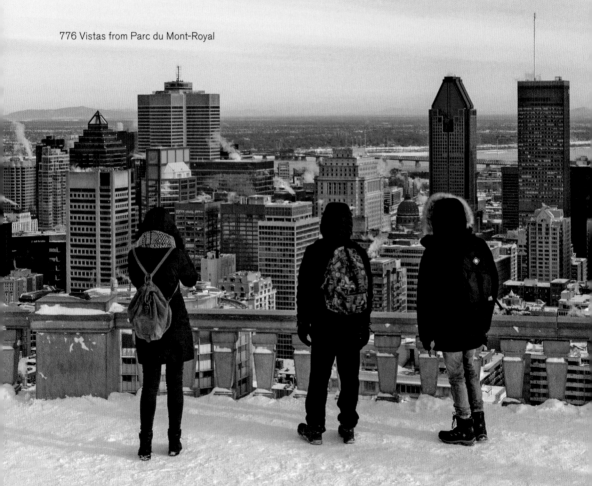

777 Ice hockey at the Bell Centre

779 Montreal International Jazz Festival

MONTREAL, QUEBEC
778 Have a laugh at the world's mightiest comedy festival

Founded in 1983, the Just for Laughs comedy festival quickly became a huge industry event, drawing hopeful comedians, established names, and comedy bookers and agents from around the world. It now runs for a month every July, and most shows are open to the public.

MONTREAL, QUEBEC
779 Admire improvisation at the world's leading jazz festival

During the last week in June, millions of music fans flock to Montreal to see their jazz heroes at the Montreal International Jazz Festival. What started as a small blues and jazz festival in 1978 is now the premier event on the jazz calendar, with multiple venues and global stars headlining.

THROUGHOUT CANADA
780 Look up for a Canadian goose

This large goose with a pale brown body and black neck is a frequent visitor to lawns and parks. Look up, too, to see them flying in perfect V-formation.

PASTURES AROUND OTTAWA RIVER, QUEBEC
781 Learn about the milk snake

Because milk snakes are often seen around barns, it was thought that they drank milk. In fact, barns provide hunting grounds for the real prize—mice!

782 Entering the Hôtel de Glace

783 Poutine to go

QUEBEC CITY, QUEBEC

782 Spend the night on ice

Perverse as it might sound, there's something cozy about spending the night in an ice hotel. Wrapped up in your warmest gear and snuggled into an arctic sleeping bag, you're cocooned in a room sculpted out of ice. Quebec's Hôtel de Glace opens each winter with a new theme for its rooms and a stunning new Grand Hall to awe visitors. There's even a chapel that hosts weddings. Far from a "survival" experience, a stay here is a luxury option, with cocktails served in glasses made from ice in one of the most stylish bars you'll ever frequent.

QUEBEC CITY, QUEBEC

783 Sample the local poutine

Poutine is a hearty dish of french fries and brown gravy with chunks of cheese curd thrown in. Little known outside of Canada, it originated in the Quebec area in the 1950s and, as with many great food combinations, several chefs have laid claim to its invention. These days it's found on the menu at greasy diners, hipster hangouts, and even high-end restaurants, many of whom like to add their own spin to the three fundamental ingredients. However you sample it, savor the comfort it brings as well as the delicious flavors.

QUEBEC CITY, QUEBEC

784 Snap the world's most photographed hotel

With its steeply gabled roof and numerous turrets, Château Frontenac looks like a French château has been transplanted directly from the Loire Valley to Old Quebec. That was exactly the intention of the Canadian Pacific Railway, which built the hotel. It was part of a series of ornate hotels designed to encourage wealthy travelers to try out new railroad lines. To take your own photo of the hotel, head to the Citadelle de Quebec, the Observatoire de la Capitale, or cross the river to Lévis.

QUEBEC CITY, QUEBEC

785 Descend from the château to Basse-Ville

Step back in time on the beautiful historic streets of Quebec City's Basse-Ville (Lower Town). This was the location of Quebec's original settlement on the banks of the St. Lawrence River. A funicular car takes visitors down to the ancient streets that are sprawled around the base of the steep cliff and are perfect for exploring.

784 Château Frontenac, pictured in winter

QUEBEC CITY, QUEBEC

786 Prepare for Lent at the Carnaval de Québec

Some cities have Mardi Gras; Quebec has the pre-Lent Winter Carnival, or Carnaval de Québec, an annual celebration that usually takes place in February or March. Enjoy the ceremonies, outdoor banquets, parades, and ice sculptures, or watch ice canoe races as you sip hot *caribou* (a local mulled wine).

QUEBEC CITY, QUEBEC

787 Get a bird's-eye view of falls bigger than Niagara

Montmorency Falls Park is around 7 mi (12 km) from central Quebec. Standing at 270 ft (83 m), the eponymous falls are taller than their Niagara cousins. You traverse the mouth of the falls on a suspension bridge, and there are also several staircases that allow photography from various vantage points.

SAINT-ANDRÉ-DU-LAC-SAINT-JEAN, QUEBEC

788 Brave a real-life bat cave

This isn't, as some might imagine, a superhero's secret lair, but it's still a thing of wonder. Located in the Trou de la Fée cave park, this three-chambered cavern is the protected home of the town's bat population. Guided tours offer a safe introduction to these lovable mammals.

SAINT-PERPÉTUE, QUEBEC

789 Get piggy at a pork festival

Every August, the residents of this town go whole hog when it comes to celebrating their favorite food. A monthlong program of activities and parties known as the Festival du Cochon focuses on all things porcine, with concerts, races, and an almost endless variety of pork-based products for visitors to sample.

EAST QUEBEC

790 See the birthplace of Quebec wine

The signposted Brome-Missisquoi Wine Route covers around twenty wineries across Quebec's picturesque Eastern Townships. Drive or cycle around the Appalachian foothills to visit the wineries, and don't miss the hundred or so Amis de la Route des vins restaurants, hotels, spas, and other attractions that all add to the experience.

MINGAN ARCHIPELAGO NATIONAL
PARK RESERVE, QUEBEC

791 Wander among limestone monoliths

Located off the coast of eastern Quebec, the Mingan Archipelago National Park Reserve encompasses around 1,000 islands and islets. It's a popular spot for city dwellers to explore nature, especially for spotting the large numbers of seabirds that populate the region, including the Atlantic puffin. The gorgeous hiking trails across many of the islands are framed by very special rock formations, too. By chance of erosion, striking limestone monoliths are carved into the landscape, some dating back 450 million years.

ACROSS QUEBEC

792 Explore Quebec by bike

For lovers of the outdoors, it's hard to beat the swathes of forest, glorious water views, plentiful wildlife, and innumerable lakes and rivers of Quebec. And what better way to enjoy it than from the saddle? Winding more than 3,000 mi (4,828 km) through the province, Canada's Route Verte ("Greenway") is a network of interconnecting cycle routes through a huge, varied area. With urban trails in and around metropolitan Montreal and Quebec City, and tracks following the majestic St. Lawrence River before heading out into remote areas to the north, the route also borders the United States at Vermont, Maine, and New York. As with many long-distance routes, hard-core cyclists aim to pedal every inch of it, but it's perfectly possible to follow an independent itinerary and tackle sections at different times. Check online to plan your trip— numerous websites offer accommodation suggestions, maps, and advice.

792 Cycling Quebec's Route Verte

AVALON PENINSULA, NEWFOUNDLAND
AND LABRADOR
793 Be the first to see the sun

Rise in the morning to the first rays of sun
hitting North America. With nothing between
you and Europe but sea, Cape Spear is the
easternmost point on the continent, and offers
spectacular views of whales and icebergs.
A boardwalk leads to the area's oldest remaining
lighthouse, perched on a rugged cliff.

FOGO ISLAND, NEWFOUNDLAND AND LABRADOR
794 Listen to the ocean from your bathtub

Every room of the ultramodern Fogo Island Inn in
the wilderness of Atlantic Canada has ocean views.
Perched atop the jagged rocks of Newfoundland's
northern coast, the hotel has a strong commitment
to local fishing, boatbuilding, and artisan cultures.
Soak in a massive tub while listening to the ocean
crashing into the rocks below.

794 Fogo Island Inn, on the wild Atlantic Coast

GANDER, NEWFOUNDLAND AND LABRADOR

795 Visit the airport that inspired a Broadway musical

In its heyday, Gander International Airport was a busy departure hub for transatlantic air travel. It has a modernist, almost avant-garde interior design that's like no other, the polished wood finish creating a glamorous vintage ambience. Many planes were diverted here on 9/11, an event that inspired a Broadway musical, *Come From Away*.

GROS MORNE NATIONAL PARK, NEWFOUNDLAND AND LABRADOR

796 Marvel at glacial landscapes

This park is stunning for hikers, canoeists, and day-trippers, but truly fascinating for geologists. The Long Range Mountains formed 1.2 billion years ago when tectonic plates collided. They've stories to tell of continents rifting and drifting, magma welling up, glaciers advancing and retreating, and sea levels rising.

796 Western Brook Pond, in Gros Morne National Park

L'ANSE AUX MEADOWS, NEWFOUNDLAND
AND LABRADOR

797 See a village predating Columbus

Long before Columbus, Norse adventurers
had sailed from Europe and set up camp in the
Americas. We know this thanks to settlements
such as this eleventh-century Viking village, now a
UNESCO-protected area. Excavated wood-framed
buildings matched those in Greenland, and some
have been re-created to show what life was like a
thousand years ago.

FORTEAU, NEWFOUNDLAND AND LABRADOR

798 Get an education at a remote museum

The small Labrador Straits Museum, founded in
1978 on Canada's remote eastern edge, celebrates
the region's rich local heritage. Through its exhibits
and artifacts, a story is told about the lifestyle
of the First Nation people who have lived along
the coastline, the early European settlers, and the
present identity of the communities that continue
to thrive here.

ST. JOHN'S, NEWFOUNDLAND AND LABRADOR

799 Climb Signal Hill for the views and the history

Signal Hill—where flag signals were once sent to
ships at sea—offers great views of Newfoundland's
coastline. It's also where the very first transatlantic
wireless message was received, sent all the way from
Cornwall, and is the site of North America's final
battle of the Seven Years' War. Enjoy the history
and the view, just don't forget your semaphore.

SAINT-PIERRE AND MIQUELON, NEAR
NEWFOUNDLAND AND LABRADOR

800 Island hop around a very European archipelago

Although off the Newfoundland coast, these islands
are a French Territory, so you'll need your passport
to visit. Once there you can enjoy evocative scenery
and of course French culture. Soak up the imported
food and wines, and brush up on your French. The
islands also reside in their very own time zone.

CAMPOBELLO ISLAND, NEW BRUNSWICK

801 Visit the Roosevelt family's summer retreat

In Roosevelt Campobello International Park there's
a single cottage, built in 1897. It was a wedding gift
to Franklin and Eleanor Roosevelt, and it's set on
almost 3,000 ac (1,200 ha) on the southern tip of
Campobello Island. It's been beautifully preserved,
and makes for a tranquil, scenic visit.

KOUCHIBOUGUAC NATIONAL PARK, NEW BRUNSWICK

802 Pitch your tent on Kelly's Beach

The landscape here offers a wealth of diversity,
including salt marshes, sand dunes, lagoons, and
golden beaches. Harbor seals and gray seals make
up some of the more interesting inhabitants, and
the region is a bird-watcher's paradise. Establish
your camp on Kelly's Beach for glorious scenery
and a chance to connect with nature.

803 Watch giant icebergs sail by

Each year, icebergs break off from the mainland in Greenland and the Canadian Arctic. These icy giants float past the northeastern coast of Newfoundland and Labrador, colloquially known as Iceberg Alley. The icebergs are around 10,000 years old, and some 400 to 800 can float by in any given spring, making them much easier to spot than whales.

804 Kayaking at high tide in the Bay of Fundy

BAY OF FUNDY, NEW BRUNSWICK

804 Kayak on some extreme tides

Located halfway between the North Pole and the Equator, the Bay of Fundy has several notable features. Visitors may spot a variety of whales (humpback, minke, and finback), and find dinosaur fossils on the beach. Its main distinction, though, is its extreme tidal range, with a difference of 52 ft (16 m), compared to a global average of 3 ft (90 cm). This has resulted in some outstanding rock formation, and a fascinating place to explore by kayak.

CHARLOTTETOWN, PRINCE EDWARD ISLAND

805 See Canada's longest-running musical

In 1908, L. M. Montgomery published an engaging novel about a young orphan making her way through society. It was called *Anne of Green Gables*, and was set in a place inspired by a small community on Prince Edward Island. In 1965, a musical adaptation premiered at the Confederation Centre of the Arts here, and its popularity has meant that it's performed every summer, making it the world's longest running annual musical.

PRINCE EDWARD ISLAND

806 Overindulge in fall flavors

Every September, Prince Edward Island is awash with foodies who arrive for the monthlong, island-wide Fall Flavours culinary festival. The island is renowned for its lobsters, oysters, mussels, and potatoes, and these staples, together with a multitude of other gourmet delights, are celebrated across more than sixty food-based events. Many high-profile Canadian chefs fly in to show off their skills, and seafood fans in particular will find themselves in foodie heaven.

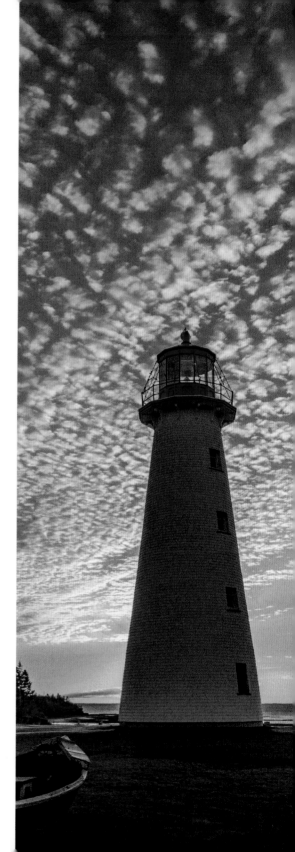

ACROSS PRINCE EDWARD ISLAND
807 Bike the Confederation Trail

This former rail network once ran tip to tip across
Prince Edward Island, but in 2000 was reinvented as
a biking and walking trail. Its 270 mi (435 km) can
be biked at a fairly relaxed speed over about five days.
It presents a charmingly bucolic landscape, through
woodlands and farmland, without any serious inclines.
There are also plenty of picturesque village stops to
choose from.

PRINCE EDWARD ISLAND
808 Take to the skies with a parasail

The summer months are perfect for soft adventure
and outdoor pursuits on Prince Edward Island. With
around 1,600 mi (2,500 km) of rugged coastline to
explore, kayaking and sailing are both extremely
popular. However, to get a real sense of the island's
natural beauty, why not take to the skies instead?
Strap yourself into a parachute and ascend as a
speedboat takes you safely around for a bird's-eye
view of PEI's wonderful bays and beaches.

POINT PRIM, PRINCE EDWARD ISLAND
809 Admire a picture-perfect lighthouse

The beautiful lighthouse at Point Prim has kept
seafarers safe since 1845. Apart from the mechanisms
of the light, little about this iconic structure has
changed since its inception. It was operated by a
keeper who lived in this lonely location until 1969,
when automation took over and the keeper's cottage
became a visitor center. Climb the steep stairs and
sense the history of the lighthouse, the responsibility
of its keepers, and the power of the sea crashing against
the rocks below.

809 Sunrise at Point Prim

810 Views of Cape Breton Highlands National Park

CAPE BRETON ISLAND, NOVA SCOTIA

810 Hit the Cabot Trail

Who doesn't love a road trip? And one that brings you back to the start is even better. The Cabot Trail is a 185-mi (298-km) loop around the northern half of Cape Breton Island. It passes remote fishing villages, winding rivers, and the stunning Cape Breton Highlands National Park. All along the route you'll want to stop and indulge. In Baddeck there is the Bras d'Or Lake, where you can sail and fish, or head into its surroundings for hiking and horseback riding—even dogsledding in cold weather. As you hit the west of the island, stop to appreciate the local craft of rug hooking and grab a souvenir to brighten your home. You'll end up where you started, but full of sea air and memories.

PEGGY'S COVE, NOVA SCOTIA

811 Photograph a Canadian landmark

There's been a lighthouse at Peggy's Cove since 1868, and the classic red-and-white version that stands now is an iconic sight. Tourists flock to this stretch of granite coast, with several scenic observation points in and around the area over which the lighthouse stands guard—St. Margaret's Bay.

SABLE ISLAND NATIONAL PARK RESERVE, NOVA SCOTIA

812 Meet a colony of wild horses

Sable Island is one of the remoter national parks in Canada. This long, thin island is situated some 100 mi (150 km) off the coast of Halifax, and is only reachable via air or boat from the city. Once there, however, visitors can revel in some truly untamed landscapes, perfect for dramatic photography. Its residents—a colony of around 500 feral horses that have lived on the island since the 1700s—are also very photogenic.

JOGGINS, NOVA SCOTIA

813 See signs of life from 300 million years ago

The sheer strength of tides in this part of the world constantly lay bare the ocean floor, and when they recede, new fossils become visible. The UNESCO-protected Joggins Fossil Cliffs are awash with stones revealing details of life in the Carboniferous Period, dating back 300 million years. Guides can help interpret the fossils, but be warned— they can't be removed by members of the public.

HALIFAX, NOVA SCOTIA

814 Investigate the Halifax waterfront

The Nova Scotian capital has a proud seagoing past— nowhere more apparent than on its historic waterfront. The area has been made accessible for pedestrians, with more than a couple of miles of boardwalk. Firsthand accounts of the waterfront's story are available at two excellent museums: the Canadian Museum of Immigration at Pier 21 and the Maritime Museum of the Atlantic. There's also a wealth of stores and restaurants to choose from—or, if you want to venture out onto the water, Dartmouth is just a short ferry ride away.

LUNENBURG, NOVA SCOTIA
815 Visit old Lunenburg

Nowhere in Canada is quite like Lunenburg. Its colorful wooden buildings have a Scandinavian feel, but they were in fact built by the British in the eighteenth and nineteenth centuries. The town has a swagger to its step—possibly from its history as a rum-running base during Prohibition—and an independent spirit neatly symbolized by a copper cod weather vane on top of the church steeple.

VARIOUS SITES IN CANADA
816 Indulge your chocoholic side

Canadians have a real affinity for chocolate. The country's oldest chocolate factory is located in St. Stephen's in New Brunswick, and the town honors this fact with a chocolate festival every August. Or if a warm hot chocolate against a cold backdrop is more your thing, head to Vancouver, where the Hot Chocolate Festival takes place every January.

ACROSS CANADA
817 Relax for four days on a train

Canada is big. The distance from Toronto to Vancouver, for example, is 2,700 mi (4,400 km). While you could spend a few days driving that distance, it's much more civilized to secure a seat on Via Rail's *Canadian* and complete the route over four days. Appreciate incredible scenery whizzing past your window in one of its pleasingly retro steel coaches.

817 The *Canadian*'s dramatic route

820 Fortress of Louisbourg—"Gibraltar of the North"

WESTERN SHORE, NOVA SCOTIA
818 Search for treasure

According to legend, there could be anything from a stack of gold to the Holy Grail itself buried in the ground on Oak Island, just off Mahone Bay. The only way to see for yourself is to book a tour with the company that owns the island, while their guides tell you the whole story.

THROUGHOUT CANADA
819 Meet the world's best-dressed police

With their wide-brim Stetsons, scarlet jackets, and flash of yellow down the side of their pants, there's no doubt that Canadian Mounties are the best-dressed police force around. For a true pleasure, get up close to one and shake his or her hand.

NOVA SCOTIA
820 Admire the Fortress of Louisbourg

Cape Breton's rugged shoreline is impressive in its own right, but it's also home to an eighteenth-century fortress, built to protect Quebec against British invasions. Costumed interpreters re-create the French courts of the past, bringing the fort's history to life.

819 Royal Canadian Mounted Police wearing the Red Serge

BURNTCOAT HEAD, NOVA SCOTIA
821 Take a walk on the ocean floor

The world's highest tides have been recorded coming in and out at Burntcoat Head, part of Nova Scotia's remarkable Bay of Fundy. Thanks to these vicissitudes, visitors to Burntcoat Head Park can take part in an unusual activity—walking on the ocean floor. Guides are on hand to point out any natural points of interest and to make sure that you don't get caught when the tide comes back in.

THROUGHOUT CANADA
822 See the best lumberjacks around

Monty Python may have made fun of lumberjacks, but seeing them show off their skills in real life is a different matter. It's an incredibly skilled profession and requires an impressive combination of coordination, strength, and endurance. There are several regional lumberjack shows (as well as logging shows in general), and demonstrations crop up at country fairs across the country.

6

MEXICO
and the
CARIBBEAN

ENSENADA, BAJA CALIFORNIA, MEXICO

823 Discover Ensenada's gastronomy and wine scene

Located on the coast of Mexico's top wine region, Ensenada isn't only known for its surf, but also for its excellent wine and food scene. Explore the restaurants and wine bars of this city and fall for the laid-back charm of Mexican wine country.

TODOS SANTOS, BAJA CALIFORNIA SUR, MEXICO

824 Eat tacos in Todos Santos

Todos Santos is a Baja California gem. Until the 1980s it lacked a tarmac road, so it avoided the worst of tourism developments, despite its stunning white beaches and charming cobblestone streets. It's fast becoming a mecca for foodies, and while there are many great restaurants, don't overlook the street food—in particular freshly made fish tacos.

CABO SAN LUCAS,
BAJA CALIFORNIA SUR, MEXICO

825 Choose between Lover's Beach and Divorce Beach

These evocatively named beaches in Cabo San Lucas literally back onto one another, but they couldn't be more different. Lover's Beach is sheltered, secluded, and perfect for a cooling swim. Divorce Beach, on the other hand, faces the Pacific, and has crashing waves, strong currents, and riptides.

825 Divorce Beach, seen from Lover's Beach

GULF OF CALIFORNIA, MEXICO
826 Revel in a marine mammal paradise

Nestled between the mainland and the Baja California Peninsula is the Gulf of California, where boat trips to the islands are often escorted by dolphins. You'll also be rewarded with sightings of California sea lions, blue-footed boobies, ospreys, and marlin and yellowfin tuna leaping out of the water. At certain times of year, humpbacks, gray whales, and blue whales appear—all drawn by the rich source of plankton.

GULF OF CALIFORNIA, MEXICO
827 Count the world's rarest marine mammal

The vaquita ("little cow" in Spanish) is a small, stocky porpoise that lives only in the north end of the gulf. It's threatened by illegal fishing using gill nets, so is now critically endangered; scientists believe there are as few as sixty individuals remaining. They're often seen in shallow waters, usually solo, and will retreat if approached. So if you're lucky enough to spot one, report it to help monitor its survival.

SONORAN DESERT, MEXICO
828 See a desert icon

The saguaro is the king of the cactus family, living for up to 200 years and reaching 60 ft (18 m) tall. It grows only in the Sonoran Desert straddling Mexico, Arizona, and California, and even here, only where winter temperatures don't drop below freezing. Between April and June, saguaros produce crowns of large white flowers that open for one night, then close the following afternoon. That short window is their only chance to be pollinated.

826 Sighting a whale shark

829 Views over Copper Canyon

CHIHUAHUA, MEXICO
829 Ride through Copper Canyon

Considered the most dramatic train ride there is, the Ferrocarril Chihuahua al Pacifico (Copper Canyon Railway) is a 404-mi (650-km) delight, crossing thirty-six bridges as it chugs through the mountainous interior of northern Mexico's Pacific Coast. Highlights include sheer canyon walls, huge waterfalls, and desert plains. The journey is set up to savor the vistas of the Sierra Tarahumara. Be sure to stop off along the way; the Indigenous people in the canyon are as interesting as the views.

CHIHUAHUA, MEXICO
830 Check out an underground kitchen

Locals have known about the spectacular cave systems at Grutas Nombre de Dios and Grutas de Coyame since the sixteenth century, and they were likely used in the past by Indigenous people for ceremonial purposes. Now you can explore the seventeen underground chambers by joining a guided tour. The cavern that has been called *la cocina* (the kitchen) features rock formations that look like various food items, including popcorn and a beer mug.

CHIHUAHUAN DESERT, MEXICO
831 See a hopper heat up and cool down

The black-and-yellow western horse lubber grasshopper is a handsome beast, but it also has a clever survival strategy. It uses the black coloring of its body to draw in the sun's heat and maintain an optimum body temperature of around 97°F (36°C), even if the temperature of the surrounding desert is lower.

MAZATLÁN, SINALOA, MEXICO

832 Celebrate Carnaval, Mexican style

When huge, multicolored marionettes (*monigotes*) appear in the center of Mazatlán, you know Carnaval is coming. When it arrives, for the six days leading up to Lent, you can't miss it. It's one huge, family-friendly street party of parades, parties, food, lots of beer, and fireworks exploding out of giant effigies.

COAHUILA, MEXICO

833 Discover the oldest winery in the New World

It might surprise you that the oldest winery in the New World is actually in Mexico. Casa Madero, established in 1597 in Parras de la Fuente, was the first winery to open its doors—since the arrival of the Spanish—and the first vines on the continent. Taste New World wine history at this historic *bodega*.

CENTRAL VOLCANIC SLOPES, MEXICO

834 See a volcano rabbit

This rabbit earns its name from the fact that it lives on the slopes of only four volcanoes: Popocatépetl, Iztaccíhuatl, El Pelado, and Tláloc. It is one of the smallest rabbits in the world, with rounded ears and hardly any tail. Instead of thumping its foot as other rabbits do when it senses danger, it squeaks.

832 Celebrating Carnaval in Mazatlán

MARIETAS ISLANDS,
NAYARIT, MEXICO

835 Spend the day on a beach in a crater

A gaping hole on the surface of one of the lush green Marietas Islands, in the state of Nayarit, leads to a secret beach known as the Playa del Amor, or "Beach of Love." There is sun, shade, and crystal clear water, so pack a picnic because you won't need to move from here all day.

ZACATECAS CITY, ZACATECAS, MEXICO

836 Grab a drink undergound

When it comes to bars with a difference, Bar Mina el Eden could be high up your list. It is 1,049 ft (320 m) underground in a former silver mine, and you have to take a four-minute trip in a mining train to reach it. Raise your glass to the many miners who worked and suffered here.

CENTRAL, EAST, NORTH MEXICO

837 See if roadrunners live up to their name

These birds can reach speeds of 26 mph (42 kmh) for short sprints. In fact, they are better on the ground than in the air, tending to fly only for short periods if they really have to. They're usually found in pairs—they mate for life—in fairly barren land, such as deserts and canyons.

835 Hideaway beach, Playa del Amor

XILITLA, SAN LUIS POTOSÍ, MEXICO
838 See a garden that pays homage to Dalí

Edward James was an art collector who lived here in the 1940s. His love of surrealism was so keen that he created Las Pozas, a garden of sculptures that's now open to visitors, where you'll see columns that become flowers, mysterious gates, and spiral staircases that lead to nowhere.

PUERTO VALLARTA, JALISCO, MEXICO
839 Take in tropical scents at the Vallarta Botanical Garden

Set in the lush Sierra Madre Mountains, these botanical gardens are a treasure trove of plants, teeming with biodiversity of all kinds and magnificent birdlife. Leave the stunning manicured gardens for a hike in the native forest and even a swim in the river.

PUERTO VALLARTA, JALISCO, MEXICO
840 Take to the streets for open-air art

Many towns have their own *malecón*, or boardwalk, but here the seaside is akin to an art museum, with street art on all sides. A dozen huge bronze and stone sculptures line the street, portraying everything from dragons to seahorses.

TEQUILA, JALISCO, MEXICO
841 Sample tequila where it's grown

As you arrive in the town of Tequila, through fields full of gray-blue agave plants, you'll notice a trace of the liquor hanging in the air. This small town has almost as many distilleries as it does churches. There's no better place to discover how it's made—and taste it!

GUADALAJARA, JALISCO, MEXICO
842 Drown in the flavors of a local snack

Regional sandwiches don't come more sloppily tasty than *tortas ahogadas*, or "drowned sandwiches." A regular sub is smothered in spicy chili sauce, so grab a handful of napkins and join the locals, who wolf them down, especially on game days.

GUADALAJARA, JALISCO, MEXICO
843 Head to a *charreada*

Mexican vaqueros were the precursors to American cowboys, and their horse skills are legendary. Experience the high energy atmosphere of a *charreada*, where men and women show off impressive lasso skills—and horse dancing, too.

GUADALAJARA, JALISCO, MEXICO
844 Strike the right note with local folk tunes

Elevate your mariachi listening experience by seeking out live concerts in this city. The music originated here, and is taken very seriously. It's much more moving than your local Mexican restaurant, guaranteed.

GUADALAJARA, JALISCO, MEXICO
845 Be in*spired* by Guadalajara Cathedral

The second-oldest cathedral in Mexico (constructed 1618) has a striking neo-Gothic design. Visitors are rewarded with another feature, though— the double spires that grace this beautiful basilica.

838 Las Pozas, Xilitla

846 Vivid colors of historic Guanajuato City

850 San Juan Parangaricutiro church

GUANAJUATO CITY, GUANAJUATO, MEXICO

846 Let colorful streets make you smile

In the eighteenth century, the wealth of minerals in the surrounding hills made this Mexico's richest city—and it has the architecture to prove it. Color is as popular today as it was then, and the city's cobbled streets are painted in vibrant hues, best seen from the lookout of El Pipila, the local hero of Independence.

GUANAJUATO CITY, GUANAJUATO, MEXICO

847 Value life at a museum of the afterlife

Mexico has a rich tradition of honoring the dead. Remember that on a visit to the Museum of the Mummies, which features around fifty mummified bodies. Many were disinterred when relatives couldn't pay a "perpetual burial" tax and it was discovered that the city's climate led to natural mummification.

SAN MIGUEL DE ALLENDE, GUANAJUATO, MEXICO

848 Discover an expat artist colony

San Miguel de Allende is an arty town. Its two art schools were both founded by expats, one Peruvian and one American, and they have drawn many foreign artists. Lose yourself in Fabrica La Aurora, an art and design center with over forty galleries, where you can watch artists at work and buy their creations.

851 Morelia's Callejón del Romance

PARÍCUTIN, PEÑA DE BERNAL,
QUERÉTARO, MEXICO

849 Visit a chapel at the end of a path

Peña de Bernal is a rock rising 1,150 ft (350 m) from its surroundings. According to legend, it could contain a snake guarding the secrets of existence or giant amethyst crystals that exude magnetic energy. Who knows? But it does have a winding footpath that ends at a tiny chapel halfway up the rock.

MICHOACÁN, MEXICO

850 See a holy site that is rising from the ashes

In 1943, a volcanic eruption covered two villages in lava and ash. Everyone was safely evacuated, but the lava continued to flow for eight years. It's an eerie place to visit, not least because of the local church, which still half stands, appearing out of the cooled rock—a resilient, holy site for many Christian pilgrimages.

MORELIA, MICHOACÁN, MEXICO

851 Stroll down the Alley of Romance

It's a romantic spot, with pink stonework, bubbling fountains, and blooming bougainvillea. And many couples who visit the Callejón del Romance hope to make their love last forever by fastening a padlock to the ironwork in the alleyway. There's no guarantee it works, but a stroll down this pretty street makes you feel that life's for loving.

MONARCH BUTTERFLY BIOSPHERE RESERVE, MICHOACÁN, MEXICO

852 See a mass of monarchs all at once

The migration of monarch butterflies from mid-November to March every year is a phenomenon of nature. Every year they breed in the United States and Canada before flying in their millions to overwinter in Mexico—journeying 1,800 mi (2,900 km). They head to the same 200 sq mi (520 sq km), navigating using the time of day, based on their own circadian rhythm and the sun's position. Their arrival in this reserve is a spectacular sight, thick carpets of monarchs covering the ground and trees. And then, come March, they leave.

MICHOACÁN, MEXICO

853 Study a pocket gopher

The pocket gopher is so called because of the large pouches in its cheeks. Unlike a hamster's, these pouches are external to the gopher's mouth; it uses them to store the roots and tubers that it burrows underground to find. When it burrows, it seals its lips with its big digging teeth still on the outside.

MICHOACÁN, MEXICO

854 Get crafty with your souvenirs

In 1572, a bishop tried to create a utopian society for the local Purépecha people, based on craft communities around Lake Pátzcuaro. More than thirty disciplines flourished, and today those traditions produce wonderful ceramics, woodwork, and textiles. Browse the local markets for stunning pieces that you won't find anywhere else.

MEXICO CITY, MEXICO

855 Sate your appetite for history at a historic cantina

Cantinas evolved from men-only drinking dens to more general spaces to eat, drink, and socialize. Some of the oldest still thrive; head for the elaborate grandeur of Bar La Opera (dating to 1876) or the unpretentious tradition of El Tío Pepe (1890).

MEXICO CITY, MEXICO

856 Visit la Casa Azul

When an accident left the Mexican artist Frida Kahlo housebound, she turned to her garden for inspiration. The grounds of her cobalt-blue walled house are filled with the bright flowers and native trees of the country she loved. Pots and beds overspill, and climbing vegetation bursts from walls and railings in the property grounds.

XOCHIMILCO, MEXICO CITY, MEXICO

857 Alter your view of history

At almost 500 years old, the church of San Bernardino de Siena is a national monument and one of the oldest in the country. Travel back by half a millennium and inspect the original altarpiece in this tiny church, dating back to the Renaissance and unlike any other in its design, as well as its renowned image of the Child Jesus, the Niñopa.

856 La Casa Azul's plant-filled courtyard

XOCHIMILCO WETLANDS,
MEXICO CITY, MEXICO

858 Look after a piece of Mexico

Southeast of Mexico City lie the stunning canals and islands of Xochimilco. They were created as a farming system by the Aztecs 500 years ago and are now hugely important for wildlife and agriculture. But they're in danger from pollution and rapid urbanization. Join a trip to monitor the water quality and wildlife and help preserve the area for future generations.

MEXICO CITY, MEXICO

859 See a game at Estadio Azteca

Opened in 1966, the Estadio Azteca is one of the most iconic soccer stadiums in the world— and Latin America's largest— and has played host to some memorable matches over the decades. With a capacity for more than 80,000 fans, the atmosphere is always electric. See Mexico's national team or top league team Club América play here.

858 Xochimilco wetlands

MEXICO CITY, MEXICO

860 Catch your breath at the Biblioteca Vasconcelos

In one of the most polluted urban environments on Earth, the reading areas of the botanical gardens that have been integrated with this giant steel, concrete, and glass library offer visitors much-needed respite from the sprawling cityscape. The garden houses more than 168 species of tree, most being endemic to Mexico, while the library itself is of epic proportions—a light-filled space that is a panacea for body and soul.

MEXICO CITY, MEXICO

861 Munch on toasted grasshoppers

Arriving at San Juan Market, you'd be forgiven for thinking it's just another food market, with colorful stalls and cheap places to eat. But look more closely, and you'll notice that the stalls sell more high-end, exotic merchandise. There are imported Italian hams and French cheeses, and specialist meats such as iguana and crocodile, but best of all are the fried grasshoppers. Try them and see what you think.

860 Biblioteca Vasconcelos

CULTURAL INSTITUTIONS OF MEXICO CITY

Soumaya Museum

Jumex Museum

Palacio de Bellas Artes

863 Diego Rivera's Tláloc (rain god) Fountain

862 See how many museums you can visit

Deciding which of Mexico City's many cultural institutions to visit can be tricky. There are more than 140 cultural spaces in town, ranging from the well-known Palacio de Bellas Artes or the Diego Rivera Mural Museum to quirkier institutions such as the Caricature Museum or Shoe Museum. Choose your route and wear comfortable shoes.

863 Breathe in the air at a city park

The Bosque de Chapultepec dates back to the city's beginnings— the lungs of the city and used to supply its water. It's where Toltecs worshipped, Aztecs built palaces, Spanish viceroys took summer retreats, and Mexican presidents established residences. Discover the old water tank, decorated with Diego Rivera's fabulous reclining fountain.

864 Soak up the scent of jacarandas

Every spring the streets of Mexico City turn purple with the flowers of jacaranda trees. It might not receive nearly as many likes as the Japanese city of Kyoto and its famous cherry blossom, but it should; Mexico City has thousands of the trees, and they're a truly beautiful sight to behold.

867 Arched walkways overlooking the Palacio Nacional's central courtyard

MEXICO CITY, MEXICO

865 Wrestle with a *lucha libra* show

It's hard to decide whether *lucha libre*—Mexican wrestling— is a sport or a dance. Wrestlers wear fabulous costumes with their trademark masks, while deploying acrobatic moves, and fights are often choreographed, with a preordained winner. That in no way lessens the spectacle, which is a perfect combination of skill, storytelling, and spandex.

MEXICO CITY, MEXICO

866 Wonder at the weird axolotl

The axolotl, or Mexican walking fish, is a kind of salamander that retains some of its larval characteristics (such as frilly gills) in adulthood, giving it a strange appearance. It has a gelatinous texture and short little legs. This wonderful creature is sadly critically endangered and was only rediscovered in the wild in 2014.

MEXICO CITY, MEXICO

867 Learn Mexico's history from a building

Spectacular inside and out, Mexico's Palacio Nacional is more than 660 ft (200 m) long. Its architecture features great stairways, courtyards, and balconies, and additions over the years partly tell the history of the country. This is told in full in the stunning interior murals by Diego Rivera, which took twenty-five years to finish.

869 Teotihucán's stepped pyramids, seen from the Pyramid of the Moon

OUTSIDE MEXICO CITY, MEXICO

868 Visit a ring of peace

The *Espacio Escultórico* (*Sculptural Space*) is a piece of land art created by a group of six sculptors in 1979 on the campus of the National Autonomous University of Mexico. It is a perfect circle of sixty-four concrete wedges, built around a mound of lava left behind after the eruption of the Xitle volcano. Stand inside it and soak up the tranquility of this ancient landscape.

TEOTIHUACÁN, STATE OF MEXICO, MEXICO

869 Abandon yourself to the lure of Teotihuacán

In the 1400s, the Aztecs found a huge abandoned city full of pyramids, temples, plazas, and palaces, with its main street aligned with the Cerro Gordo volcano. They called it Teotihuacán—"the place where the gods were created." Visit to sense the mystery and magic of its impressive buildings.

TAXCO, GUERRERO, MEXICO

870 Buy some silver jewelry in Taxco

The streets of Taxco are almost literally lined with silver— with stores every few steps. The precious metal was mined here from the sixteenth century until relatively recently, and the talents of silversmiths passed down through generations. Even if you're not on the hunt for an heirloom, it's a beautiful setting to learn about silver.

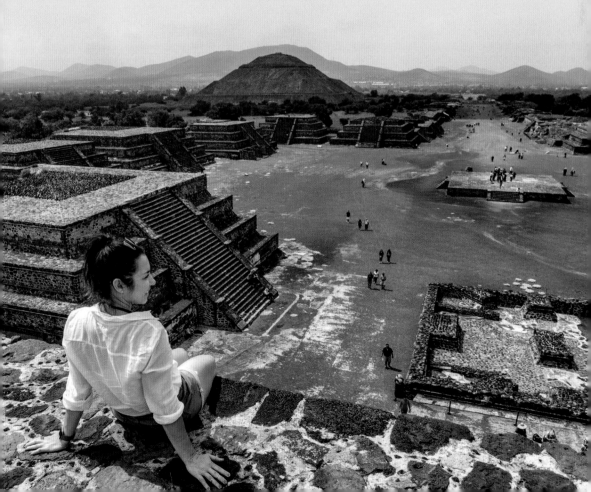

PUEBLA, MEXICO

871 Don't awaken a sleeping giant

Although dormant, the huge Iztaccíhuatl volcano still
looms large on the skyline here. Join experienced guides
on an intermediate-level hike up the foothills and to within
a few thousand feet of the snowy summit. Look back out
over the stunning views of the "smoking mountain" of
Popocatépetl and the Valley of Mexico.

875 Tlacotalpan's historic port

PUEBLA CITY, PUEBLA, MEXICO

872 Seek out a saucy accompaniment for your meal

Many stories tell of the origins of mole poblano, but it's clear that the delicacy was born here. Considered a national dish, this dark, rich sauce has more than twenty ingredients, and graces even more recipes than that. Try it with tamales or as an accompaniment for any local dish.

PUEBLA CITY, PUEBLA, MEXICO

873 Satisfy your sweet tooth at Calle de los Dulces

Imagine living in a town with a thoroughfare called "Sweets Street." Locals here don't have to imagine, as the Calle de Los Dulces is a three-block haven of stores selling every kind of confection. Be sure to try *camotes*, Puebla's signature treats, made from sweet potato.

PUEBLA CITY, PUEBLA, MEXICO

874 See and believe an urban legend

For years, there was an urban myth about secret tunnels beneath the city of Puebla. Then in 2015 they were found. Tall enough to ride through on horseback, the tunnels link Fort Loreto to the city center.

VERACRUZ, MEXICO

875 Give a porting chance to a historic town

It's not often that an entire town is recognized as a UNESCO World Heritage Site. Tlacotalpan is such a place, and day-trippers will love exploring its sixteenth-century architecture and historic urban design.

VERACRUZ, MEXICO

876 Learn what goes into your cup of Joe

It takes a perfect blend of altitude, temperature, and rainfall for coffee plants to thrive, and happily Veracruz has all three. Head to the hills to learn just what it is that makes your morning coffee taste so good.

878 Day of the Dead costumes and makeup

SIERRA NORTE, OAXACA, MEXICO

877 Discover a commonwealth of mountain villages

High up in the Sierra Norte are eight Zapotec villages linked by hiking paths and trails and a communal approach to safeguarding the rich natural resources around them. The villages, known as the Pueblos Mancomunados (Commonwealth of Villages), run a joint ecotourism project that allows visitors to learn about life in a mountain village while embracing the magnificent views and rich biodiversity all around.

OAXACA CITY, OAXACA, MEXICO

878 Celebrate Day of the Dead

Día de los Muertos is a national holiday (November 1 and 2) in Mexico, dedicated to honoring the dead through the living. It derives from the Aztec belief in Mictlan—a kind of limbo between life and death, from which spirits can make a trip home once a year. To help them find their way, tombs and altars are decorated with food and drink offerings. In Oaxaca City, the fun starts a week before November 1, with the opening of the festive markets. To see decorated graves and tombs, head to the Panteón General cemetery, or try Xoxocotlán Cemetery, just outside the city.

879 Oaxaca City colors

880 Oaxacan mezcal bar

OAXACA CITY, OAXACA, MEXICO
879 When in Oaxaca, shop local

Oaxaca City is full of color. Not just the building facades but the stores and stalls brimming with vibrant fabrics, woven rugs, painted wooden toys, and fabulous ceramics. The state is home to more of Mexico's Indigenous groups than anywhere else, and they come together here to sell their beautiful craftwork.

OAXACA CITY, OAXACA, MEXICO
880 Learn about a misunderstood liquor

If your experience of mezcal is downing tequila shots in a karaoke bar, then prepare to be reeducated. This region produces the world's best mezcal (of which tequila is a type), distilled to produce a smoky, peppery liquor. Head for top tasting rooms such as La Mezcaloteca, where the botanics are fully explained.

OAXACA CITY, OAXACA, MEXICO
881 Try a Mexican pizza

Traditional Mexican cuisine is on UNESCO's list of the Intangible Cultural Heritage of Humanity, and they don't mean Taco Bell. Oaxaca's street food is fresh, tasty, and varied and some of the best in the country. Try the *tlayuda*—a crispy corn tortilla base topped with refried beans, meats, cheeses, and veg. It's called a Mexican pizza by some, and it's just as messy to eat.

OAXACA CITY, OAXACA, MEXICO
882 Be mesmerized by a church ceiling

The Templo de Santo Domingo is beautiful on the outside, with baroque carvings on symmetrical towers, but inside it's phenomenal—cave-like walls and ceilings that are utterly covered with gilded, bas-relief decoration. A former monastery next door is now an art museum, which has led to interesting installations outside the church.

HIERVE EL AGUA, OAXACA, MEXICO
883 Bathe in a natural mineral pool

It's never been said that Hierve el Agua inspired the movie *Frozen*, but it's possible. Two huge waterfalls appear to be frozen on the mountainside. In fact, when the area petrified, the minerals in the water turned to stone. Above them, natural mineral pools offer amazing views over the mountains—and softer skin.

SANTA MARÍA DEL TULE, OAXACA, MEXICO
884 Stand beside the world's widest tree

Dwarfing the adjacent church, the Árbol del Tule holds the honor of being the world's widest tree. It is a Montezuma cypress—or ahuehuete—with a trunk measuring 31 ft (9.4 m) across. Local legend claims it was planted 1,400 years ago by Pechocha, a priest of the Aztec god of the wind.

ZIPOLITE, OAXACA, MEXICO
885 Strip off on a nudist beach

Do you dare to go bare? It's difficult to understand why there's such a difference between a skimpy bikini and your birthday suit, but there is. At a nudist beach, surrounded by other naked people, you'll realize that being naked isn't such a big deal. Have your first experience at Playa Zipolite—Mexico's first and only legal nudist beach.

883 Natural pools in Hierve el Agua

885 Naked swimming at Playa Zipolite

PUERTO ESCONDIDO, OAXACA, MEXICO
886 Get swept up in world-class surf in Puerto Escondido

The beach breaks on Playa Zicatela are known as some of the gnarliest around—come here to watch the pros rather than to test your own limits. With 10-ft (3-m) waves forming perfect tunnels, it's high-octane stuff, so it's fortunate that you can find plenty of other ways to chill in the laid-back beach town, from yoga sessions to friendly beach bars.

THROUGHOUT OAXACA, MEXICO
887 Shop for stylish black pottery

Oaxaca's distinctive black pottery—*barro negro*—has found its way beyond the borders of the state, and the country, to grace dinner tables and museum shelves around the world. The clay, found outside the town of San Bartolo Coyotepec, has been used for centuries, and originally pieces had a dull gray finish. In the 1950s, local potter Doña Rosa Real developed a technique to create a shiny black finish.

886 Oaxaca's "Hidden Port," Puerto Escondido

889 Pedestrianized street in San Cristobál de las Casas

TAPIJULAPA, TABASCO, MEXICO

888 Fish around for dishes that are hundreds of years old

This region has a proud ancient history, reflected not least in its cuisine. It's a rare chance to dine on pre-Hispanic dishes, mostly seafood and freshwater fish. Try delicacies such as tropical gar (*pejelagarto*), grilled with limes and chilis, or baby shark (*cazón*).

SAN CRISTOBÁL DE LAS CASAS, CHIAPAS, MEXICO

889 Tour colonial architecture

The custard-colored baroque cathedral here presides over the town's plaza like a warm hug of perpetual sunshine. Construction began in 1528, but it was completely overhauled in the eighteenth century. The city is full of colorful colonial architecture—much of it located on traffic-free streets—making it a wonderful place to soak up the past.

PALENQUE, CHIAPAS, MEXICO

890 Uncover a Mayan ruin

Like most of Mexico's Mayan ruins, those at Palenque were once completely hidden beneath the jungle canopy. It's phenomenal how well they've survived the ravages of nature and the clumsy attempts of early explorers who bashed down walls to see what was inside. Today, the site reveals intricate artworks and hieroglyphics as well as impressive temples, pyramids, and palaces.

IZAMAL, YUCATÁN, MEXICO

891 Be dazzled by an all-yellow city

There are many colorful cities in Mexico, but Izamal tops them all. Every building here is yellow. All of them. The uplifting paint job happened in 1993 as a way to spruce up the colonial town before a visit from the pope. The story goes that yellow was chosen as a link to the town's Mayan origins and worship of the sun god Kinich Kakmo. Whatever the reason, it's very cheerful.

YUCATÁN, MEXICO
892 See the splendor of Chichén Itzá

Chichén Itzá was the epicenter of the Mayan empire from 750 until 1200. Its main temple, El Castillo, has 365 steps and demonstrates the Mayans' sophisticated knowledge of astronomy. Visit at an equinox to watch a snakelike shadow form and join a stone serpent head at the pyramid's base.

MERIDA, YUCATÁN, MEXICO
893 Stay in the lap of old-school luxury

Between the seventeenth and nineteenth centuries, elegant country estates (haciendas) were built across this region, each with its own distinctive architecture and ambience. You can stay at some of them and experience their old-school style: Uayamon, for instance, dates back to 1685; Temozon is even older.

VALLADOLID, YUCATÁN, MEXICO
894 Cool down in a city water hole

Cenotes are water holes that form when a cave roof collapses, exposing the groundwater below. Many such water holes are hidden deep within the lush Mexican jungle. However, in Valladolid, Cenote Zaci is unexpectedly located right in the center of the city, just blocks from the main square.

892 El Castillo at Chichén Itzá, seen against the Milky Way

894 Cenote Zaci in Valladolid

RÍA LAGARTOS BIOSPHERE
RESERVE, YUCATÁN, MEXICO
895 Admire the rosy hues of Las Coloradas

The same little creatures that turn flamingos pink are responsible for the vibrant pink salt lakes of Las Coloradas. The lakes are man-made to harvest salt, but the color is all natural as the water evaporates and the concentration of algae, plankton, and shrimp gets stronger.

QUINTANA ROO, MEXICO
896 Indulge in a tropical yoga retreat

The Caribbean coast of Mexico has everything the modern beach bum could desire: white beaches, palm trees, Mayan ruins, and yoga. Yes, yoga! There are countless retreats and classes to choose from in this part of the world, and surely few more relaxing places to perform your sun salutations.

ISLA CONTOY,
QUINTANA ROO, MEXICO
897 Wing your way to a bird haven

Isla Contoy is a protected island—uninhabited and free of development. Only guided day trips are allowed, and visitors are able to spot more than 200 species of birds among the island's lagoons, mangroves, and forests, including pelicans and cormorants.

895 Salt lakes of Las Coloradas

ISLA HOLBOX, QUINTANA ROO, MEXICO

898 Get back to nature at the Casa Las Tortugas

The Italian couple who fell in love with the raw beauty of this unspoiled island on Mexico's Riviera Maya have created an environmentally conscious hotel on the beach, surrounded by lush vegetation and colorful birds. Lodge in a traditional Mayan bungalow for a luxurious eco-vacation.

ISLA MUJERES, QUINTANA ROO, MEXICO

899 Follow the sun to an island where the day starts early

The easternmost point in the easternmost region of Mexico is Punta Sur on Isla Mujeres. The island has a colorful past, full of piracy, military skirmishes, and lawlessness. Today, though, it's a tranquil escape where you can experience Mexico's earliest sunrise.

CANCÚN, QUINTANA ROO, MEXICO

900 Watch sailfish hunt

With their swordlike bills and arching fins, sailfish are one of the most distinctive fish in the sea. They are also prolific hunters. They form packs and round up sardines, driving them toward the surface. They put their bills into the midst of the shoal and slash them back and forth, injuring individual sardines that they then pick off and eat. Tours from Cancún from February to April look for circling seabirds to know a hunt is underway, and it's possible to watch this amazing sight with just a mask and snorkel.

898 Isla Holbox's sandy coast

CANCÚN, QUINTANA ROO, MEXICO

901 Go bargain hunting at a bazaar

You might notice that there's a distinct lack of written prices in and around Mercado 28 in downtown Cancún. The daily market is a large, open-air complex where you can buy everything from traditional crafts to tacky souvenirs. Stall holders are prepared for haggling, so bring your best negotiating skills and prepare for some friendly bartering. You'll hopefully walk away with a few bargains.

CANCÚN, QUINTANA ROO, MEXICO

902 Visit an underwater museum

The Underwater Museum of Art, off Cancún, is the world's first underwater contemporary art museum. Don your wetsuit and swim silently around life-size human sculptures, perhaps joined by reef fish or even a turtle. It's so magical, every coastline should have one. And for those who don't dive, the sculptures can be seen by snorkeling or from a glass-bottomed boat.

COZUMEL, QUINTANA ROO, MEXICO

903 Croc and roll at a nature reserve

This island has its areas of relatively busy tourism, but getting back to nature is easy with a visit to Parque Punta Sur, a 250-ac (100-ha) eco-park that's a haven for some of the area's most charismatic wildlife. See exotic birds and sea turtles, and observe crocodiles from the safety of a lookout tower.

COZUMEL, QUINTANA ROO, MEXICO

904 Cleanse yourself inside and out with an ancient steam ceremony

The Mayans may be an ancient civilization, but many of their ideas and traditions live on. You can engage in one of their healthier practices by signing up for a guided temazcal ceremony, popular in this region. The word means "steam house" and through phases of cleansing, the saunalike room takes on a holy, ceremonial ambience.

COZUMEL, QUINTANA ROO, MEXICO

905 Encounter life below the surface off Cozumel

Just a short hop from the mainland is the island of Cozumel: flat, verdant, and with a coral reef teeming with life. Put on your mask and snorkel, lower your head, and let the water fill your ears as underwater life fills your vision. Fish gently nudge the colorful corals, starfish slowly scoot across the sand, and a ray or a turtle might even pass by.

COBA, QUINTANA ROO, MEXICO

906 Don't ruin your trip by missing out on Mayan history

Chichén Itzá is a world-famous attraction, but it can be busy and time-consuming. There's a great alternative at Coba, just outside Tulum. Here lie similar ancient Mayan ruins, built between 500 and 900 CE. Climb the majestic pyramid and peruse ceremonial and spiritual areas, including Macanxoc structures by the nearby lagoon.

TULUM, QUINTANA ROO, MEXICO

907 Swim through the world's largest underwater cave system

The Yucatán Peninsula is based on a bedrock of limestone, and over the years this has been dissolved by water to leave a maze of caves and tunnels below the surface, as well as many cenotes—sinkholes filled with water. In Tulum, you can swim through this cave system, marveling at the stalactites and stalagmites as you go.

THROUGHOUT MEXICO

908 Try the local pulque

Though not technically beer (or brewed for that matter), this cloudy fermented beverage is a regional speciality that beer lovers will find worth seeking out. The milky, viscous liquid is made by fermenting the fresh sap of certain types of agave plants. It clocks in at around 4 to 6 percent ABV and is sold in pulquerias throughout Mexico.

TULUM, QUINTANA ROO, MEXICO

909 Witness natural splendor

If heaven exists in Mexico, then the Sian Ka'an Biosphere Reserve, a UNESCO World Heritage Site, is close to it. A biosphere containing 200 conservation projects has resulted in a near paradise, replete with protected natural areas, diverse wildlife from monkeys to crocodiles, and twenty-three Mayan archaeological sites.

905 Snorkeling off Cozumel

TULUM, QUINTANA ROO, MEXICO

910 Explore the only Mayan ruin on a beach

The ancient Mayans knew what they were doing when they sited Tulum overlooking one of the most beautiful beaches on Mexico's Caribbean coast. Who wouldn't want to live here? Explore the dramatic ruin in a place that was built as a seaport for trading jade and turquoise.

GULF OF MEXICO

911 Witness the ocean turn red

The "red tides" that occasionally turn the sea orangy red are caused by algal blooms. The sight can be impressive, but take care as they can be toxic.

910 Tulum's Mayan ruin

VIÑALES, CUBA
912 Take a guided hike through the Viñales Valley

You'll be spoiled for choice when it comes to hiking trails in this popular region in the west of Cuba, so make the decision easier by joining a local tour or hiring a guide. This stunning region is renowned for its mogotes—imposing limestone monoliths that tower over the stretches of sugar cane plantations and tobacco fields below. As well as enjoying the magnificent scenery, you'll have the chance to explore underground cave systems and sample sugar cane syrup, fresh from the farmers.

VIÑALES, CUBA
913 It's close *and* cigar at a tobacco farm

The farmers around here tend to grow sweet corn in the dry season and tobacco in the wet season. It's the latter that has become globally famous for its quality, and many farms have visitor centers where you can not only buy a genuine Cuban cigar, but you can roll your own under expert supervision. Perfect for a gift or to smoke yourself.

913 Horseback riding in Cuba's tobacco region with JMC Viñales Aventura

HAVANA, CUBA

914 Get your car appreciation motor running in a vintage model

Since the Cuban Revolution, US sanctions have meant that American car sales in Cuba are nonexistent. So Cuba has become a living car museum, people fixing up vintage models again and again to keep driving them. Many of these old cars are used for taxi services, so you can ride in a fifty-year-old cab.

HAVANA, CUBA

915 Get perspective on the old town

In Old Havana there is a camera obscura hidden away on the rooftop of Gómez Villa. Venture up for a visit to a 360-degree panoramic view.

914 Vintage car in Havana

LIVE ARTS IN THE STREETS OF OLD HAVANA

Musicians in Callejon de Hamel

Salsa in Parque Central

Gigantería theater performers

916 See the artistic transformation of Old Havana

The area around the alley of Callejon de Hamel was once rundown and ugly, but local artist Salvador Gonzáles Escalona has changed all of that, filling it with colorful, surrealist paintings and sculptures. Visitors to the old town are also entertained by a variety of performance arts. The Gigantería theater ensemble, for example, parades through the streets, preserving Afro-Cuban carnival traditions.

917 Mix some history with your drinks order

As with most cocktails, the exact origins of the mojito are unclear, but the cocktail was definitely invented in Havana. "Mojo" means "little spell" and it's likely that slaves in the sugarcane fields first mixed a version of the rum and mint drink. The bar La Bodeguita del Medio makes the boldest claim to being the first to serve it, but you can order one anywhere in the city and know it's authentic.

918 Dive down to a wreck

With its dazzling, well-preserved reefs, plunging sea walls, and swim-through caves, Cuba is a destination apart for divers. The Bay of Pigs is found in a rarely visited area on the south of the island, where you can dive and relax without being swamped by other people. Here, you'll find the wreck of *El Jaruco*, deliberately sunk in 1994 to provide an interesting dive site. The lack of currents at Maria la Gorda makes for a relaxing experience, as you explore eighteenth- and nineteenth-century Spanish galleon and pirate wrecks in clear waters.

919 Play dominoes in the street

People playing dominoes in the parks and public areas of Cuban towns and cities is commonplace. Follow the distinctive click-clack sound of the tiles to join in—but brush up on the slightly variant Cuban rules first.

920 Help map the biodiversity of Cuba

Cuba is one of the world's biodiversity hot spots, with around 20,000 species of animals and 7,500 species of plants within its shores. However, for a number of years it has been cut off from international research, and little is known about the current state of play of these species. Join scientists at the Lomas de Banao reserve to document this magnificent island and know that you're part of protecting species for the future.

921 Get a buzz from a bee hummingbird

A reasonably regular sight at Playa Larga, the bee hummingbird is just 2½ in (6 cm) long, making it the world's smallest bird. Its small-scale perfection is mesmerizing.

OFF CUBA

922 Feel the thrill of hooking a big game fish

Hemingway captured the drama of big game fishing perfectly in *The Old Man and the Sea*. The book came from his love of the sport: the waiting game, the luring of the majestic blue marlin or a sailfish, then the skill and the battle of reeling it in. Hook your big game fish in the Caribbean.

NASSAU, THE BAHAMAS

923 Get hot to trot on a beach

The beaches of Nassau are world-class, and have been featured in countless commercials and movies. One of the most cinematic ways to appreciate them is to take a horseback-riding trail through the forests and along the coastline of Coral Harbour and Adelaide, skirting the natural lake of Corrie Sound.

NASSAU, THE BAHAMAS

924 Party with the locals

Although its eighteenth-century origins are lost in the mists of time, on December 26 and January 1, a huge music and dance celebration called Junkanoo takes place. Lose yourself in West African rhythms and don outlandish costumes to mix with the locals, as parades and parties take over the entire island for a couple of days.

923 Horseback riding on a Nassau beach

927 Dolphins off Blue Lagoon Island

NASSAU, THE BAHAMAS
925 Enjoy seafood accompanied by poetry

Fried snapper, grilled grouper, grilled shrimp, lobster tails, fish chowder—the list of traditional Bahamian seafood is long and lovely. Head to Arawak Cay, where sit-down restaurants, beach shacks, and street vendors serve it up all day long. Hang out by the storytelling porch to enjoy a tale or two while you eat.

TIGER BEACH, THE BAHAMAS
926 Learn to love sharks, not fear them

A certain movie is perhaps single-handedly responsible for giving sharks a bad name. But if you get the chance to swim alongside Caribbean reef sharks with a professional guide, you can't help but be awed by their streamlined efficiency and sense of majesty. If you also consider that far more people are killed by dogs than sharks each year, you will realize that a fear of these fish is misplaced. Cultivate a healthy respect for them instead.

BLUE LAGOON ISLAND, THE BAHAMAS
927 Seal your love for Bahamanian beaches

This island is home to arguably the best beaches in the Bahamas. The ocean is turquoise, palms frame hidden lagoons, and the area attracts exotic wildlife such as dolphins and sea lions. Jump on a guided tour to meet these charismatic residents up close.

BIG MAJOR CAY, THE BAHAMAS
928 See a wild pig swim

Big Major Cay offers a unique welcome to its visitors; the population of feral pigs living on this island likes to swim out to meet boats arriving at the aptly named Pig Beach!

THE BAHAMAS
930 Sample some conch

Pronounced "conk," conch is the national food of the Bahamas—a firm white shellfish that you should order steamed or deep-fried with veggies and citrus flavors.

DEAN'S BLUE HOLE, THE BAHAMAS
929 Dive into a deep, deep blue hole

Sinkholes that form on the ocean floor are known as "blue holes." The deepest is in China. The second deepest is here. At 663 ft (202 m), Dean's Blue Hole has plenty of opportunities for exploration at every level. Snorkelers can get a sense of it, while scuba divers can head down deeper into the more open caverns.

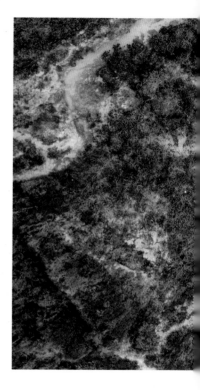

928 Big Major Cay resident

929 The depths of Dean's Blue Hole

931 Starfish Point

STARFISH POINT,
CAYMAN ISLANDS
931 See the real stars at this hidden beach

Starfish are one of the ocean's more mysterious species, and this glorious beach on the north side of the Cayman Islands is a grand spot to get to know them more. The waters here are home to photogenic red cushion sea stars, and taking a day trip will introduce them to you, against a beautiful backdrop.

HELL, CAYMAN ISLANDS
932 Journey to some devilish outcrops

The heat can definitely be an issue here, but the facilities mean that you can take shelter and get refreshments. Hell in this case is a weird corner of the Cayman Islands, covered in dramatic black limestone rock formations that are worth a few photos. There's also a post office so that you can send your postcards from Hell.

934 Floyd's Pelican Bar

935 Gliding along the Martha Brae

CAYMAN ISLANDS

933 Test yourself on the Mastic Trail

Not many tourists undertake this hike on Grand Cayman, but those who do are greatly rewarded. As the last untouched forest on the island, the swathe of vegetation is a far cry from the golden beaches nearby. You'll see indigenous flora and fauna as you are led along the trail by an expert guide. Alternatively, you can guide yourself; expect to be walking for around three hours, and wear sturdy footwear.

NEGRIL, JAMAICA

934 Try a watering hole surrounded by water

About a mile (1.6 km) from the coast, there's a shack raised up on stilts. Hop on a boat and you'll discover what's perhaps the world's coolest drinking hole, Floyd's Pelican Bar. Food and cocktails are all available, and the dress code is as casual as you care to be. People tend to stay a while.

TRELAWNY, JAMAICA

935 Raft down the Martha Brae River

It's not exactly whitewater here, and the sleepy rafts are more akin to a gondola. Hop on a 30-ft (9-m) bamboo raft, expertly steered by a qualified captain, and take a leisurely one-hour tour down the river on this beautiful island. You'll find picturesque swimming spots along the way.

936 Sunrise on Doctor's Cave Beach

MONTEGO BAY, JAMAICA

936 Dance the night away in the Caribbean

Where better to take in the sounds of reggae than where it all began: Jamaica. The weeklong Reggae Sumfest festival, held each July in Montego Bay, is one of the world's great musical gatherings, bringing together a relaxed vibe, sunshine, and a passion for partying. After dancing all night, you can revive yourself at the palm-fringed Doctor's Cave Beach, with a refreshing dip in crystal waters.

FALMOUTH, JAMAICA

937 Create an eerie glow in the sea

There aren't many places to reliably witness bioluminescence, but the Luminous Lagoon is one of them. Trail your hand in its waters by night and watch it leave a path of light. This natural phenomenon is caused by millions of tiny microorganisms (dinoflagellates) that thrive in the blend of salt and fresh water created as the Martha Brae flows into the lagoon. These cause a glow when the water is agitated.

MYSTIC MOUNTAIN, JAMAICA

938 Get sled astray as you descend on rails

Mystic Mountain lets you see Ocho Rios and the surrounding region from a different angle. It's an eco-friendly attraction that includes chairlifts up through the forest canopy and a zip line down for the more adventurous. There's also a mechanical bobsled on tracks, so you can pay homage to the team from the famous movie *Cool Runnings*.

ORACABESSA BAY, JAMAICA

939 Enjoy a bonding experience on a cinematic beach

James Bond movies have been filmed all over the world, but this location is one of the most alluring. If you're rich, you can stay at GoldenEye, where Ian Fleming wrote many of the novels. For the rest of us, James Bond Beach is a scenic spot where the locals hold regular festivals, but it can be enjoyed any time.

943 Coffee country in Jamaica

COASTS AND MOUNTAINS OF JAMAICA
940 See Jamaica's most beautiful bird

The red-billed streamertail is a stunner. Both sexes have a bright red bill and iridescent green body, but the male also sports long, glossy black tail feathers that are twice the length of its body. It's a type of hummingbird, and when it hovers in front of flowers or feeders, searching out nectar, it's a sight to behold. Its beautiful appearance has also earned it the names of "scissortail" and "God bird."

KINGSTON, JAMAICA
941 Go up to bat for a memorable sporting experience

Even if you have little interest in cricket, the sporting occasions at Sabina Park are worth the price of a ticket. Home to the Kingston Cricket Club and the venue for international matches, the ground comes alive on match days, and it's an excuse for a party with 20,000 people against the backdrop of the Blue Mountains.

KINGSTON, JAMAICA
942 Get up, stand up, and tour the home of a musical legend

Bob Marley brought reggae to the world. Although his life was cut tragically short, his legacy lives on at the Bob Marley Museum. Built around his former home and recording studio, it's a shrine to the man's talent and international reach and is filled with rare memorabilia and more.

BLUE AND JOHN CROW MOUNTAINS NATIONAL PARK, JAMAICA
943 Percolate on a chance to drink some of the world's best java

The Blue Mountains just outside Kingston have a very special bounty—some of the world's best coffee. Conditions are perfect for coffee growing, but limited space means that the product is in high demand. Head to the source for tours and tastings.

944 Visiting Citadelle Laferrière
on horseback

CAP HAÏTIEN, HAITI

944 Saddle up to visit a pioneering castle

Citadelle Laferrière is a dark
stone castle that sits atop a
hill just outside of Cap Haïtien.
Built in 1820, the fortification
is the first example of African-
influenced colonial architecture,
and it has an imposing, almost
Gothic appearance. It is now a
UNESCO World Heritage Site,
and visitors are required to use a
4x4 or a horse to make the climb
to its walls.

ÎLE-À-RAT, HAITI

945 Escape the rat race

Île-à-Rat redefines the paradise
island getaway. It's secluded,
remote, and it takes less than ten
minutes to walk around the fine
white-gold beach ringing the
lushly forested interior. Rent a
boat taxi from Labadee and pay
extra for the fisherman to rustle
up a fresh lobster lunch on the
beach. Christopher Columbus
is said to have used Île-à-Rat as
a lovers' hideaway—it's easy to
see why.

946 Jacmel at Carnival time

JACMEL, HAITI

946 Dicover Jacmel's colorful charms

The old town center of Jacmel is brimming with mansions, coffee depots, wrought-iron balconies, and peeling facades. Lovely beaches such as Ti Mouillage are nearby, as is Bassin Bleu, a series of waterfalls and pools where only a few visitors are permitted each day. Book a hotel with old-world charm and visit in late January to catch the sights and sounds of Jacmel Carnival.

SAUT-D'EAU, HAITI

947 See the voodoo that you do so well

Locally known as "Sodo," this commune is located around Haiti's highest waterfall, Le Saut. Both Christian and Vodou traditions claim it as a holy site; an apparition of the Virgin Mary is said to have appeared here in 1891. Annual festivals celebrate the miracle, and even if you don't buy into the story, it's a place to learn more about Vodou or just appreciate the waters.

CHALK SOUND, TURKS AND CAICOS

948 Chalk it up to experience at a lagoon

The turquoise of the waters around Chalk Sound is so vibrant it almost looks fake. Designated a national park, it's a highly scenic natural lagoon with cute limestone islands and a great spot for leisurely kayaking, canoeing, or paddleboarding. It's a twisty drive to get there, but you'll be rewarded with a motor-free environment.

950 Whale watching in Turks and Caicos

PRINCESS ALEXANDRA NATIONAL PARK,
TURKS AND CAICOS

949 Grace one of the world's most pristine beaches with your presence

Grace Bay has much to recommend it. There's
the small matter of it being regularly voted the
best beach in the world, the soft white sands and
flawless waters obvious to any visitor. Below the
surface, too, a gorgeous barrier reef system attracts
divers from around the world.

SALT CAY, TURKS AND CAICOS

950 Watch a majestic humpback whale migration

In the winter season, humpback whales migrate
from the northern Atlantic to warm Caribbean
waters. For reasons unknown, in a millennia-old
tradition, many come to this specific region to
mate and give birth. Visitors can watch pods of
whale families swim by, calves and mothers,
in a heartwarming natural display.

PUERTO PLATA,
DOMINICAN REPUBLIC
951 Ride the Caribbean's only cable car

The Caribbean region only has one fully operational cable car, and it's here. The *teleférico* has been a tourist attraction since 1975, and is still going strong. Hop into the car and be whisked up 2,600 ft (790 m) in just ten minutes, the lush green plains and vibrant ocean greens all visible as you climb the slope of Mt. Isabel de Torres.

PLAYA EL LIMÓN,
DOMINICAN REPUBLIC
952 Discover a coconut-lined beach

Take the scenic Highway 104 west through the mountains to the tourist-free hidden beach of Playa el Limón. This 2-mi (3-km) stretch of virgin Atlantic coast is lined with coconut trees leaning into the ocean. You are likely to have the spot to yourself; if not, the drive alone will justify the trip to this stunning stretch of coastline.

SANTO DOMINGO,
DOMINICAN REPUBLIC
953 Wander along sixteenth-century streets

The Colonial City (Ciudad Colonial) is the most historic neighborhood of Santo Domingo, the oldest continuously inhabited European-established settlement in the Americas. Walk around the sixteenth-century Cathedral of Santa María la Menor, and see the stunning architecture of the National Pantheon and more.

951 Puerto Plata's cable car

THROUGHOUT THE
DOMINICAN REPUBLIC
954 Partake in a Presidente on home turf

First brewed as a dark lager in 1935 in Santiago, the classic Caribbean Presidente pilsner was transformed into its current pale lager formula back in the 1960s. Clean and crisp, it's the perfect foil for sunny beaches and hearty Dominican stews, snacks, and sandwiches.

SAN JUAN, PUERTO RICO
955 Discover a rum old time

There are dozens of world-class brands of rum that originated in the tropical climes of the Caribbean. Bacardi is perhaps the best known, and you can visit Casa Bacardi to see for yourself how it became so successful. Take a tour, learn some history, and enjoy sampling the city's biggest success story.

SAN JUAN, PUERTO RICO
956 Color yourself impressed by San Juan

San Juan is the second most populous metropolitan area in the Caribbean, and while there are historic sights such as the Cathedral of San Juan Bautista, the city is worth visiting just for its architecture. Cobbled streets take you past a succession of brightly colored houses, each more charming than the last.

956 Colorful streets of Old San Juan

957 El Morro's strategic harbor location

SAN JUAN, PUERTO RICO
957 Keep guard at El Morro

Follow the cobblestone streets of Old San Juan to the sea, to the Castillo San Felipe del Morro. Standing guard at the entrance to the harbor to protect the island from pirates, privateers, and foreign states, the fort has seen off all sea-based attacks, falling only in 1598 when the Earl of Cumberland took it by land. It's a steep climb, but a cooling ocean breeze awaits at the top. Explore the barracks, dungeons, passageways, secret staircases, and ramparts, or simply sit inside one of the domed *garitas* (sentry boxes) and watch the ships come and go.

EL YUNQUE NATIONAL FOREST, PUERTO RICO
958 See the forest and the trees in a one-of-a-kind woodland

There are lots of forests in the US National Forest System, but only one of them is tropical, and that's El Yunque. The foliage is incredibly lush and green, and hiking through the landscape brings you past scenic, junglelike waterfalls, and along twisting rivers. Spot parrots and the forest's most famous resident, the coqui frog.

CULEBRA, PUERTO RICO

959 Give tanks for the memories on a beach

There are plenty of great beaches in this corner of the world, and Flamenco Beach has those golden sands and clear waters. But it also happens to have old World War II tanks rusting on the sands—formerly used for bombing practice, and now used for the backdrop to unusual beach selfies.

ST. JOHN, US VIRGIN ISLANDS

960 Visit an old sugar plantation

Sugar plantations, with their imported slave labor and fatal impact on the Indigenous people, define the Virgin Islands' history and development. Confront the past by paying a visit to the Annaberg Plantation on St. John, where you'll encounter ruins of a factory, slave quarters, and a windmill.

ST. THOMAS, US VIRGIN ISLANDS

961 Tackle 99 steps

The US Virgin Islands' capital city, Charlotte Amalie, is full of colorful colonial buildings and steep, steep streets. One such street, known as 99 Steps, in fact contains 103 steps built of bricks that came over from Denmark as merchant-ship ballast. It rises prettily between buildings, bordered by flowers, and offers stunning views over the harbor.

ST. CROIX, US VIRGIN ISLANDS

962 Dane to visit a National Historic Site

One of the few "urban parks" in the region, Christiansted National Historic Site commemorates Danish development of these islands in the eighteenth and nineteenth centuries. Six historic structures still stand, and you can educate yourself about those times while admiring the colorful neoclassical architecture.

US VIRGIN ISLANDS

963 Hoist the mainsail for maritime adventures in paradise

The Caribbean in general is a wonderful place for sailing, but the US Virgin Islands are close to perfection. Conditions are consistently good year-round, there are endless island inlets and coves to explore, and the short distance between them makes for relaxing sailing. Charter a boat and head out for picnics, scuba diving, or just island hopping.

963 Sailing in the US Virgin Islands

FLAMANDS BEACH, ST. BARTHS

964 Beach to their own at an endlessly romantic spot

With low hills decorated with succulents and an alluring crescent of white sand against calm, turquoise waters, Flamands is the filet of the island in terms of beaches. Its seaweed-free sands are an idyllic picnic spot, and it's a supremely walkable, half-mile stretch—hard to beat for a romantic backdrop.

964 Flamands Beach

GUSTAVIA, ST. BARTHS

965 Shop 'til you drop

Gustavia, on St. Barths, owes its name to King Gustav III of Sweden and the period in its history when it was a Swedish colony. Now, it's a top destination for the well-heeled tourist and has the shopping to match. Designer stores from Louis Vuitton to Hermés, Cartier, and Bulgari throng the main street—all duty-free.

BAIE DE ST. JEAN, ST. BARTHS

966 Don't be late to the party at an all-day rager

St. Barths is a glamorous, upscale destination, where many people (celebrities included) come to wind down. It can be sleepy and low key, and that's why most people choose it. Every Sunday, though, day club Nikki Beach cranks up the energy levels with an all-day beach party you can attend in your bathing suit.

ANTIGUA AND BARBUDA

967 Explore a dark world beyond the beaches

Just beyond the pink sands of Barbuda, there's a subterranean world to discover. The limestone cave system has many deep caverns that can only be explored by serious cavers, but there are a few that you can visit. Head for Two Foot Bay, with its bats and iguanas, or Indian Cave, for ancient petroglyphs.

ANTIGUA AND BARBUDA

968 Face the audacity of slope of the highest peak

Once known as Boggy Peak, the tallest point in Antigua was renamed in 2009 to honor the forty-fourth president of the United States. Mt. Obama requires a half-day hike to ascend the 1,500 ft (460 m) along 4 mi (6.4 km), but you'll be rewarded with beautiful views over mango and papaya groves.

968 Lush landscape of Mt. Obama

HALF MOON BAY, ANTIGUA
AND BARBUDA

969 Quench your thirst at Smiling Harry's

Enjoy a drink from this rustic beach shack at the mouth of a cove, which is also famous for its Antiguan fare. Then clamber over the rocks at the cliff end of the beach for a natural mud bath.

ST. MARYS, ANTIGUA
AND BARBUDA

970 Spot a feral donkey

The last sugar factory on Antigua closed in the 1970s, and so the last of the plantations' working donkeys became unemployed and were released to live freely. Large populations of feral animals now live in the wild, entertaining tourists while frustrating farmers, for whom the pickup has long been the preferred beast of burden.

ANTIGUA AND BARBUDA

971 Enjoy the naked beauty of the Hawksbills

Four secluded beaches—Royal Palm Beach, Sea Grape Beach, Honeymoon Cove, and Eden Beach—make up the Hawksbill beaches, which are privately owned but publicly accessible. These coastal stretches are more tranquil than other spots on the island, but be aware that on Eden Beach, clothing is considered optional!

970 Feral donkey on Antigua

973 View of Scotts Head, start of the Waitukubuli Trail

MORNE TROIS PITONS NATIONAL PARK, DOMINICA

972 Explore Dominica's tropical highlands

Luxuriant forest wraps around the volcanic features of the eponymous Morne Trois Pitons to create Dominica's wildest landscape. Relax on idyllic deserted shores fringed with coconut palms, and cool off beside the Emerald Pool, before swimming deep into the Titou Gorge with its prehistoric ferns.

ACROSS DOMINICA

973 Retrace the footsteps of slaves

Few people have completed the full 115 mi (185 km) of the Waitukubuli Trail, Caribbean's first long-distance walking trail. Running the length of Dominica, through rain forest and over mountainous ridges to a boiling lake, the trail takes a week to hike and follows paths that were used by runaway slaves escaping the coastal plantations.

MALGRETOUTE, ST. LUCIA

974 Heal yourself in a mud bath

St. Lucia's volcanic activity is dormant, but there's still enough going on to create hot springs, bubbling mud pools, and the unmistakeable aroma of sulfur in the air. Visit the Sulphur Springs to cover yourself in the volcanic mud—it's said to heal eczema, sunburn, and mosquito bites— before washing it off in a mountain waterfall.

974 Bathing at Sulphur Springs

977 Janti's relaxed Happy Island bar

FOND GENS LIBRE, ST. LUCIA

975 Join a hiking tour up Gros Piton

St. Lucia's two distinctive Pitons—Petit Piton and Gros Piton—are volcanic plugs whose steep green slopes dominate the landscape. A hike up Gros Piton offers fabulous views over the sea and island, the chance to see exotic birds, and the feeling of being on top of the world.

MUSTIQUE, ST. VINCENT AND THE GRENADINES

976 Mingle with the rich and famous

If spotting A-list or even D-list celebrities is your thing, then there's a good chance you might run into rock stars and supermodels at this exclusive island. Rock up to Basil's Bar and discreetly try to see who's hiding behind their Prada sunglasses.

HAPPY ISLAND, ST. VINCENT AND THE GRENADINES

977 Hit the happiness buffet at a bar

You don't need to blow out a flip-flop getting to an island life–friendly bar that would make Jimmy Buffett proud. In 2002, a guy called Janti built Happy Island as his home and bar, and you're welcome to sail out and join him for a cocktail.

978 Seclusion on Petit St. Vincent

PETIT ST. VINCENT, ST. VINCENT AND THE GRENADINES

978 Forget about the world on St. Vincent

It's easy to forget that there are other people on the island when you check in here. One-bedroom cottages are discreetly tucked into the hillside, and two-bedroom beach villas nestle along the shoreline. The island is refreshingly free from telephones and television: a quaint flag system to communicate with the staff replaces the former; wide-open ocean views replace the latter. With no Wi-Fi, either, the outside world becomes practically nonexistent, leaving you to explore the 115-ac (47-ha) volcanic island undisturbed. Guests also have access to the resort's private yacht, *Beauty*.

VARIOUS SITES ON GRENADA

979 Spice up your life on the "Isle of Spice"

It's hard to overstate the importance of Grenada's exotic spices, with the most important being nutmeg, cinnamon, cloves, and mace. Take one of the many spice tours on offer for a fascinating insight—including Belmont Estate, Dougaldston Estate, and Gouyave Nutmeg Processing Station.

GRAND ETANG NATIONAL PARK, GRENADA

980 Make variety the spice of life on a scenic hike

Nutmeg is particularly popular on this beautiful island, and it grows in the tropical rain forests of the central highlands. Join a guided tour or leisurely hike and wander through lush woodlands, spotting impish monkeys and the colorful fish of Grand Etang Lake. Make sure you start or finish your hike with a visit to Annandale Falls on the southwestern perimeter of the park.

MOUNTAINS OF GRENADA

981 Check out cheeky mona monkeys

Venture into the mountainous interior of Grenada and you will be sure to see mona monkeys. Brown-backed, white-bellied, and with a stripe of black in between, they are often spotted storing food in their cheeks.

980 Grenada's Annandale Falls

MOLINERE BAY, GRENADA

982 Prepare to be floored by beautiful art on a seabed

Created by artist Jason deCaires Taylor in 2006, the Molinere Underwater Sculpture Park is thought to be the first of its kind. Scuba-qualified visitors can dive to a depth of 15 ft (4.5 m) and see around seventy-five eerily beautiful works, from solitary figures to a ring of children holding hands. Many are also visible to snorkelers and even guests on glass-bottomed boats who prefer to stay dry.

HOLETOWN, BARBADOS

983 Stand where the English first did

Blown off course between South America and England, Captain John Powell and his crew found themselves on Barbados. They erected a cross, scratched the King's name into a tree, and so claimed the island for England. Two years later, in 1627, Powell's brother returned with a group of settlers and established Holetown. Stand at the Holetown Monument (which unfortunately has the wrong dates) and imagine yourself an explorer.

982 Molinere Underwater Sculpture Park

HARRISON'S CAVE, BARBADOS
984 Make tracks to a trail below ground

There are some amazing cave systems to explore on foot, but the exquisite trail within Harrison's Cave is so big that it has electric trams. Hop on board and see the cave's crystallized limestone walls and deep pools, and gasp as the trail opens up into the 45-ft (13.7-m) high Great Hall.

ANDROMEDA BOTANIC GARDENS, BARBADOS
985 Enjoy exotic species

This botanical garden was established in the 1950s. It offers winding paths through 6 ac (2 ha) of tropical plants, including trees not found anywhere else in the Caribbean. There are hundreds of different plant species, including orchids, heliconias, bougainvilleas, and ginger lilies.

EASTERN FORESTS, BARBADOS
986 Blink and miss the world's tiniest snake

As thin as a piece of spaghetti, the Barbados threadsnake is so tiny that it could coil itself up on a coin.

985 Andromeda Botanic Gardens

987 Barbecued fish at Oistins

OISTINS, BARBADOS

987 Don't look for bigger fish to fry on Fridays

To fit into the social scene on Barbados you need to know where the movers and shakers go, and that's the Friday night Fish Fry at Oistins Bay Garden. Bring along a healthy appetite for some freshly prepared seafood and feel the party starting up around you.

BARBADOS

988 Crop around the clock at a harvest party

There are some huge parties in these parts, but none compare to the Crop Over festival. The festival's origins date back to 1687, when it was established to celebrate the end of the harvest. It now rages for three months, celebrating the culture of the whole island.

PORT OF SPAIN, TRINIDAD AND TOBAGO

989 Let your hair down at a pulsating party

The mother of all good times, in a corner of the world that is famous for its festivals, is the Trinidad Carnival. Join in with its riot of calypso, steel bands, and soca, all wrapped in extravagant costumes in the lead-up to Lent.

TRINIDAD AND TOBAGO

990 Discover your true colors

There are many Hindu residents here, and just after the more famous Carnival at the start of Lent, they have their own party: Phagwa. Colored powders are thrown in joyous celebration, so wear white and be prepared to be doused in all manner of shades.

TUNAPUNA, TRINIDAD AND TOBAGO

991 Spill the tea over a civilized afternoon snack

There's been a tearoom at Pax Guest House since 1932, and the tradition lives on. Visitors can sit back on the veranda and sample teas, homemade breads, jams, and jellies while looking out across verdant fields.

CARONI SWAMP, TRINIDAD AND TOBAGO

992 Count all the ibis you can

Most plentiful in the breeding season, vividly colored, long-billed scarlet ibis are a wonder to behold. Mating pairs will nest in the same tree. Together with the cocrico, they are Trinidad and Tobago's national bird.

990 Riotous times at Phagwa

TRINIDAD FORESTS, TRINIDAD AND TOBAGO

993 Monitor ocelots

Very little is known about local populations of these wildcats, which are around twice the size of domestic cats. However, the island of Trinidad, where ocelots are not overshadowed by other bigger cats, offers a perfect place to study them.

PENAL, TRINIDAD AND TOBAGO

994 Bathe yourself in a mud volcano

A volcanic eruption in 1852 exposed underground vents to the Earth's surface here. Activity these days is confined to much safer mud volcanoes, where visitors can literally soak up the natural benefits in a spa treatment with a difference.

VARIOUS SITES ON ARUBA

995 Discover the cool powers of the aloe

Aruba first discovered aloe in the mid-1800s; back then it was used as a laxative. The plant took to the dry soils and the country was soon the world's main supplier of aloin resin. Visit a plantation to learn about its other uses and age-old harvesting techniques.

994 Mud bathing at L'eau Michel Mud Volcano

998 Swimming with turtles off Little Curaçao

SAN NICOLAS, ARUBA

996 Dip your toes in at Baby Beach

A perfect half-moon of a beach, Baby Beach has both soft white sand and shallow, protected waters making it ideal for, well . . . babies. The calm waters make it a popular spot for snorkeling, too—you'll see parrotfish, angelfish, and eels.

ACROSS ARUBA

997 Tour Aruba in a golf cart on steroids

Buckle up at the wheel of a 4x4 UTV (utility task vehicle) for a tour of Aruba that makes the journey as good as the destinations. Aruba's UTVs are like supercharged golf carts, and they will have you smiling away as you take in the island's landmarks and experiences.

LITTLE CURAÇAO, CURAÇAO

998 See no one on Little Curaçao

The only signs of this island's past as a quarantine station for slaves and a phosphate mine are a lighthouse, shipwrecks, and abandoned homes. Otherwise it's entirely abandoned and uninhabited, apart from a slowly expanding resident turtle colony.

RINCÓN, BONAIRE

999 Discover the only time you can spike a drink

The Cadushy Distillery is the only distillery on the island, and it makes some wonderful rums and other liquors. What you must try, though, is its speciality, which is a rare cactus liqueur. At 80 proof, it packs a real punch. Ask the guide to mix a cocktail, or take a shot for the full experience.

THROUGHOUT BONAIRE

1000 See a flock of pink flamingos

Such is Bonaire's link to flamingos that it has a pink airport called Flamingo Airport. Until recently there were actually more flamingos than humans living here. The stylishly kitsch birds can be seen all over the island. Catch them during their courtship displays for fabulous shows of head-bobbing, wing-flapping dancing.

1000 Flamingos of Bonaire

INDEX

IMAGE CREDITS

The publisher would like to thank the following for the permission to reproduce copyright material.

Front cover: Kristin Addis @ bemytravelmuse
Spine: My Good Images/Shutterstock
Back cover (top to bottom): Row 1L Intricate Explorer/Unsplash; Row 1M f11photo/Shutterstock; Row 1R Ed Dods/Shutterstock; Row 2L Matej Kastelic/Shutterstock; Row 2M Caleb Fisher/Unsplash; Row 2R Tara Lowry Photography; Row 3L Wisanu Boonrawd/Shutterstock; Row 3M Gateway Arch; Row 3R TLF Images/Shutterstock; Row 4L Abigail Marie/Shutterstock; Row 4M Ela & Greg, Screw It. Let's Ride! www.screwitletsride.com; Row 4R Photostock by LEEM/Shutterstock; Row 5L Starcevic/iStock; Row 5M Penn's Cave, Pennsylvania, USA; Row 5R VIA Rail Canada

Alamy: 58–9 H. Mark Weidman Photography; 64–5 BLM Photo; 70R Cavan Images; 78–9 Cavan Images; 95 Danita Delimont; 101 Jon Arnold Images Ltd; 124B Bill Grant; 137 Tom Till; 151TR Spencer Grant; 157 Tim Graham; 185 M. Timothy O'Keefe; 214 Zachary Frank; 221 Jeffrey Isaac Greenberg 14+; 232–3 directphoto.bz; 263 Jerry and Marcy Monkman/EcoPhotography.com; 277 Boomer Jerritt/All Canada Photos; 294 Alan Dyer/Stocktrek Images; 298L Blaine Harrington/agefotostock; 300 Ken Gillespie Photography; 307 David Giral; 309 Henry Georgi/All Canada Photos; 392 Tim Whitby; 402 SEAN DRAKES

AgeFoto: 320L RENAULT Philippe; 327 Robert Postma

Dreamstime: 159L © Robbiebrewer

Getty: 12–13 Menno Boermans; 15 Neil Rabinowitz; 20 Island Memories Photography; 26 San Francisco Chronicle/Hearst Newspapers via Getty Images; 27 Brent Stirton/Staff; 42 Mitch Diamond; 46 Pete Ark; 63 John P Kelly; 66R Denise Truscello; 80–1 Vonkara1; 96 peeterv; 105 David Howells; 141 Seth K. Hughes; 143R Murat Taner; 154–5 Douglas Keister; 159R Jared C. Tilton / Stringer; 161 Raymond Boyd/Getty Images; 163TR Patrick Smith; 163B Bloomberg; 167R Joe Murphy; 168 Terry Wyatt; 173 Carmen Mandato/Stringer; 178 Roberto Machado Noa; 179 Jeff Greenberg; 201 Mladen Antonov/AFP via Getty Images; 202–3 Drew Angerer; 207T The Washington Post; 207BR The Washington Post; 222 Jumping Rocks; 223 New York Daily News Archive; 231 Timothy Fadek; 238 Roy Rochlin; 240B Atlantide Phototravel; 242L Torresigner; 243L Photograph by Arunsundar; 246 Comstock; 255 Boston Globe; 258 Robert Nickelsberg; 264–5 Jerry Monkman / Aurora Photos; 288TR NurPhoto; 292–3 AscentXmedia; 301 Paul Souders; 310TL Cole Burston; 320R Amy Muschik / EyeEm; 322–3 aetb; 346 Peter Adams; 357 Michael Runkel/robertharding; 369 Michele Westmorland; 380L Poppy Hollis; 384 John Seaton Callahan; 385 THONY BELIZAIRE/Staff; 396 Severine Baur; 401 Bob Thomas/Popperfoto

iStock: 87 htrnr; 98–9 ricardoreitmeyer; 106 TR bkkm; 122 scgerding; 174 Marje; 190 zimmytws; 213L milehightraveler; 220R jimfeng; 247 kickstand; 248 jtyler; 306 Zofca; 310TR Steven_Kriemadis; 343 ferrantraite; 354 eddygaleotti; 355 Starcevic; 361 Joel Carillet; 377 Liukov; 381 mgcatfish; 389 felixairphoto; 399 Anfisa Tukane; 400 Flavio Vallenari; 405 VanWyckExpress

Shutterstock: P11 907Shots; 16 saraporn; 17 Dudarev Mikhail; 21 Wonderful Nature; 24L satit sewtiw; 24L Kondratuk Aleksei; 24R Christian Heinz; 28 maxseigal; 35TR Marco Bicci; 41 EliteCustomAdventures.com; 44R arkanto; 48 Cory Woodruff; 50 CSNafzger; 54TL Abigail Marie; 54TR kevincwalker; 54B Antonio Guillem; 55 Michelle Holihan; 56 Oleg Kovtun Hydrobio; 58 Victoria Ditkovsky; 62R Megan Mahoney Photography; 68 Baylor de los Reyes; 71 Checubus; 72 Pung; 76 Paul Brady Photography; 82–3 Impassioned Images; 85 XONIX; 86–7 Byron Banasiak; 93 Martin Hobelman; 97L RaksyBH; 106TL JasonYoder; 106B Randy Kostichka; 111 Jadie G; 114 photo.ua; 118–19 Sarah Quintans; 121L Paulo Nabas; 121R Matt Grimaldi; 124TL PhotoFlyt; 129 Joni Hanebutt; 134 Prosper106; 136 EQRoy; 138–9 Christopher Winfield; 142L kan_khampanya; 142–3 Wisanu Boonrawd; 144 Mark Taylor Cunningham; 145 Martina Birnbaum; 148R Roberto Michel; 149L Malachi Jacobs; 154L NicholasGeraldinePhotos; 155 James Kirkikis; 156 Vicki L. Miller; 158 Pierre Jean Durieu; 160 JNix; 163 TL Golden Ratio Photos; 166 f11photo; 167L jejim; 170–1 Torin Shanahan; 175L Sean Pavone; 175R ron99; 176 Gestalt Imagery; 177 Jeff Stamer; 181 Mike Workman; 182 susana valera; 184 allouphoto; 186–7 Sandra Foyt; 191L digidreamgrafix; 191R lazyllama; 192–3 Robert H Ellis; 194 TempleNick; 194–5 Malachi Jacobs; 195 Daniel Friend; 198–9 Andrew Gittis; 207BL Lewis Tse Pui Lung; 208 Orhan Cam; 209R Kristi Blokhin; 212 Vicky Faye Aquino; 219 Sandra Foyt; 226 Mike Ver Sprill; 228 Niamh Hughes; 229R travelview; 230 Matej Kastelic; 233 Diego Grandi; 240TR Aleksandr Dyskin; 245 f11photo; 250L Felix Lipov; 251 quiggyt4; 252–3 Jay Yuan; 261 haveseen; 266–7 littlenySTOCK; 270–1 Tomas Kulaja; 272L Pecold; 272R EB Adventure Photography; 272R Scalia Media; 273 Olgaradzikh; 278 Ilhamchewadventures; 280 EB Adventure Photography; 282–3 Juana Nunez; 284 norikko; 285 WildShutter; 288TL e X p o s e; 290L Ronnie Chua; 290R Ghost Bear; 291 Shawn.ccf; 297

Ed Dods; 298R Osvaldo Dauve; 299 Tathoms; 302–3 Nikolay Kachev; 304 Nick Goetz; 305 karen burgess; 312–13 Lisa Charbonneau; 314 TRphotos; 315 JHVEPhoto; 317 R.M. Nunes; 318 Marc Bruxelle; 321 Lopolo; 325 Curtis Watson; 328 gvictoria; 329 Paul Donald; 338–9 Javier Garcia; 340 Leonardo Gonzalez; 341 Eduardo Quiros; 342 AureoAu; 346–7 Luxbox; 347 Ricard MC; 349 Imke Zijm; 350 schlyx; 351 BondRocketImages; 352TL Jareth Ley; 352TR Dado Photos; 352B Richie Chan; 353 Francisco Gomez Sosa; 358 Eva Lepiz; 359L eskystudio; 360 Aleksandar Todorovic; 362 Photostock by LEEM; 363 sofiatrevi; 364 Cesar Dussac; 365 David Merino; 366–7 zstock; 374TR Lesinka372; 376 May_Lana; 378 HelloRF Zcool; 379 Jim Schubert; 380R Jam Travels; 383 Photo Spirit; 386 Nickolas warner; 387 MLIN; 388 Soto.Creativo; 390–1 Candis Bridges; 395 fokke baarssen; 397 BlueOrange Studio; 398 Landscapeography; 404 Gail Johnson

Unsplash: 1 Gianandrea Villa; 2–3 Drif Riadh; 4–5 Alyssa Teboda; 18–19 Kalen Emsley; 22 Steve Alama; 23 Johannes Andersson; 25L Matthew Brodeur; 25R Clarisse Meyer; 29L Yang Liu; 32 tatonomusic; 35TL Amogh Manjunath; 35B Brandon Nelson; 36 Lance Anderson; 38 George Cox; 40 Clarisse Meyer; 43 Chelsea Audibert; 44L Derick McKinney; 45 Roberto Nickson; 49 Karsten Winegeart; 52 Nic Y-C; 59 Nicole Geri; 66L feelingvegas; 67 Andrew Broderick; 70L Intricate Explorer; 73L Jake C; 88–9 Jeromey Balderrama; 90 Alyssa Teboda; 94 Laura Seaman; 120 Ian Scargill; 126 Benjamin Rascoe; 127 Muzammil Soorma; 128 Blake Guidry; 151TL Steve Saunders; 151B Rosie Kerr; 152 Lia Raby; 169 Rollalyn Ruis; 172 Christopher Alvarenga; 180 Drew Darby; 183 Nichlas Andersen; 188 Gene Gallin; 204–5 Mark Tegethoff; 209L Caleb Fisher; 210–11 Doug Kelley; 215 Benjamin Rascoe; 217

Michael Browning; 227L K Chessyca; 227R Jordan Finnerty; 229L Reno Laithienne; 232 Matej Sefcik; 234 Robert Bye; 236 Julien DI MAJO; 240TL Benjamin Voros; 241 TAALAI DJUMABAEV; 242R Patrick Robert Doyle; 254 Taylor Rooney; 256–7 Kevin Long; 262 Omri D. Cohen; 268–9 Patrick Tomasso; 279 Nikita Taparia; 286–7 Andy Holmes; 306–7 Sandra Ivleva; 335 Nic Amaya; 336–7 Hugo Doria; 344 Mike Bacos; 356 Victor Moran; 359R Marlon Michelle Corado; 364–5 Earth; 370 Anna Sullivan; 372–3 Florian Wehde; 374B Daniel Sessler; 394 Patrick Jansen; 416 Kwan Fung

WikiCommons: 84 State Historical Society of North Dakota http://statemuseum.nd.gov/; 110 Kbh3rd; 132–3 Jeremy Thompson; 394–5 Aneil Lutchman

Also: 7, 8–9 Jenn Marino @lifenaturlvr; 10 Amber Basgil @brunch_n_babes; 29R www.willamettevalleytour.com; 30 Bend Brewing Company; 31 Cyrano de Bergerac (2006) in the Oregon Shakespeare Festival's Allen Elizabethan Theatre. Photo by T. Charles Erickson; 37 Brad Coy; 57 Jenn Marino @lifenaturlvr; 61 Tempest Tours www.tempesttours.com; 62L Janet Jain @yo_chuma; 69L Solitude Mountain Resort; 69R Bureau of Land Management; 73R Western River Expeditions; 75 Jessica Springer – Well Planned Adventures; 77L thomas e. mccracken copywriting & creative thomasemc.com; 77R Matteo Malacaria @simumatti; 86 Nikki @nikspiks2017; 97R Rema Alameddin @remabobeema; 100–01 Matt Meier; 103 Bella Bender @bellabender; 104 Christine Warner; 108 Ray Tong; 109 Gateway Arch; 112 Courtesy North Dakota Tourism; 115 Nick Brown @nickbynorthwest; 116 Jenn Marino @lifenaturlvr; 123 Ashley Cooper @gone_rogue2020; 124TR Ela & Greg, Screw It. Let's Ride! www.screwitletsride.com; 131 Toboggan at

Pokagon State Park, Steuben County Tourism Bureau; 146 National Park Service; 147 Kevin @kaptography; 148L Evan Ingram @katsuobushi_killa; 149R Mark Chesnut @mundera www.MarkChesnut.com; 164 Maker's Mark, Chihuly Glass instalment, Kentucky Distillers' Association; 165 Shaker Village of Pleasant Hill; 196 Image for Cass Scenic Railroad provided by Walter Scriptunas II www.scriptunasimages.com @scriptunasphoto; 213R Scott Beale; 216L Penn's Cave, Pennsylvania, USA; 216R Segway Tours of Gettysburg; 218 JR P; 220L Visit Philadelphia; 224–5 Duncan Rawlinson; 235 Sabina Trojanova; 239L Betty Tsang; 239R Wally Gobetz; 243R Janice Persico @mommawanderer; 244 Andrew Evans // @RoamingTravelers; 250R Emmanouela Vokri @emmanuela_vo; 274–5 Ken Spence www.kenspence.com.au; 281 Vancouver Lookout; 288B Tara Lowry Photography; 295 © Tamsin Payne; 310B Jim Nix; 316 NASA; 319L François Lacasse/Club de hockey Canadien inc.; 319R Éole Wind; 324 Alex Fradkin, Fogo Island Inn; 330 @adammacgregor; 332–3 VIA Rail Canada; 334 Christopher Walzak @prophotographiccapebreton @capebretonphoto; 371 www.jmcvinalesaventura.com; 374TL Richard Bogle; 378–9 SNSF Scientific Image Competition; 381 mgcatfish; 382 © Peter Brown, Fleming Villa www.theflemingvilla.com; 389 felixairphoto; 393 Aneil Lutchman; 399 Anfisa Tukane; 400 Flavio Vallenari; 403 Lisa Ramdeen, X-Perience Local Ltd.; 405 VanWyckExpress

AUTHOR BIOGRAPHIES

Kath Stathers

Kath is a writer and editor who lives in London with her partner and two children. Her career as a travel writer has taken her everywhere, from Iceland to the deserts of Dubai, and her work has appeared in national UK newspapers, including the *Times* and the *Guardian*, as well as a number of magazines. Kath's never happier than when on a new adventure, whether it's going to the top of the Sagrada Família in the center of Barcelona (which she recently ticked off her bucket list) or exploring the wildernesses of South America. Still on her to-do list are to see the northern lights and to learn how to surf.

Paul Oswell

Paul is an award-winning travel writer. Born in Lancashire, England, he now lives in New Orleans. He has been widely published across newspapers and magazines such as *Condé Nast Traveler* and the *Guardian*, reporting from all seven continents (yes, including Antarctica!). Paul specializes in writing about the United States and North America, with a particular fondness for the Deep South, where he has made his home. He is currently planning a bucket-list trip of his own: traveling across the United States by train. He is also determined to master the art of making a decent pot of gumbo.

The northern lights in Yellowknife, Canada